TEACHING GLOBAL DEVELOPMENT

Teaching Global Development: A Curriculum Guide

EDITED BY

William Savitt
of the
Interfaith Hunger Appeal
Office on Education

UNIVERSITY OF NOTRE DAME PRESS

Notre Dame   London

Library of Congress Cataloging-in-Publication Data

Teaching global development : a curriculum guide / edited by William
    Savitt.
        p.   cm.
    Includes bibliographical references (p.) and index.
    ISBN 0-268-01882-0
    1. International education—Curricula. 2. Economic development—
Study and teaching (Higher) 3. Acculturation—Study and teaching
(Higher)   I. Savitt, William, 1962– .
LC1090.T42   1993
370.11'5—dc20   93–24718
                                                                        CIP

CONTENTS

PART THREE: ANNOTATED BIBLIOGRAPHY

FOREWORD

Teaching Global Development is the result of the shared commitment to global education of the agencies of the Interfaith Hunger Appeal (IHA): Catholic Relief Services, Church World Service, Lutheran World Relief and The American Jewish Joint Distribution Committee.

IHA was founded in 1978 as a united fund campaign for the major Catholic, Jewish and Protestant relief and development agencies working in the developing world and to sensitize the American public to the condition and causes of global hunger and poverty.

In 1985, our board of trustees mandated Interfaith to shift primary focus to its awareness and education initiatives. With limited resources, we decided to focus our efforts on "multipliers of influence"— policy makers, business leaders and, above all, educators. After considerable evaluation and debate we agreed that IHA could maximize its impact by working to support and encourage undergraduate faculty members. In their hands lies the next generation of our nation's leadership.

The IHA Curriculum Development Project is anchored by biennial institutes for college and university professors. These institutes were cosponsored by institutions whose experience and commitment provided proper context for interdisciplinary faculty development: Institutes have been held at Colgate University, the University of Notre Dame and the University of Massachusetts. Spelman College will be site of the 1994 seminar.

In addition to the present volume, the IHA Office on Education offers a range of supporting programs that further facilitate undergraduate curriculum development:

Development TeachNet, a quarterly publication now in its fifth volume. The publication has been expanded to include essays, annotated syllabi, bibliographies and other pedagogical resources.

The Matching Funds Grants Program provides financial means for college faculty to organize development education projects at their home institutions.

The Town Meeting at HBCUs program brings together faculty from Historically Black Colleges and Universities and other development educators in a series of smaller conferences designed to foster curriculum development and resource sharing, and to build regional networks of development education faculty.

Teaching Global Development is conceived as a practical guide for undergraduate faculty interested in teaching about international development and global hunger/poverty issues. As such, it focuses on pedagogical technique and strategies for curriculum development and reform. The objective of the book is to provide undergraduate teachers with the skills they need to develop courses and teach them well. As with all IHA programs, this volume emphasizes the potential of situating development studies in interdisciplinary or core curricula.

In producing this guide, IHA's Office on Education has convened some of the most advanced and creative thought presently available in the field of development education. This book is only possible through the contributions of highly reputed scholars who have unselfishly served the Academy with the motivation of bringing the undergraduate to a higher understanding and appreciation of the plight and challenges of other cultures.

Teaching Global Development is offered in the hope that it can help you in the classroom and in the conviction that injustice abroad is the concern of teachers at home and that education in the North is as important to a more just future as development in the South.

Msgr. Robert J. Coll
Executive Director
Interfaith Hunger Appeal

ACKNOWLEDGMENTS

From its institutional and intellectual roots *Teaching Global Development* is a collaborative project, made possible only by the support and participation of many people and organizations.

The contributors earn first thanks for their commitment of time, effort and intellectual resources. It is the ensemble of voices, each distinctive in its own right, which makes this a cohesive and effective book.

Thanks are due to the sponsoring agencies of Interfaith Hunger Appeal—Catholic Relief Services, Church World Service, Lutheran World Relief, and The American Jewish Joint Distribution Committee. IHA and its education program are expressions of the common concern of these agencies for ending hunger abroad and enhancing global awareness at home.

The Development Education Program of the United States Agency for International Development has contributed invaluable guidance and financial support to this project. David Watson, Theresa Graham, Tracy Doherty and Beth Hogan of US AID have been instrumental in its realizaton.

A crack team of researchers deserves recognition for the Annotated Bibliography. Leading the unit was the superb Ted Proferes, who made a mighty contribution at a critical moment in the process. Other major contributors included Andrew Dunn, Allan Potofsky and the IHA staff.

Virginia Saponaro of IHA merits an enormous expression of gratitude for her consistent support, good grace and friendship. My colleagues at the Office on Education, Paula Bottorf and Peter Cenedella, were likewise necessary preconditions for the successful completion of the book. Peter edited the Syllabus section and made a fundamental contribution to the realization of this book and to the development of the IHA Office on Education. Philip Gourevitch was an indispensable collaborator during the early stages of the project. Thanks also to David Rivera, Jr., Margaret Shute and Marie Emsworth of IHA.

Vigorous thanks and a large debt are owed to Sarah White, who provided keen conceptual criticism throughout the evolution of the project and reviewed late stages of the manuscript with exceptional insight. This is a much better book for her participation.

We would also like to thank James Langford, director of the University of Notre Dame Press. His enthusiastic support for the project since the beginning and his patience and interest throughout have made the process more pleasant and more productive. Thanks as well to Jeannette Morgenroth, our editor at the Press, who reviewed the manuscript with great care and offered many suggestions to improve it.

Norman Barth, Executive Director of Lutheran World Relief, was president of IHA when we began to prepare the manuscript. His stalwart support for our work mirrors his commitment to the whole of the development enterprise and shepherded the Office on Education through difficult times.

Finally, special thanks are due to the two people at the very heart of our organization. Donald M. Robinson, a founding father of IHA and its current president, has been our most resolute supporter and a constant source of guidance. This book is just one of many results of his abiding commitment to global development, global education and a more just world. Finally, deepest thanks to Monsignor Robert J. Coll, executive director of IHA. Msgr. Coll was the motive force behind the creation of the Office on Education and has been its engine ever since. His energy, vision and loyalty have made this work possible.

PART I

Essays in Development Education

INTRODUCTION

The Interdependent Patriot: Education for the Global Citizen

William Savitt

From the Pledge of Allegiance to campus speech codes to the debates on multiculturalism, the great controversies in U.S. education today reflect the recognition that schools make citizens and frame the values of our nation's civic culture. Perhaps this reality is frankly acknowledged at the elementary level: many school districts still grade students on "citizenship practices," an omnibus category which includes such virtues as working well with others and joining the line promptly in order of height. But formal education's role in citizen making is sometimes unwelcome or unfamiliar to those who work in colleges or universities, milieux whose self-identity emphasizes the neutral transmission of knowledge rather than moral education.

Nevertheless, a generation of dispute over multiculturalism and internationalization yields the transparent lesson that curriculum and morality, culture and power are hopelessly tangled issues, necessarily thrashed out on campuses of higher learning. The fundamental stake is not one canon or another, this course or that. The fundamental stake is the citizen of the future, the depth and breadth of our national vision, the civic culture and civic values that will define our public discourse in the next century.[1] The present volume endeavors to facilitate more and better teaching about global issues, particularly development issues, in the conviction that such education is already and increasingly prerequisite to responsible, mature citizenship. We begin with perspectives on several current issues in global education and higher education.

3

Education for the Global Citizen

As our subject is *Teaching Global Development*, and our audience undergraduate educators, we can scarcely avoid the controversy surrounding multiculturalization and internationalization efforts on college campuses. For our purposes it is necessary to recognize the similarities and differences between these movements, and to evaluate them above all as effective agents of curricular change, of which those of us concerned to implement development studies can take advantage.

Though closely related and frequently conflated, multiculturalism and internationalization are distinct movements. Curricular internationalization alone is a limited achievement, involving increased knowledge of—but not necessarily increased respect for, or engagement with—other nations, cultures and peoples. It is entirely possible to imagine, for example, a business curriculum focused on international issues which fails to move students from their cultural starting blocks and could indeed promote a predatory attitude toward other cultures. Indeed, traditional pedagogies in international relations often fail to shift students' perspectives or challenge their worldview.

The effectiveness of multiculturalism in this connection may be likewise limited. Because of its cultural emphasis, it can bypass issues of political and economic justice—the sinews of power relations at the core of the development equation.[2] A multicultural approach, no matter how challenging, does not guarantee understanding of interdependence. And in some contexts, it neither illuminates the dimensions of, nor inculcates a concern for, global crises such as famine or chronic hunger.

While each approach has merit, neither alone adequately addresses the requirements of development educators. It is at the confluence of these movements that the curriculum for the Global Citizen—the slogan of the IHA Office on Education since its founding in 1989—can emerge. The achievement of global citizenship, the development of both a sense of global belonging and a series of global civic values, constitutes a fundamental objective of our curriculum development efforts.

What are these civic values? At the very least they entail a sense of shared interest and shared engagement; an acceptance of the individual and national responsibilty that comes along with a community of the planet; and a recognition of the ways in which all cultures contribute to the common good. In short: participation, engagement, respect—the same virtues of citizenship that underlie any democratic regime. There is considerable and perhaps legitimate concern that the failure of these virtues endangers the well being of our Republic. A like failure of global citizenship could well undermine a broader community in the increasingly interdependent world of the future.

The concept of global citizenship provides a means of fusing multiculturalism and internationalization in common cause for increasing the curricular visibility and viability of what is called, more often in the informal than formal education sector, "development education."

Globalism and the US Interest: Doing Good by Doing Well

The idea of global citizenship, like global education and international development aid itself, has been resisted and sometimes criticized on the grounds that engagement abroad represents a failure of commitment to this country and its needs. And there will always be a student population that remains unresponsive to moral considerations, however compelling. It is therefore important that we arm ourselves in the battle for the curricular agenda with arguments that can appeal across the ideological and political spectrum.

Fortunately, however, we need not rely solely on the language of altruism, fairness, respect and justice to win curricular change: even the crudest calculus of self-interest points to the need for global education. Recognition of interdependence is no longer the purview of social reformers alone. Dozens of critical issues of great public concern—including continuing ecological violence, AIDS and other communicable diseases, refugeeism and illegal immigration, and drug trafficking—are now evidently and indisputably international problems requiring global solutions. Moreover, there is growing recognition that we must act cooperatively, or at least with a global strategy, in the world economy, as the economic health of the U.S. is profoundly affected by global economic trends. The bottom line is that development education makes good sense: the U.S. can no longer function effectively without global awareness, quite apart from the ethical imperative of engagement. The transformation of the globe has created an analogous need for transformation of the curriculum, without which students will arrive in any realm of endeavor lamentably unprepared to achieve.

No doubt there will remain those who reject on nationalist grounds the idea of global citizenship. This false patriotism, however, constitutes the last refuge, not of the scoundrel, but of the naif. Ignorance of the global context imperils not only our moral presence and our cultural awareness, but our national security as well. It is in this spirit that IHA works to promote education for the global citizen—not as a division or attenuation of the imperative to national allegiance, but as its logical extension in an increasingly interdependent world. No treason for the loyal American, global citizenship is in fact a patriotic duty.

The Transformation Debate:
Utopia and Its Enemies

If development education demands self-reflection on our role as U.S. citizens in the global milieu, it at the same time requires ethical reflection on individual responsibility and response to development's challenges. The problematic of "transformation," still more current in the informal than formal education sector, is a place where these two levels of analysis converge, offering substantial pedagogical potential.

The transformation argument has emerged as a critical response to traditional assumptions that development for everybody can be simultaneously achieved in a harmonious way. The ravages of structural adjustment and the discourse on sustainable development have led many to conclude that the promise of such development cannot be kept within the prevailing environmental and political climate. One solution to the conundrum: a radical transformation of geopolitical and development policy on the one hand, and a radical transformation of personal attitudes towards growth and quality of life on the other— in brief, a transformation of values, or the emergence of what a leading proponent of transformation calls "a new human consciousness."[3]

Is wholesale reordering of our public institutions and personal value systems a necessary precondition of effective development? This is a question that development educators would do well to ask themselves and their students, because transformation at bottom carries an "inner dimension": it calls for individual ethical reevaluation. Here transformation meets pedagogy. Any student who tackles development studies must confront, at some point, the interdependent impact of human lifestyles and the culturally constructed notions of community, individual, and the "good life" which inform them.

And if, as its proponents argue, transformation is necessary not only to spur sustainable development but to maintain viable social and ecological world systems, an essential restructuring of how we as a society and we as individuals organize ourselves to meet human needs will be necessary. Arguing along these lines, the late Carroll Joy maintained that for people truly to learn development and to respond sensibly to contemporary international issues, they must go through a "cognitive crisis." Otherwise, many people will simply reject or ignore information inconsistent with their received worldview and modes of thought— modes of thought that undergird global violence, war and injustice.[4]

There are, of course, sharply divergent views. It is always simplest, goes the response, to call for the complete transformation of human beings. But real development will take place in the real world, by women and men trained to grapple with people, values and institutions as they are, not as they ought to be. Though progress has been fitful, decades of development work have yielded clear and important benefits. Transformation as seen from this perspective overlooks the enduring sway of the present. Act pragmatically and make progress in the context of the day; avoid tragic (or self-righteous) refuge in lofty, probably unreachable, prescriptions for individual and political regeneration. The argument is a poignant restatement of the age-old quarrel between reformers and revolutionaries.

This debate is not rehearsed here in order to advocate one side or the other. Rather, the question provides a "way in" to the classroom at a personal level. Learning development means facing ethical dilemmas and weighing the pragmatic against the ideal. Educators can employ the transformation argument to explore the chasm that often exists between undeniable facts and underlying belief systems. In any context where interdependence is on the table, tensions between values, beliefs and lifestyles, on the one hand, and the staggering proportions of global poverty on the other, can help bring hunger and development home. And exploring these tensions can begin to show the kinds of cost involved in introducing social justice on a global scale.[5]

An Instrumental Approach

As the discussion above shows, our approach is instrumental: the key for global educators is to creatively use debates, controversies, problematics as levers for course design and curriculum development.

Opportunities for new courses and access to required or general education catalogue listings are scarce commodities, and development educators must be willing to work hard, within the political arena of the academy, to secure them. Faculty might find that taking advantage of internationalization or multiculturalization programs provides the means to the end of curriculum development, albeit with some compromise of development content or interpretive focus. Similarly, occasionally frustrating, often stimulating, collaborations across fields or across disciplines may be the prerequisite for gaining a wider student constituency. The academy is a conservative institution, and the pace of curricular reform is always slow: resourcefulness, opportunism and flexibility may be the prerequisite of successful curriculum development.

Without such an instrumental approach, development education risks falling into the most dangerous trap of all: preaching to the converted. Students with global awareness or finely calibrated moral sensibilities will always be drawn to development education. But a new climate in many schools now challenges faculty to widen the circle, to broaden the constituency for thinking and acting about development. *Teaching Global Development* is designed to facilitate, in whatever small way, this formidible, inviting, urgent task.

* * *

Teaching Global Development: A Curriculum Guide is conceived of as a how-to manual for undergraduate faculty interested in teaching about international development or global hunger/poverty issues. Our objective has been to create a practical compendium of pedagogical techniques and strategies for course development and curriculum reform. The volume endeavors to be at once a readable meditation on the state of the development education art and a reference to be thumbed through often while crafting a syllabus.

The guide consists of three parts. First, Essays in Development Education assembles six perspectives on our curricular and pedagogical agenda. The essays are designed to resonate with instructors across the disciplinary spectrum, both experienced development teachers and newcomers to the field.

Second, Annotated Syllabi features a range of course outlines selected for quality and representativeness from a variety of disciplinary perspectives and levels of sophistication. The annotations represent a guided tour through the varieties of development education, drawing attention to course design, use of texts, pedagogical technique and the lessons of teaching experience. The courses are educational success stories with wide relevance to the development education community.

The final section offers a selected, annotated bibliography of the literature on development. Faculty are invited here to browse through the vast and variegated literature of the field, guided by notes indicating the substantive and interpretive thrust of texts and ideas for their effective classroom use. Readers are also referred to other bibliographies and data bases for information not included here due to limitations of space.

Unifying the sections of the volume is the commitment to practical support of educators in the development field. This book is meant to be a tool—handy, helpful and versatile. We urge you to use it often, and to expect to find answers to your questions here.

The first part of *Teaching Global Development* comprises readings unified by the theme of pedagogical utility. Because development education is practiced in such a variety of disciplinary and institutional settings, it is no simple task to isolate issues which span the field and have real teaching value. But the series of problematics engaged below offers a broad sweep and should prove stimulation for anybody teaching about the Third World.

The problem of morality is a good example. No matter what the analytic angle, issues of good and bad, right and wrong are never far from the surface when confronting the problem of North and South. Steve Commins's "Development Ethics: Costly Choices" is a clear-eyed assessment of the issue. Moving past the easy consensus that today's world is replete with condemnable injustices, Commins argues that humanitarian development action is itself a complex moral kiosk, in which values and interests must be weighed, with winners and, necessarily, losers. A clutch of case studies and discussion topics will allow faculty to integrate Commins's nuanced approach to development ethics into a variety of classroom contexts.

"Are There Still Competing Paradigms of Development?" asks Jim Weaver in the title of his contribution, and he argues the question in the negative. A frank reappraisal of the state of the debate in development economics, this essay will be of interest to economists and non-specialists alike. Weaver concludes, provocatively and with some

regret, that the real competition is now within the hegemonic capitalist model and not between contending paradigms. At the same time,
Weaver has crisply surveyed the field of development economics, historically and thematically, in a way which allows teachers to bring a
current and solid framework of economics to any development course.

Bob Keesey's "Incorporating the Humanities in Development Education" persuasively makes the case for doing just that. Arguing on
practical and threoretical grounds, Keesey relates with vigor the utility
of various "literary" inputs in development education. The essay is
rather like a journey, not simply through the evolution of Keesey's
teaching strategies, but across the intellectual ties that bind the social
sciences and the humanities. It's a fun ride, and it's much more than
that: the ample citations and reflections on teaching experience allow
teachers to pick and choose the items most suitable for inclusion in
their own syllabi.

"Reaching the Course Guide: Towards Sustainable Curriculum
Development," by Godfrey Roberts, is part calculated strategy and part
exhortation. An experienced teacher who serves as an assistant dean at
Rutgers University, Roberts has participated in the course development process from both sides and has in the process achieved a privileged perspective on the problem. Here he uses his experience to the
benefit of the global educator, offering the results of a faculty survey
and numerous tips for course implementation to render the process of
administrative and colleague approval a bit easier.

Kathleen Maas Weigert's essay, "Student Activism and Pedagogy: A
Reciprocal Relationship in Development Studies," explores alternative pedagogies to show that student interest in global hunger and
poverty can contribute to curriculum development and effective
teaching. Undergraduate social commitment can be harnessed to good
classroom effect, Weigert argues, if faculty are willing to step out of the
traditional teaching mold and draw on student energy.

If there are students who bring to campus a commitment to issues of
global hunger and poverty there is at least an equal number of students
who arrive in college classrooms with no education at all about the
Third World. The perceptions of these students are thus shaped by the
institutions of mass media. We do not always consider the role of
media in informing—or misinforming—students at all levels, and the
final essay of part 1, "Development Education and Mass Media," by
James Gentry and Lillian Rae Dunlop, is included in the conviction

that this element of student education deserves critical engagement. Noting that the Western press often leaves its consumers with negative images of the Third World, Gentry and Dunlop investigate why news from the South is so intermittent and crisis oriented; reflect on varying cultural constructions of news and the global information order; and offer an extended and pedagogically stimulating discussion of classroom approaches to development news.

Conceived with the intention that faculty, irrespective of discipline or institution, will find pedagogical value here, this collection draws together experienced development educators with hard-won lessons from the field. A variety of perspectives, one goal: more and better development teaching.

NOTES

1. A fuller analysis of the controversy over multiculturalism and internationalization is precluded by limitations of space, and is at any rate rendered off-point by the instrumental approach argued below. For a fine discussion of some of the issues raised here, see Karamcheti and Lemert, "From Silence to Silence: Political Correctness and Multiculturalism," in *Liberal Education*, 77:4, September/October 1991, pp. 14–18.

2. See, for example, the remarks of Eugene D. Genovese and Elizabeth Fox-Genovese, quoted and discussed in William Reddy, *Money and Liberty in Modern Europe* (Cambridge: Cambridge University Press, 1987), p. 52.

3. David Korten, *Getting to the 21st Century: Voluntary Action and the Global Agenda* (West Hartford, CT: Kumarian Press, 1990), p. 5.

4. See *Ideas & Information*, nos. 16 and 18–20, for perspectives on the transformation debate. See also Betty Reardon's contribution to Daniel Thomas and Michael Klare (eds.), *Peace and World Security Studies: A Curriculum Guide*, 5th edition (Boulder, CO: Westview Press, 1989); Elise Boulding, *Building a Global Civic Culture: Education for an Interdependent World* (New York: Teacher's College Press, 1988); and Gerald L. Gutek, *American Education in a Global Society: Internationalizing Teacher Education* (New York: Longman, 1993), especially chapter 2 for an enormously sensible discussion of the debate.

5. Educators may find that the sober synthesis to this debate advanced by Gutek (1993) is an effective model for presenting the problem in the classroom.

SOURCES

Boulding, Elise. *Building a Global Civic Culture: Education for an Interdependent World*. New York: Teacher's College Press, 1988.

"Controversy Erupts Over Cautionary Note." *Ideas and Information about Development Education*. 20: Summer 1991.

"An Editorial Cautionary Note." *Ideas and Information About Development Education*. 19: Spring 1991.

Gutek, Gerald L. *American Education in a Global Society: Internationalizing Teacher Education*. New York: Longman, 1993.

"An Interview with Carroll Joy." *Ideas and Information about Development Education*. 16: Summer 1990, p.8.

Korten, David C. *Getting to the 21st Century: Voluntary Action and the Global Agenda*. West Hartford, CT: Kumarian Press, 1990.

_____. "Development as Transformation: The Agenda." *Ideas and Information*. 18: Winter 1991, p 6.

Liberal Education. 77:3, May/June 1991. Special Issue on Multiculturalism in the Curriculum.

Liberal Education. 77:5, November/December 1991. Special Issue on International Education.

"A Mandate for Change: Hunger and Curriculum Development." *Hunger TeachNet*. 3:4, June 1992.

Thomas, Daniel C., and Micahel Klare, eds. *Peace and World Security Studies: A Curriculum Guide*. 5th edition. Boulder, CO: Westview Press, 1989.

Ethics and Development: Costly Choices

STEPHEN K. COMMINS

In a West African village, a committee has been formed to guide the planning of an irrigation system for the community's farm land. The purpose of the new water system would be to provide a more secure agriculture base for each farming cycle. When the irrigation program was discussed at the community meeting, it was received with widespread approval by those present at the meeting. After further meetings, however, two sources of opposition to the plan emerged from groups not involved in the initial planning: fishermen and pastoralists. Their objections came from the belief that they would be economically hurt by the loss of water from the river normally available for fishing and the watering of animals. If their concerns are not included in the planning process, they are threatening to create disturbances to block the irrigation system. . . .

The government of a West African country is facing a deadline on accepting a proposed structural adjustment program supported by the World Bank in coordination with the International Monetary Fund and bilateral donors. An agreement on the program would mean that the country will be able to reschedule its debt obligations, receive a fresh infusion of aid from several developed countries, and be eligible for a new, low-interest adjustment loan from the World Bank. There is, however, a price to be exacted in the form of economic shocks which will include increased unemployment through the dismissal of government workers, the devaluation of the country's currency, and the drastic reduction in funds available for health and educational programs. Diverse organizations, ranging from unions to grassroots urban groups, have raised the threat of mass protests if the agreement is signed. . . .

13

Introduction

The 1992 United Nations Conference on Environment and Development, the "Earth Summit," brought together thousands of official delegates and interested observers to debate proposals and alternatives for alleviating poverty and addressing problems of environmental degradation. While Rio de Janeiro prepared for its international visitors, street children by the thousands were swept off the streets and hauled out of the city. This made the locale more acceptable for visitors, but what does it say about the value of these children? Is development for international conferences or for the needs of the poor? The simple act of removing street children from sight is a stark, painful reminder that development is not just about numbers, it is about people and values. This essay attempts to link the question of ethics with the practice of development, to identify some of the issues that render complex the apparently simple ethical imperative to foster economic justice, and to provide resources on development and ethics for educators.

Two types of ethical questions frame the discussion to follow: first, What is good development? and second, How can we make informed choices between various costs and benefits in development work? Obviously, there are other ethical questions which could be fruitfully explored. One is whether alleviating hunger should be a priority of governments and international organizations, and how high that priority should be compared to other needs. Another is to explore the ethical premises of different economic models that have dominated development approaches. These issues will not be directly tackled here but will be implicitly addressed as underlying questions.

During the 1990s, the complexities of a multipolar global political economy will make the process of choice in development more difficult. What one observer has called the "Leninist extinction" has shifted the world's axis from East-West to North-South. In a rapidly changing and increasingly interdependent global environment, the decisions made about international development policies and programs become ever more urgent. These choices reflect implicit and explicit values, which are often obscured from planning processes. Further, development policies, programs and projects all have costs (sometimes hidden) as well as benefits for individuals and social groups. When considering the wider context of development decision making, students—and teachers—must be aware that the process includes not only verifiable information, but contingency, uncertainty and the choice between divergent values.

The simple ethical imperative in development is that it should be done, that hunger and poverty must be alleviated. The complex, pedagogically fruitful questions revolve around *how*, not *whether*, to alleviate poverty. It is in choosing which trade-offs to make, and which costs to bear, that ethics play a role beyond a more general question of whether to alleviate poverty. This essay argues that in identifying ethical issues that occur within fluid systems of political, economic and environmental relations, and in suggesting ways of approaching the ethical dilemmas that arise, teachers can integrate an ethical dimension into all varieties of development education and leave their students better equipped in their thinking about hunger and poverty.

Ethics and Development

Pedagogical Approaches

Students are often introduced to the ethical or moral dimensions of world hunger and poverty in terms of the responsibility of those with resources toward those who are less fortunate. Or, students explore the need for a just redressing of the imbalance between the "rich" and the "poor." In contrast, the ethical questions reviewed in this chapter do not consider whether something should be done about global poverty. Rather, this essay presumes that presenting ethical issues in the *practice* of development can broaden understanding by enabling students to surface their hidden assumptions or mental models, and also provide them with a systemic and dynamic framework for interpreting development issues.

As students begin to consider ethical issues that arise in development practice, they also can take the opportunity to examine and question their own perspectives and premises. What one colleague has called the "primacy of perspective" is a good beginning point for working with students in ethical reflections. Their mental models, as frameworks for interpretation, will significantly affect how they view a particular situation and what type of ethical questions they are likely to consider. Thus, if population growth is viewed as the primary problem to be addressed, this will shape priorities in one direction. Conversely, if environmental degradation, or land tenure relations, or the need for free markets, or (now more rarely) the need to nationalize industries are the most important issues, then different decisions are likely to emerge. In examining the ethical issues raised by development decisions, students come to grips with their own unvoiced assumptions.

Along with surfacing mental models, an ethical approach to the *practice* of development can help students perceive the process from a systemic and dynamic perspective. One difficulty in understanding any particular development situation is that the observer's image is most often a quick snapshot that misses as much as or more than it reveals. This static vision serves as a poor and usually misleading substitute for a web of relationships and historical factors, so that the observer is placed in a position rather like trying to interpret the whole of *War and Peace* after reading just two brief passages. For the practitioner, or the student, to understand development processes and to grapple with ethical questions in a thorough rather than superficial way, a "systems-thinking" perspective is essential. Often, development and environment problems are interpreted in a linear, short-term cause and effect fashion. This has a number of unfortunate consequences:

1. The underlying causes of a particular problem or context are either not understood or misunderstood;
2. The choices made regarding the best ways for improving lives of people in specific situations are sometimes the wrong choices, due to consequent misinterpretations;
3. The development programs that emerge from linear interpretations do not work and may even reinforce the negative socioeconomic and environmental patterns.

The lack of a systems approach often means that important costs will be overlooked or underestimated, and that the impact of a program or policy will not be clearly understood. It is a rare instance when there is a simple, free-standing solution to a development problem. Integrating a systems approach with ethical reflection can illuminate development issues and provide a clearer basis for understanding the underlying relations that make hunger and poverty seem irremediable.

What Role for Ethics?

The relative paucity of literature on ethical aspects of development challenges the teacher to use available resources creatively. For if development ethics is a field that has not had wide visibility, its importance is nonetheless broader than is often presumed. Ethics can help provide the criteria for making difficult decisions and determining clearly the costs incurred. The task for ethics in development education is to engage students in addressing hard choices—in confronting practical issues and not just abstract goals.

As ethical reflection leaves the high ground for the messy work of development, the student will be asked to surface mental models and to question simple linear thinking. Even when development *goals* become clear, ethical reflection must continue to address the inevitable conflicts between individuals and communities over particular policies and programs. Communities are not harmonious gatherings of noble peasants or unspoiled, pre-industrial cultures. Internal tensions within communities, as noted in the opening vignette on the West African village, must be factors in decision making and cost-benefit analyses. In this way, ethical reflection can help students work through the basic questions facing development practitioners:

> What is good development in *this* situation?
> How and on what basis should decisions be made?
> What are the highest priorities?

Constructing this development ethics involves four tasks:

1. the elaboration of a consciously critical position as to the goals of development;
2. the analysis of development processes from the inside and the "isolation" of the values and countervalues latent in those processes;
3. the preparation of guidelines for different sectors of behavior whose importance to development processes is critical: normative strategies in a variety of domains;
4. and, most importantly, the development of a coherent theoretical framework in which partial and fragmentary ethical constraints can be unified around a few central and interrelated analytical concepts. (Goulet, 12)

Ethics in Practice

A basic role for ethics is to help people decide how to act in a given situation. A traditional interpretation of ethics is that it can help in determining or identifying "What is the good?" This becomes much more difficult in the practice of development, as there may be competing goals or competing goods. A deceptively simple question can also help the process of ethical reflection:

What are the signs of good development?

This is a question that provokes thinking about values as well as practical outcomes. Answers will vary widely depending upon the mental models or the prime perspective that individuals or organizations bring to the question. Some may say that good development is primarily found in modernization, improved technology and cultural change. Others may highlight equity and the reform of unjust political or economic systems. The demise of the Eastern bloc has raised the banner of the market, along with its related values of efficiency and reduced role for the state. The Earth Summit highlighted the problems of the environment and, perhaps, the impossibility for economic security or improvement without preserving and regenerating environments. More recent attention has been given to the building of local capacities for sustainable development, what Chambers has called capability, equity and sustainability. A concomitant goal is democratization when this is understood as more than the ballot box—when it comprises institutions that represent and serve the needs of the poor. In the end, perhaps there is no single answer but, rather, many questions that can frame the search for the "good" in "good development":

> Who is involved in the decision making?
> Who is benefiting?
> Who is losing?
> What are the short- and long-term costs involved?
> What is happening to the least and the last?
> What are the changes in gender relations?
> What is the impact on the environment for the future?
> Who is bearing the costs?
> What is the impact on the local or national polity?
> Who will benefit in three or five years?
> In ten or twenty?
> What organizations exist to sustain any gains for the poor?

Thorny questions are often more helpful than quick answers. Any discussion of development and ethics is likely to founder on a shoal of abstractions or easy answers unless issues are concretized. The following situations neither limit the purview of ethical decision making nor constitute a complete review of areas of action. The intent is to move consideration of ethics out of the theoretical and into the practical, where, as Berger noted, the pyramids of sacrifice are ever ready to claim more victims of seemingly good intentions.

Practical Problems

What follows is a selection of practical issues and problems in contemporary development. These cases also represent pedagogical opportunities: in guiding students through such specific issues (and many others), teachers can move beyond a narrow definition of ethics to introduce into the classroom a wider set of ethical questions.

Environment and Development: Goals in Conflict?

A good place to start looking at costs and choices is with the concept "sustainable development," which has gained wide currency in development organizations over the past few years. As with many other well-intentioned visions of a better world, the ideal in practice raises many complications. The basic premise of sustainable development is that the needs of the present generation should be met without compromising the ability of future generations also to meet their needs in turn. This vision holds that resolving poverty should go together with preserving or regenerating the environment. In practice, the goal of sustainable development is difficult indeed, both at community and international levels.

One problem is in terms of priorities for sustainability and development. The 1992 Earth Summit highlighted the differences in perspective between North and South, as well as between national governments and grassroots or Non-Governmental Organizations. For the developed countries, the Earth Summit was about the environment, and not a place to consider international economic and trade relations, debt, aid levels, or the role of transnational corporations. Developing nations in turn were unhappy with the exclusion of economic issues and the emphasis on global warming and other problems that carried an implicit message that they would never be permitted to develop along the lines of earlier models.

Many important questions were skirted, most pointedly population growth and consumption patterns. The Earth Summit was unable to broach the question of how high population growth rates in the South can be balanced with meeting human needs in the context of finite resources. Nor was it possible to question seriously the United States and, to a lesser extent, Japan and the EEC countries on how the wasteful consumption patterns of developed countries could be fundamentally changed. Beyond either North or South, there were Non-Governmental Organizations (NGOs) present that questioned the capacity of existing nation-states to resolve the world's development and environment problems. The NGOs wondered whether the governments as represented could make the changes necessary for sustainable development, because their own internal operations were so divided. As one observer noted: "The chief problem with an integrated approach to development is that all governments, to one degree or another, speak with forked tongues."

Sustainable development remains a goal with unanswered questions: Can governments make the changes necessary in their structures and operations? Is international cooperation possible on the issues raised at the Earth Summit? Is it possible to deal with population growth *rates* at any global forum that invites a cohesive, rather than fragmentary, response?

The Haiti Embargo

The election of Father Jean-Bertrand Aristide as president of Haiti in early 1991 was taken as a sign of hope for Haiti's poor. Haiti is the poorest country in the Western Hemisphere, and it has long been ruled by cruel tyrants and a corrupt security force. Aristide's election was hailed outside of Haiti by its neighbors, many of whom were embarking on new experiments with electoral democracy, as a sign of hope and possibility for a better future. When the Haitian military overthrew President Aristide in September 1991, its actions were met with nearly universal condemnation by other governments. In order to force the military to return power to President Aristide rather than to civilian allies, the Organization of American States approved an embargo aimed at bringing about the requisite political changes. The results of the embargo, however, did not squeeze the elite, but instead brought disaster to the poor.

The ironic and tragic result of the embargo has been to enrich the elite who have been able to control the black market for smuggled goods. Meanwhile, prices of virtually every commodity that the country imports leaped after the beginning of the embargo. Fuel prices rose to over 7 dollars per gallon, while the price of rice nearly doubled. The rise in transportation costs meant that farmers were forced to sell their fresh produce only at local markets, where there were very low prices due to the flood of goods that could not be shipped to the cities. Some farmers had to watch their crops rot, leading to an erosion of their savings.

The embargo cut medical supplies and other basic necessities. Unemployment has risen and food shortages have increased. Without employment or opportunities to sell foodstuffs, the people have been forced to cut down trees for the production of charcoal. This had led to increased deforestation in a country already suffering from a long history of denuded hills and soil loss. NGOs have watched in great sadness as the work of years of forestry programs has been lost while desperately poor families cut through reforested areas.

What were the alternatives for the OAS? What limited the response to action that resulted in greater poverty and suffering? How has Haiti's history and economic structure shaped the ways in which the embargo has affected the country? How has the historic role of the United States in the Caribbean constrained the types of response that might be made to the coup? How has the history of U.S. intervention affected the OAS actions?

Structural Adjustment

Since the early 1980s, the load of external debt carried by many African and Latin American countries has been a matter of major concern to both governments and development organizations. While the threat to international banks has given Latin American debt greater prominence, the debt of many African countries is greater as a percentage of their Gross National Product. Efforts to reduce African debt have been linked to the reform of African economies through a process called "structural adjustment."

Structural adjustment programs are designed to promote a long-term goal of making an economy efficient and able to compete effectively in the global economy. This means such changes as emphasizing agricultural production and improved prices for farmers, cutting government spending and subsidies, and reforming tax systems. In theory, the national economy becomes consequently more open to foreign investment and the climate improves for domestically owned businesses.

The goal of improved economic efficiency comes with a human cost. Deep cuts in government spending mean that civil servants are put out of work with few alternative jobs at any wage. Along with the civil servants, thousands of employees from state-owned industries are put out on the street. Subsidies for urban food consumers and health services are subject to reduction or elimination. Cuts in subsidies for education and public transportation will have a particularly negative impact on the standard of living of urban residents.

The high cost of structural adjustment—especially for the most vulnerable—has been recognized by the World Bank (belatedly, according to critics). Both Non-Governmental Organizations and UNICEF have documented the negative impact of structural adjustment programs on poor people in many countries. In recognition and response to this criticism, the World Bank has created programs for supporting social systems (health, education, nutrition) within a broader structural adjustment framework. Does this resolve the basic cost of structural adjustment? Are there alternatives that are based upon other premises than that of the Bank and the IMF that could also provide balance and then growth to the economies of poor countries?

Demographic Trap

The question of how population growth affects poverty has a long and controversial history dating from the writings of Thomas Malthus nearly two hundred years ago to the more recent works of Paul Ehrlich and Garret Hardin. On one side of the debate are those who argue that until population growth is curbed, all efforts at alleviating poverty are counterproductive because there are continually more mouths to feed. The critics of this view contend that only when poor people have economic security will they be willing to lower their family size.

A new voice has recently added intensity to this debate. Maurice King, a doctor with extensive experience in international health and development programs, wrote a starkly challenging paper entitled "Human Entrapment in India." In this paper, King argues that the "demographic trap" had closed, limiting any hope for the future in a number of regions, including Bangladesh, Pakistan, Kenya, Nigeria and perhaps parts of India. The argument holds that it is too late for these countries to overcome the imbalance between high population density, high population growth rates and high fertility on the one hand, and diminished environmental and economic capacity on the other. King goes on to argue that neither family service nor child survival agencies could address the demographic trap because it undermined their programmatic rationale.

In particular, he criticizes UNICEF for its unwillingness to accept the possibility that saving children's lives will not eventually lead to smaller families. King notes that if it is true that in some regions the lowering of the child death rate does not lead to lower birth rates, then there are inherent ethical conflicts that must be faced. He points especially to the conflicting values of equity, the greatest good for the greatest number, the sanctity of human life and the value of the individual child. He challenges UNICEF and other child-focused organizations to admit that saving lives today may create greater problem and suffering in the future.

King's paper raises difficult issues, particularly the direct challenge to the focus on child survival. The lack of success in the most intensive population control/family planning programs makes his challenge even more daunting. India and China, the countries with the largest populations in the world, have both attempted draconian programs of population control. Under Indira Gandhi in the 1970s, India mandated the forced sterilization of men who had two or more children. China has attempted to address its population pressures through a series of measures to encourage one-child families. This goal has been modified in recent years, but at its height one of the negative results was an increase in female infanticide, as many families preferred to have a boy if they were limited to one child.

The debate offers enormous potential to spark classroom debate: What is the right balance between child survival and family limits? What are the ethical costs of saving children now? Or not? Of sharply and forcibly restricting family size—Or not?

The Poor and the Poorest

Beginning in the 1970s, international development organizations gave increasing attention to the needs of those termed the "poorest of the poor." Robert McNamara, then president of the World Bank, highlighted this group by speaking of the burden of their absolute poverty. For a number of years, the World Bank and bilateral donors turned their attention to targeting the needs of the poorest sectors of developing countries. During the 1980s, policies and programs shifted to a wider framework of adjustment, economic efficiency and agricultural reform. Concern for the poorest remained an area of interest within the international development community, but it has also been an area fraught with difficulties.

Many development organizations, especially NGOs, include in their statements of purpose a goal of reaching the "poorest of the poor." This phrase is more than rhetorical flourish; it is partly rooted in the recognition that many benefits of traditional development progams went to middle-income groups or the better off among the poor.

But change often proves much more difficult in practice than in theory, and many well-intentioned development programs reach no further than the "accessible poor." In planning programs, many NGOs make choices about whether to serve communities that are relatively accessible to ports, cities, roads and other networks, or to reach out to more isolated groups. The commitment to reaching the "poorest" points to the more isolated, poorer communities, but the commitment to reaching more people at less cost would make the accessible communities a greater priority.

Should NGOs and others concentrate on providing their resources to people in the greatest need or to the most people in some need?

Tail Enders

Investment in irrigation systems has been a major part of development strategies in a number of Asian countries. The construction and utilization of irrigation systems may provide benefits for farmers who find themselves constrained by lack of an assured supply of water for their crops. Increased production and certain access to water may also promote investment in cropping systems and land improvement. From practical experience it is apparent, however, that there are also difficulties associated with irrigation systems, including saline deposits and siltation of water systems. The ecological problems have become widely known in recent years, but there is a very different type of problem with some irrigation projects that illustrates how unintended consequences create unintended winners and losers.

When an irrigation system in India is built with a main channel and controlled side channels, it can create problems for "tail enders." These are the farmers who are located at the end of the branch channels, whose farms often do not receive the amount of water necessary for their crops. In the system, the tail enders find that they do not receive as much water as their neighbors who are closer to the main

channel. This may occur because of poor controls on the water allocation, silting in the smaller channel, poor planning, or theft of water at
more accessible points of the canal.

The result is that tail enders are often forced to work secretly at
night, sneaking out to the canal sluice gate in order to let water into
their canal. This is difficult work; it costs them their sleep and forces
them to run the risk of stepping on snakes or disturbing their neighbors. They could also pay the canal gate operators to allow them more
water, but why should they be the ones to bear more of the cost? This
is a simple problem at one level, yet the number of tail enders who
exist at the end of canals, roads, health systems and the like is large.
How can projects and programs be designed at the start to take into
account this systemic problem?

Non-Governmental Organizations

An increasing disillusionment with the politics and apparently poor
results of official foreign aid programs has led to a focus on Non-Governmental Organizations (NGOs). NGOs are said to be more closely
in touch with local communities, more flexible in their programs and
projects, less bureaucratic in their management, and more open to the
participation of poor people in the planning and implementation of
development efforts. They are often idealized by observers in the
United States, who see them as development providers preferable to
either bilateral or multilateral aid.

Yet there are many difficulties with NGOs and their operations that
indicate that their situation is far more complex and occasionally problematic. NGOs are very diverse in size, organizational structure, goals
and their particular understanding of development work. They have
different funding systems, a wide spectrum of willingness to address
political or economic questions, and significant differences in how
they relate to counterparts in low-income countries. Some important
issues can emerge from looking at the actual operations of NGOs, as
these organizations have increasingly moved into the international
spotlight as favored development agencies.

NGOs raise money from either public or private donors. Fund raising is a significant constraint on NGOs, because they are dependent
on the interests held by donors or messages that they use to encourage
donors to give. The line between encouraging giving and marketing
poverty is a thin one, and more than once NGOs have been guilty of

"famine pornography": a message that demeans and exploits the suffering of others in order to raise money. One way in which NGOs have sought to overcome the charge of paternalism is through development of partnerships with organizations based in developing countries. The difficulty that emerges in these relationships is quite simple: Who makes the final decisions on projects and accountability? Where does the power really reside?

Another difficult area for NGOs concerns the violation of human rights by governments where the NGO or its partners operate. If a government is killing or torturing its citizens, should the NGO protest? If it does, what will happen to its ability to operate in that country? What will happen to indigenous organizations that receive money from that NGO? With the pressure from the bottom up for the democratization of many countries, what can NGOs do to support this opening without being thrown out of a country? Or should they care that they might be thrown out for the right reasons? Is it better to stand on principle and lose the capacity to promote economic justice? Or to continue development work but compromise on principle—and perhaps tacitly sanction abuse?

Bias of Bureaucracy

An area that is often overlooked in the consideration of development ethics has to do with the priorities and constraints that exist *within* any development organization. This is as true for a small Non-Governmental Organization as it is for the World Bank or the U.S. Agency for International Development. All organizations have operational rationales, both explicit and implicit; and all organizations have limits on how far staff can move beyond the scope provided by boards, donors, management policies and others in the chain of command.

Furthermore, no matter how grassroots and flexible an organization claims to be, it is still in the "helping" business with some bureaucracy to satisfy. This is a fundamental dilemma facing development practitioners, no matter what their institutional affiliation. How can they break free both of their own systems and of their own biases to put the needs of the poor first?

One of the most widely used terms in international development today is "participation." This implies allowing the active involvement in planning and even in decision making by poor people themselves. In practice, participation runs against the grain of most organizational systems, as well as against inherent professional biases (however subtle) of development workers. As one commentator has noted:

> In the real world, the "haves" like to see themselves as beneficent and have others see the world the same way in which they do. Academics, government planners and officials, development consultants, and specialists involved in the business of development all claim to be working to improve the lot of the Third World masses. Yet the masses are rarely consulted about their needs and aspirations or queried about ways they think that one should go about the development process. (Gellar)

Robert Chambers has written powerfully about the need for reversals, for development professionals to "put the last first" in their thinking and in their practice. It is only through a fundamental shift in development biases that the ethical issues raised in this paper will become central to development decision making in the future.

Seeing What Best to Do

The complexities of development decisions necessitate finding approaches which make it more likely that poor people and communities will have some voice and influence in decisions affecting their lives. There are no simple formulas that resolve the conflicts between communities, classes, castes or gender groups. Nor is there any quick way to make it possible for a well-intentioned government or donor agency to determine the choice that benefits the most people with the fewest "losers." There are processes, which often demand more time and compromise, that may make it possible to lessen costs and increase benefits in efforts aimed at alleviating hunger and poverty. These processes themselves carry values, including a concern for the poor and the least, an appreciation of the time that it takes for "good" development, and an affirmation of the human over the technical.

This section is intended to provide teachers and students with the opportunity to identify ways in which potentially effective approaches have emerged for addressing development problems. It includes both some brief examples of alternative paths and two processes for making choices in development practice. The processes cannot be abstracted from the broader issues identified in this chapter, but they can be useful tools for seminar work or research projects that link specific problems with these exercises.

Participation and Structural Adjustment

During the 1990s, the pressure for reduction of debt burdens and financial imbalances will continue to place on some governments the necessity of seeking external financing for different types of adjustment efforts. When structural adjustment programs are designed and implemented, it is essential to go beyond the social amelioration targets that seek to buffer the pain of adjustment. The full social cost to the losers of adjustment programs must be identified by local NGOs and partner agencies, so that the potential options are clearly weighed and understood.

Structural adjustment programs need to have more than a narrow set of fiscal goals. The involvement of different affected groups can help create alternative models for structural adjustment. At the same time, grassroots groups in low-income countries can work in partnership with NGOs in the North for the reduction of debt through forgiveness by creditors. The harsh truth is that a number of countries have had their debts forgiven or reduced when it was politically favorable to do so. The participatory process can allow for the linking of organizations that have seen the price of adjustment on the poor, and that can challenge donors to act through more sensitive and sensible programs.

Democratization

Alan Fowler has identified the process of democratization as an area where NGOs can have a significant impact in the future shape of Southern politics and economic development goals. NGOs, through their work at the community level, can cooperate in strengthening the building blocks of civil society. Democracy is far more than access to the ballot box: it involves participation in decision making, civil and political rights, freedom from violence and torture, and some form of open access to the poor. Given the tremendous poverty and hunger in many developing countries, it also means the accountability of national and international development programs to the intended beneficiaries.

Involvement in democratization processes carries risks for both local and international NGOs. Building up the capacity of communities to articulate their goals is conflictive, both within the community and with governmental authorities. It is not a venture to be undertaken lightly or naively. Such efforts will be most effective when they stem from a wider vision of development and a thorough understanding of the need for leaving behind something more than a well or a health care clinic. It will come from a sense that one of the questions to be answered in good development is this: Do poor people have more power, capability and sustained resources for change than they did before?

Participatory Rural Appraisal

A new approach to working with low-income communities is called Rapid or Participatory Rural Appraisal. This approach is based on a recognition that rural communities are far from static—rather, they are linked to wider networks of increasingly rapid change. Organizations must therefore gather insight and information swiftly, sensitively and cost-effectively if they are to operate in such rural environments. This model holds that outsiders should learn from the community first, rather than coming in with their prepackaged answers.

The RRA/PRA activity is first to determine who needs to be heard in a community, valuing the views of poorer men, women or the landless. PRA occurs in a listening place where there is time for the participants to discuss, debate, probe and evaluate the description being made of their community. A PRA group can use a wall, a floor, or the ground itself to draw maps that describe their community: its rainfall by season, crop growing patterns, the river's depth, land tenure, income and debt cycles, death and mortality patterns. These maps will be discussed, haggled over and refined. The end result is a picture of the community which, while far from perfected, provides a valuable starting place for answering the question: How do poor people describe their lives, their community and their priorities?

PRA allows outsiders to listen and learn first, before producing the great plans and visions for improved livelihoods. Through the use of interviews, walking around the community with the less powerful people, through mapping and through meeting with groups, PRA provides for a fundamental reversal: learning from the least. A fundamental end result, and a key basis for decision making, comes from understanding how the poor themselves see their community, and what they believe are the criteria for their well being.

All of this can repay analysis in the classroom. New approaches in the field demonstrate the diversity and complexity of rural community life in the South and highlight the notion that all benefits exact their price. In the process of exploring this approach, students will come to realize that Southern communities are not monolithic, that development is not a simple, linear process, and that development ethics consists of confronting—and making—costly choices.

Conclusion

There are no quick fixes or easy roads to alleviating hunger and poverty. Policies and projects cannot be created and implemented in a political-economic, historic and environmental vacuum. The factors that create and sustain poverty and hunger are complicated, situation specific, and call for regular questioning of the basic premises of development work.

Such basic questioning is perhaps the single most important ethical component of the development process. Without an ability to ask hard questions, *especially* about one's own views, it is likely that little will change or be accomplished. One of my brightest colleagues commented that after over a decade of international development work, the answers were fewer, the questions better.

Sometimes the questions are simple, the answers hard. It is grappling with both the questions and answers that provide the learning for a better-fed, more secure future.

> "Me father died of starvation in the black '47. Maybe you've heard of it?"
> "The Famine?"
> "No, the starvation. When a country is full o' food and exporting it, there can be no famine. Me father starved dead; and I was starved out to America in me mother's arms."

The ethics of development become especially visible when the complete breakdown of social, political and economic systems lead to famine. Famines, however, are not "natural" events, they are the result of a complex set of issues, many of which are development issues having little do with rainfall or climate. When the last and the least have value, famines can be prevented. When the last and the least are put first, then the ethics of good development become clearest, and the answers to the hard questions of poverty and environment are nearest.

SOURCES

Bass, *Camping with the Prince and Other Tales of Science in Africa*. Boston: Houghton Mifflin, 1990.

Berger, Peter. *Pyramids of Sacrifice*. Garden City: Anchor Press/Doubleday, 1974.

Chambers, Robert. *Rural Development, Putting the Last First*. New York: Longman, 1984.

Elliott, Charles. *Comfortable Compassion*. New York: Paulist Press, 1987.

Fowler, Alan. "Non-Governmental Organisations as Agents of Democratization: An African Perspective." *Journal of International Development*, forthcoming 1993.

Friedmann, John. *Empowerment*. Cambridge: Blackwell Publishers, 1992.

Gellar, Sheldon. "The Ratched-McMurphy Model: A Critique of Participatory Development Models, Strategies and Projects." African Studies Association meetings, December 1983.

Goulet, Denis. *The Cruel Choice*. New York: Atheneum, 1971.

King, Maurice. "Health Is a Sustainable State." *The Lancet*, 366/8716, September 15, 1990.

Lipton, Michael. *Why Poor People Stay Poor*. Cambridge: Harvard University Press, 1976.

Scott, James. *Weapons of the Weak: Everyday Forms of Peasant Resistance*. New Haven: Yale University Press, 1985.

Sen, Amartya. *Poverty and Famines*. New York: Oxford University Press, 1981.

Senge, Peter. *The Fifth Discipline: The Art and Practice of the Learning Organization*. New York: Doubleday, 1990.

Are There Still Competing Paradigms of Development?

JAMES H. WEAVER

Introduction

A little over a decade ago, Kenneth Jameson and I published a book entitled *Economic Development: Competing Paradigms*, and in 1989 I co-authored a related article on "Competing Paradigms of Development."[1] The book and article laid out the traditional, orthodox, neoclassical or capitalist paradigm of development, spelling out three versions of that model—Smithian, Malthusian, and Keynesian—and outlining development strategies that had emerged within that paradigm. The radical political economy paradigm was presented in two versions: dependency theory and neo-Marxism were considered along with different socialist development strategies. When I was asked to write the present essay, I asked myself, Are there still competing paradigms of development?

In a word—No. There is really only one paradigm of development today. The orthodox paradigm has won. Socialism has failed in all of its different forms—in the Soviet Union, in Tanzania, in India. China still has many of the trappings of a socialist economy but has introduced numerous market mechanisms into the system. And so, although it may be painful for those of us on the left to admit it, we must be honest before the facts. Very few people study Marxism today to try to figure out how to develop. And not many people look on the former Soviet Union or China as models of a good society.

This is not to say that the capitalist paradigm and the strategies it has generated have produced good societies. Far from it. But today's debate involves only advocates of different development strategies *within* the capitalist paradigm.

There does seem to be widespread agreement concerning the goals of development, namely broad based sustainable development (BBSD).

33

And there is an emerging strategy that tries to modify the capitalist system to overcome some of its worst flaws—a strategy I call "capitalism with a human face."

This essay examines the capitalist paradigm from a variety of perspectives. I present the traditional capitalist paradigm in its Smithian, Malthusian and Keynesian variants; discuss three capitalist development strategies; explore capitalism with a human face; give the radical critique of the capitalist paradigm; examine some empirical evidence for the orthodox prescription; and draw a few conclusions.

The Traditional Capitalist Paradigm

What is a paradigm of development? Thomas Kuhn[2] introduced the concept of a "paradigm" as a comprehensive worldview shared by a group working on or thinking about a particular topic. A paradigm of development responds to four key questions:

1. What are the value assumptions about human nature, the good life, and the good society?
2. What are the goals of development and what measures do we use to tell whether or not these goals are being achieved?
3. What is the general methodology? This includes a theory of development as well as particular tools for analysis of developing countries.
4. What strategies are suggested for attacking the problem of economic development? Here worldview becomes a guide for action, engaging key institutions and public policies.

The conventional capitalist paradigm includes three versions: 1) the free market approach of Adam Smith, 2) the pessimistic assessment of Thomas Malthus, and 3) the government regulation approach of John Maynard Keynes. This paradigm dominates thinking in the United States, and its assumptions are familiar to Americans.

Assumptions

These models assume that human beings are rational, with each person knowing his or her own self-interest and acting individually in such a fashion as best to attain that self-interest. People are assumed to be hedonistic, maximizing pleasure by the consumption of material goods, and minimizing pain, including labor.

The good life, therefore, is one which enables the individual to maximize consumption and minimize labor. To achieve this, the good society should guarantee consumer sovereignty (so that individual preferences determine what is produced); efficiency (maximum output with given inputs); and stability (to avoid runaway inflation and depression).

Evolution of Development Goals and Measures of Success

The goals of development have changed over time. The 1950s sought maximum growth of gross national product per capita. Countries were classified as developed or underdeveloped (the term in use at the time) according to their per capita income. The growth rate of per capita income was the measure of how successful countries were in achieving development.

In the 1960s, an additional goal was added: structural transformation of the economy to ensure continued growth. This involved moving from an agricultural- to an industrial- to a service-based economy. It also involved moving from low productivity and uneducated labor to high productivity and educated labor, from animate to inanimate energy, and from primary to manufactured exports.

Today we combine these first two goals into a new formulation. Development requires a healthy, growing economy undergoing a structural transformation. A healthy economy requires relatively stable prices, relatively full employment of labor and capital, and external equilibrium (a sustainable balance of payments).

In the 1970s, we became concerned because poverty did not seem to decline in many countries despite rapid economic growth. So a third dimension was added to the development equation: the wide distribution of benefits to promote human development, reflected by increasing literacy and life expectancy.

The 1980s saw new concern for political development. It was argued that economic growth that benefits everyone requires a healthy civil society—intermediate institutions between the individual and the state such as unions, chambers of commerce, tenant groups and

women's groups. Further considerations included respect for human
and civil rights. Finally, effective governance, including protection of
private property, the rule of law, and open rule making, became a prerequisite of development.

The 1990s introduced a new element. If development is to be sustainable, it must be consistent with the preservation and conservation of the
environment. Various measures of environmental sustainability have
been developed, including emissions of pollutants and deforestation.

Thus, the 1990s development goal of "broad based sustainable
development" comprises each of the four aspects outlined above.

Methodology

Two assumptions underlie the conventional capitalist approach:
human wants are insatiable; and resources (such as land, oil and min-
erals), finite or fixed. The result of unlimited wants and limited
resources is scarcity, which is *the* economic problem.

While no system can fully resolve the problem of scarcity, it is
argued that capitalist institutions are the most effective at maximizing
output through the efficient use of the factors of production. This
includes the improved use of labor, through specialization and division
of labor; the creation of capital, which is central to improving worker
productivity; the effective use of land and other natural resources; the
fostering of technology, which revolutionizes not only tools but also
organizations and knowledge; and the encouragement of entrepreneurship, which is essential not only for innovation and capital formation
but also as a "want creator," creating demand for new products.

Institutions of the Capitalist Economy

There are four crucial institutions necessary for the capitalist economy to achieve development: (1) private ownership of the means of
production; (2) markets for the factors of production (land, labor and
capital); (3) the capitalist firm, organized so as to maximize profits; and
(4) markets for goods and services.

If these institutions exist, what is the role of government in encouraging development? While all those adopting the conventional capitalist paradigm embrace the above vision, there is profound disagreement on the question of the role of government—dissent articulated
most clearly in the Smithian, Malthusian and Keynesian models.

The Smithian or Free Market Approach

What should governments do to facilitate capitalist development? Adam Smith provided the answer in 1776—laissez-faire.[3] The government should do very little, for the actions of private individuals, following their own self-interest, will bring about development, guided by the "invisible hand" of competition. This does not mean that government is to do nothing, for it has several definite roles. According to Smith, development requires two things: the acquisitive spirit and domestic tranquility. The first requirement was satisfied by the assumption that all people are rational economic beings, motivated to consume. The second requirement was satisfied by "law and order," or the protection of the key capitalist institution of private property. As Smith noted, one of the main functions of government is "for the defence of the rich against the poor, or of those who have some property against those who have none at all."[4]

Another proper function of government is to enforce private contracts. If people enter into a contract, they must live up to it. By enforcing private contracts, the government protects the world of commerce from mere force and fraud, and ensures that markets do indeed function so that market transactions can be carried out.

In addition, the government has certain other roles to play. It must provide those goods which society as a whole consumes but which a private firm could not produce and sell profitably to the individuals in society. The main such "public good" is national defense. There is no way to exclude from its benefits someone who does not pay, so firms cannot earn a profit by providing national defense. This must be done by the central government using powers of taxation to spread the cost.

Government must provide for a system of money and credit, whereby the people with entrepreneurial ability can get together with the people who have the money. Since entrepreneurial activity is central to development, government's proper role is to ensure that there is a money, credit and banking system which allows entrepreneurs to obtain the needed funds. Government must provide a stable money supply.

Finally, the government must establish a system to facilitate trade with other countries. International trade is a very important element in the traditional economic paradigm, for it expands the market so a firm or a country can specialize in producing those goods in which it is most efficient and sell those goods to the whole world. From this free trade, all parties will benefit.

There are many problems with laissez-faire capitalism. In fact, no developing country has opted for this strategy in the twentieth century except Hong Kong, and Hong Kong is a colony and did not choose the strategy for itself. Nevertheless, Hong Kong's economy has performed amazingly well. The country was open to foreign investment, followed an essentially free trade policy and experienced the most rapid rate of economic growth of any country in the world from the end of World War II until the 1990s.

The Pessimistic View of the Malthusians

Unlike the optimistic view of Adam Smith, Thomas Malthus sharply questioned the ability of industrial capitalism to deal with the fundamental economic problem of scarcity. His central argument was that the persistent and widespread poverty he saw around him in the nineteenth century was symptomatic of a larger problem: a world trapped in a losing race between a fixed supply of natural resources, and people, who, unlike natural resources, could (and did) multiply. The inevitable result, of course, was that the population would eventually exceed the world's carrying capacity, leading, in the absence of regulation, to "natural" checks such as pestilence, plague, famine, disease and war.

What, then, could be done to improve the prospects for world development? The Malthusian view holds little promise. The "rational self-interest" in the capitalist paradigm is accepted, but viewed in a very different light, leading individuals to pursue short-term, self-interested strategies which, if left unregulated, can be catastrophic for future generations. Most important, the prospects for increasing resources dramatically through new technology are considered to be illusory, creating as many problems as they solve.

It is very likely that further growth in the Third World along the path followed by the already rich nations will be catastrophic for the world's ecosystem, polluting the air, water and soils to intolerable levels, and enhancing the currently destructive trend towards global warming. In short, the good life, in material terms, is not and cannot be attainable for everyone; humankind is trapped in a highly conflictual world of haves and have nots, with little prospect for substantial reductions in poverty, and a real chance to damage the globe beyond repair.

Given this analysis, the Malthusian version of the good society now becomes one which attempts to take the hard and cruel choices essential to preserve the world as a whole. These choices would include policies to produce zero population growth and zero economic growth.[5]

The Keynesian/Government Regulation Approach

The Keynesian variant of the capitalist paradigm is much more optimistic about the productive potential of market capitalism, but suggests that the free market system, left on its own, has historically led to five serious problems. First, it has been prone to instability, leading to periodic economic crises, the most spectacular of which was the Great Depression in the 1930s which led to World War II, and to the even greater depression suffered by the countries of Africa and Latin America in the 1980s. Second, it has been exploitative. In a laissez-faire system, for example, capitalist firms employ women and children in factories for long hours at very low wages. Third, the market is unable to price accurately all of the "externalities," leading private investors to ignore some investments that would be socially productive and to engage in others that can bring many costs to the environment. Laissez-faire capitalism produces great inequalities of income and wealth. Finally, the system itself often tends towards monopoly, which destroys the checks and balances of the free market competition on which capitalism depends.

Keynesians see the solutions in using enlightened government regulation to reduce these problems in order to take advantage of capitalism's productive potential without its negative side effects. This approach has been extraordinarily influential in determining public policies since World War II. Virtually all the industrialized countries committed themselves to government regulation of the economy to promote employment, growth and purchasing power, to reduce income inequality, to regulate monopolies, to ban child labor and establish minimum wage and maximum hour laws, to establish systems of unemployment compensation, social security and welfare, and to control pollution. These economic systems have been called by various names, such as the welfare state, the mixed economy, or social democracy, but the policy fundamental to them all was a commitment to prevent the recurrence of another Great Depression through the use of government spending, taxation and control of the money supply.

At the same time, a new international economic system was created at Bretton Woods in 1944, which was a further extension of Keynes's ideas. The prewar gold standard was replaced by an institution designed to regulate the international monetary system, the International Monetary Fund (IMF). Capital movements were also regulated, in part by the International Bank for Reconstruction and Development (World Bank). International trade was to be regulated by the General Agreement on Tariffs and Trade (GATT).

With respect to the less-developed countries, a whole new school of economics was born out of Keynesianism after the Second World War—development economics. Development economics has been characterized by its rejection of laissez-faire, free trade policy for developing countries. Why? The disastrous experience, during the Great Depression, of capitalist countries following the laissez-faire policies; the impressive rate of industrialization achieved by the Soviet Union during the 1930s using central planning; and the conviction that the institutions necessary for market economies to operate were not present in developing countries.

Development economists equated development with industrialization and virtually ignored agricultural transformation. Convinced that laissez-faire and free trade would not produce development, they argued for government planning, a large role for government saving and investment, protection of domestic industry and greater foreign assistance.

Three Development Strategies

What practical strategies have been tried in developing countries following a capitalist path? I shall discuss three such strategies: state-led import substitution industrialization, state-led export-oriented industrialization, and growth with equity. The Soviet strategy, by now completely discredited, does not figure here.

State-Led Import Substitution Industrialization (ISI)

In the 1950s, development economists proposed a strategy for rapid industrialization based on domestic production of goods previously imported. This approach advocated the imposition of quotas and tariffs to keep foreign goods out and to protect infant industries. It also recommended the maintenance of overvalued or multiple exchange rates in order to encourage the importation of capital, intermediate goods and raw materials, while discouraging the importation of luxury and consumer goods. Governments were advised to control and allocate foreign exchange to crucial industries, as well as to provide them with special subsidies, such as low interest rates, cheap electricity, cheap building sites, and low tax rates. ISI advocates also argued that food prices should be kept low, so that wages would not rise and cut into profits, and that agriculture, particularly agricultural exports, should be heavily taxed so that the government could redirect that revenue into industrialization. Lastly, common markets and free trade areas were promoted to achieve economies of scale and foster rapid industrialization, despite small national markets.

As a result of the ISI approach, many less-developed countries experienced extraordinarily rapid economic growth in the 1950s and 1960s. Korea, Taiwan, Brazil, Mexico and Chile all had remarkable success following these policies. By the 1960s, however, the viability of ISI came under close scrutiny by orthodox economists. ISI was heavily criticized, particularly its application to smaller countries with economies too small to justify domestic production of all or most durable goods. In addition, Korea and Taiwan clearly moved away from ISI and into a second strategy of state-led, export-oriented industrialization. There is general agreement today that countries that have followed ISI policies exclusively have reached a dead end, in spite of an initial period of high growth.

State-Led Export-Oriented Industrialization

Japan pioneered the policy of state-led export-oriented industrialization. In the 1960s, numerous imitators appeared, most notably in East Asia: Korea, Taiwan and Singapore. The crucial elements of the export promotion approach were early and successful land reform, massive education programs to create human capital, and the promotion of labor-intensive export industries by a very activist state which had a relatively high level of autonomy from interest groups such as landowners, business and labor. According to this strategy, governments should guide and plan the economy, pick those industries to be favored, encourage exports with subsidized interest and foreign exchange rates, encourage cooperation among major firms and between those firms and the government, and educate and discipline workers to provide a productive, docile and low-wage labor force.

Countries following this strategy have experienced extraordinarily rapid rates of economic growth and quite equitable distribution of income because of the rapid growth of employment that was generated in the labor-intensive export industries. Korea went from an agriculturally-based to an industrialized country in one generation. Surely, this is the most rapid structural transformation in history.

Unfortunately, the export-oriented strategy is based on a logical fallacy. All countries cannot run a balance of trade surplus at the same time. Some countries must import more than they export. The U.S. has been a remarkably open market for the exports of the East Asian countries. However, it is becoming less open and it is not clear that lesser developed countries (LDCs) can develop trading links with each other.

Growth with Equity

Advocates of this 1970s strategy emphasized the failure of previous strategies, despite rapid economic growth, to ensure that people in developing countries had access to jobs, food, shelter, housing, health care and education. Thus, this strategy emphasized various ways the government could directly provide citizens with access to these basic necessities. Emphasis was placed on agricultural and rural development, on employment generation, redistribution with growth, and the need for a new international economic order.

Sri Lanka is usually cited as the best example of a country following a growth with equity strategy. Remarkable results were obtained in life expectancy, literacy, infant mortality and other indicators of human development. However, economic growth was not sufficient to generate the government revenue to support such programs, and, by the late 1970s, the strategy in Sri Lanka had changed dramatically.

The Decline of Development Economics

Whereas the birth of development economics in the post–World War II period was based on the belief that developing economies did not have viable markets and that government planning and state-owned enterprises could promote rapid and equitable growth, development thinking in the 1980s emphasized the efficiency of the market and pointed to the many failures of government intervention.[6] Earlier development economists were derided for having ignored the necessity for agricultural transformation before industrialization.

International financial institutions (particularly the World Bank), academics and development practitioners in the 1980s espoused a return to market-oriented, free trade policies in order to promote development. The strategy came to be called structural adjustment.

Exactly what did this return to laissez-faire mean? It meant that governments should limit their activities to those that governments alone can perform. Governments should provide those public goods that the private sector will not provide and that are necessary for a market economy to function. Such public goods include national defense, protection of persons and property, enforcement of contracts, making and enforcing the rules of the game, a sound system of money and credit, some public works, agricultural research, and financing (although not necessarily provision) of public health and public education.

By the mid 1980s, it was clear that the rush to laissez-faire capitalism had not been successful. The poor in developing countries were experiencing tremendous hardships from the world depression of the early 1980s and structural adjustment programs were not ameliorating the problem. Economic growth never resumed in Latin America and Sub-Saharan Africa during the 1980s.

By the 1990s, developed countries had several severely flawed development strategies from which to choose. Laissez-faire, free trade, the Soviet strategy, state-led import substitution industrialization, state-led export-oriented industrialization, growth with equity, and structural adjustment all had serious weaknesses. It was clear a different strategy was needed. Such a new strategy is now developing, which I call "capitalism with a human face."

Capitalism with a Human Face

A remarkable convergence has taken place in the thinking of development practitioners concerning the appropriate policies for developing countries. Theoreticians and policymakers from the left and the right agree that many strategies followed to date have generally led neither to rapid economic growth nor to equity. The explanations for this failure focus largely on the role that governments have played in both internal and external policies.

In looking at the generalized failures of government, three spheres of activity merit particular scrutiny: the informal sector, the formal sector, and the rest of the world (see table 1).

The informal sector consists of those economic actors who do not have access to foreign exchange or subsidized credit from the government and are not subject to governmental regulation or taxation. It includes subsistence and small-scale farmers (especially food crop

Table 1

Three Spheres of Activity:
The Informal Sector, the Formal Sector and the Rest of the World

INFORMAL SECTOR	GOVERNMENT BARRIERS TO ENTRY INTO FORMAL SECTOR
AGRICULTURAL-RURAL AREAS: Landless workers, subsistence farmers and near-subsistence farmers Petty commodity producers—tools, beer, household goods, etc. Moneylenders Midwives—traditional medicine Retailers—shops in homes URBAN INDUSTRIAL SECTOR: Petty commodity producers—household goods, clothing, etc. Retailers—street vendors Transport—unlicensed taxis Moneylenders Urban squatters Black marketeers, smugglers Midwives—traditional medicine CHARACTERISTICS: Low income Small scale Labor intensive Little formal education Capital from moneylenders High interest rates	Licenses and permit requirements to operate a business—bureaucratic delays, red tape, corruption, bribes required Legal system makes it impossible for urban squatters to get title to homes and use as collateral for loans No access to formal sector credit or subsidized inputs, fertilizer, water, electricity Building codes make legal housing prohibitively expensive No access to foreign exchange to import inputs Low prices for agricultural products Unions closed to outsiders

FORMAL SECTOR	GOVERNMENT POLICIES	REST OF THE WORLD
STATE SECTOR	Regulations to limit foreign ownership, to reserve certain industries to state and domestic ownership, to restrict profit repatriation	Multinational corporations
Professional, managerial class		Multinational banks
Military		Agro-industries
Civil servants	Quotas and tariffs on imported goods to protect domestic firms	Exporters and importers
State-owned enterprises		International aid agencies
State-owned banks		
Hospitals	Subsidized credit, low interest rates to favored firms	
INTELLECTUALS/ACADEMICS, MEDIA	Government subsidies to state-owned enterprises	
INDUSTRIAL SECTOR	Tax holidays and loopholes for favored firms	
Import-substituting industries		
Multinational corporations		
Labor unions		
AGRICULTURAL SECTOR		
Commercial farmers		
Export agriculture		
CHARACTERISTICS		
High income		
Access to foreign exchange		
Access to import quotas, licenses		
Access to subsidized credit		
Access to urban hospitals and higher education subsidies		
Regulated and taxed by government		
Much income from rent seeking rather than production		
Capital intensive		

producers), small-scale enterprises, urban squatters, smugglers and petty traders.

The formal sector consists of those firms that do have access to foreign exchange and subsidized credit from the government and are taxed and regulated by the state. At the top of this sector is the state, which regulates prices for farm products, agricultural inputs and consumer goods; sets wages; regulates the hiring and firing of workers; sets interest rates; subsidizes credit to favored firms; allocates foreign exchange; allocates import quotas; subsidizes food; and determines which sectors are open to the private sector and to foreign capital and which sectors are reserved for domestic capital and the state. Below the state, there are other actors, including the military, the professional and managerial class, civil servants, the highly protected import substitution industries, the parastatals, those multinational firms allowed to operate behind tariff walls, and the workers of the large industrial firms.

Lastly, there are the economic actors in the rest of the world. Of primary concern here are multinational corporations, international trading companies, multinational banks and agro-industries.

It is the strict separation of these three arenas that hampers development efforts today. In most developing countries, a wall has been constructed by the government to protect the formal sector from the competition of the informal sector. Hernando de Soto has described a host of regulations and barriers—such as requirements for licenses, permits and bribes—that keep informal sector firms from becoming legitimate and competing with the formal sector.[7]

A second wall protects the formal sector from competition from the rest of the world. This wall includes quotas, tariffs, overvalued exchange rates, exchange controls and investment codes that limit foreign investment to certain sectors of the economy, limit the percentage of foreign ownership allowed, or limit repatriation of profits.

There are obviously interactions between the informal and formal sectors. Trade does take place between them and there are interactions between the formal sector and the rest of the world. Primary products are exported, and capital, intermediate goods and luxury items are imported. Nevertheless, the walls exist, and trade between the sectors is very limited. Removal of these barriers, moreover, can be difficult politically since the walls usually are kept in place by a patronage system constructed to provide benefits to government supporters through the preferential allocation of foreign exchange, import and export licenses and business permits.

The first task of a capitalism with a human face is to break down these walls. This requires orthodox macroeconomic policies—first stabilization and then structural adjustment.

Stabilization is intended to assist countries to achieve external equilibrium, which will involve reducing expenditures abroad, or increasing export revenues, or both. To achieve this, many countries will need to devalue their currencies, reduce the growth of money and credit, and reduce the size of the fiscal deficit.

Structural adjustment will involve opening the economy to the rest of the world, eliminating quotas, reducing tariffs, allowing direct foreign investment and establishing incentives for exports. It will also involve reform of fiscal and financial policy.

A free market and free trade are important but alone are not sufficient for development that is broad based and sustainable. In addition to the macroeconomic reforms enumerated above, the strategy emphasizes the creation of an enabling environment for the growth of independent organizations, rural and urban. Community activists must be encouraged to create a pluralist network of non-governmental grassroots organizations to meet self-help and service needs in the community, and business entrepreneurs must be encouraged to build firms that create a competitive marketplace providing for the needs of consumers. Such an enabling environment results from government policies that remove unnecessary risks to NGO activists and entrepreneurs; provide protection of human rights, particularly those regarding the rights of free speech, the rights to organize and assemble, and the rights of property; establish a fair, stable and open rule of law, so that organizational innovators can make plans and assess risks; create an open and responsive system of governmental decision making, so that private actors can influence policy and anticipate policy changes.

Among the microreforms are environmental policies that minimize resource use and environmental pollution, such as tax and licensing policies that charge private beneficiaries for the public costs of the environmental resources that they use; ending subsidies that artificially encourage inefficient uses of resources; creating property laws that encourage environmental conservation and that fix responsibility for environmental degradation.

The third aspect of the contemporary strategy is a greater emphasis on both human development and poverty reduction. This strategy calls for reshaping development strategies in order to generate as much employment as possible, make significant progress in human resource development and provide a safety net for those people the development strategy leaves out.

The fourth aspect is a call for rural/agricultural transformation and reform of the urban/industrial sector. Transformation of the agricultural/rural sector will require the macroeconomic reforms outlined above, as well as special efforts such as freeing farm prices, improving rural infrastructure, increasing human capital through education, introducing new technology, instituting security of tenancy, and encouraging small-scale enterprise. Urban and industrial restructuring will involve a systematic look at the constraints on increasing urban productivity. These constraints include regulations, bureaucracies and governmental corruption that block innovation and investment; environmental problems such as polluted air and water; lack of infrastructure such as sewage systems, clean water, transportation, telecommunications and electricity; and the inability of local governments to tax and provide those services necessary for private firms to operate.

The fifth component is reform of the social sectors, particularly health and education. This involves refocusing attention in governmental programs away from provision of health and education services and toward governmental financing and private provision of services. It will also involve redirecting services from urban and curative health to rural and preventive health; from subsidies to urban and higher education to rural and primary and secondary education. In many cases, reform will involve fees for service for those who can afford to pay them. Social sector reform involves reduction of food and other subsidies and targeting those subsidies to those who really need them.

These are the five elements of a successful strategy for capitalism with a human face. In addition, it is clear that broad-based sustainable development on a planetary basis will require reform of the international political economy. It turns out that the end of the cold war has left nations with less external pressure to cooperate and has increased economic competition and the tendency to think nationally rather than internationally.

The emphasis on debt repayment during the 1980s and the growing movement toward trading-blocs and protectionism are ominous reminders of the disastrous Versailles economic order that followed World War I and that led to the Great Depression, fascism and World War II. If we are going to avoid this fate, we must radically restructure the international economic order.

The United Nations needs to be given the resources to establish a standing army and be able to preserve the peace and to deal with gross violations of human rights such as have taken place in the former Yugoslavia, Cambodia, Liberia and Somalia.

International economic decision making is currently in the hands of the Group of Seven (the seven richest industrialized countries), with no representation from the developing countries. This system of decision making must become more inclusive.

We need an international bankruptcy court (just like domestic bankruptcy courts) so that heavily indebted countries can pay as much of their debt as possible and resume economic growth.

We need to strengthen and reform the international institutions established at Bretton Woods: the World Bank, the IMF and the GATT. The IMF should be restructured so that it can put pressure on countries that run balance of payments surpluses (such as Japan and Germany) to open their economies and import more. We should replace the dollar as the international reserve currency with the IMF-created special drawing rights (SDRs). GATT should be given power to enforce its rules and enable developing countries to export to the richer countries and to open their own economies to international competition.

We also clearly need new and more powerful international institutions to deal with global environmental problems.

The Radical Critique of the Capitalist Paradigm

The key to the radical approach is the concept of power. Unlike capitalists, radicals suggest that there is an inherent conflict between the rich and the poor, and that the key to development lies in a successful challenge to those in charge of the capitalist system. The nature and timing of this challenge varies, but the concept that development is essentially a political struggle is central to this view.

What do radicals have to say about Third World development and the relationships between rich and poor nations? All agree that the relations between rich and poor nations have been dominated by imperialism, but they disagree fundamentally on the implications of this relationship. Two of the most well-known views on this crucial issue are dependency theory and the neo-Marxist approach.

Dependency Theory

Dependency theorists argue that Third World underdevelopment is a direct result of the pattern of First World development. Imperialism worked to the advantage of the rich nations and to the disadvantage of the poor, systematically underdeveloping the Third World to make it serve the interests and needs of rich nations. Third World countries are underdeveloped because rich nations thrive in a market system based on exploitation of resources, both human and natural. This system requires developing countries to be dependent on the developed countries for markets for their raw materials and small manufactures and then requires further dependency on developed countries to supply them with advanced technology and luxury goods.

The economic system within the poor country mimics the world system—a very rich minority extracting wealth from a very poor majority. The roots of this inequality lie in colonial history and in the practices of multinational corporations. The result is that the social surplus which is available for investment is in the hands of the elites who send it out of the country as profits, capital flight, or to pay for the importation of luxury goods.

The key strategies in this model therefore focus on groups or nations freeing themselves from dependency. It is assumed that development can occur once the dependent relationship is broken. Four options for breaking this relationship are discussed: independence or de-linking from the international capitalist system, liberation of the poor, revolution, and a new international economic order.

The first solution is for the Third World to seek independence from the developed world and to create its own development strategies apart from the world capitalist system. Third World countries must default on their debts, free themselves from the developed world and turn inward to domestic markets and create their own South/South trading patterns.

The second solution, liberation, requires the poor to break their social, institutional, economic and political chains. Liberation comes from the poor themselves. It is their task to create a better society which is more fully human than that of their exploiters. It will arise out of the Christian base communities in Central and South America, from institutions like the Grameen Bank in Bangladesh, from the grassroots movements springing up all over the world.

The revolutionary option is espoused by groups like Shining Path in Peru or the New People's Army in the Philippines. They argue that a nonviolent transition from the exploitative system existing in those countries is not possible. Only a violent social revolution can bring a more just society.

Calls for a new international economic order are heard regularly from the leaders of less-developed countries. These calls were first heard in 1974 at a special meeting of the UN. The Bruntland Report issued by the World Commission on Environment and Development[8] in 1987 repeated the call and added sustainability of the world ecosystem as another requirement of the new order.

The debt crisis and the retrogression in living standards in Africa and Latin America during the 1980s, and the clear way in which the external world constrained development in less-developed countries, gave new impetus to dependency theory. However, the fact that countries such as Korea and Thailand have experienced successful capitalist development in spite of the constraints of the existing world order have cast doubts on this theory.

Neo-Marxist Approach

Neo-Marxists have a very different explanation for underdevelopment. While the dependency view focuses on the way goods are traded, suggesting that underdevelopment is caused by rich nations taking unfair advantage of poor nations, neo-Marxists tend to focus on the way goods are produced. Capitalism is seen as an extremely dynamic mode of production and the key to economic development. Development, then, occurs in those countries in which capitalism has been able to break down the servile mode of production known as feudalism which inhibits progressive change.

Unlike dependency theorists, who tend to explain underdevelopment in poor nations in terms of outside forces (exploitation by rich nations), neo-Marxists tend to look inward to explain a nation's level of development in terms of its own particular forces and relations of production.

England became a developed nation because it was a capitalist nation, with a capitalist mode of production, not because it exploited its colonies. The first looters and plunderers of the poor countries, Spain and Portugal, on the other hand, were not able to develop in spite of the wealth they gained through plunder, as their feudal mode of production allowed their wealth to strengthen feudal structures rather than destroy them.

India did not fail to develop in the fifteenth century because of colonialism; England had not colonized the country yet. India failed to develop in the fifteenth century for the same reasons it fails to develop in the twentieth century, because of the forces and relations of production which block capitalist development.

The real barriers to development today are the precapitalist forces and relations of production which exist in less-developed countries. "Feudal" agricultural workers have rights to land so that they can produce their own subsistence. As a result, they resist being drawn into the money economy as wage labor and therefore provide only a very limited market for capitalist production in the country. In this relatively stagnant system, it becomes impossible to develop as there is no way to increase the productivity of labor. If countries wish to develop, they must introduce capitalism and must pay the same social cost that all developed capitalist countries have paid—a violent, wrenching social transformation of their agricultural sector which forces the peasants off the land and into wage labor.

Once capitalist development has succeeded, and material abundance has been achieved, then the groundwork for socialism has been laid. And it will not be the kind of socialism attempted in the Soviet Union or China but a socialism that builds on the best of capitalism, that accepts the human rights and democratic governance that have been achieved under capitalism, but that overcomes the exploitation and inequality that inevitably accompany capitalist development. Failures of Marxist movements in Russia, China, Cuba, VietNam and Nicaragua, however, have cast serious doubts on the possibility for achieving such a vision in any country at any time.

Empirical Evidence on Development Strategies

The argument for market capitalism and free trade is not clearly supported by the empirical evidence. Table 2 presents the data on levels and growth rates of per capita income, and table 3 presents data on human development indicators for a selected group of twenty-five countries.

All of the various development strategies have been tried in Asia, with very different results. India pursued import substitution industrialization and has had rather low rates of growth and appalling results in

Table 2

GNP Per Capita

COUNTRY	GNP PER CAPITA, DOLLARS 1990	AVERAGE ANNUAL GROWTH RATE (PERCENT), 1965–1990
LOW-INCOME ECONOMICS		
Mozambique	80	-
India	350	1.9
China	370	5.8
Kenya	370	1.9
Pakistan	380	2.5
Ghana	390	-1.4
Sri Lanka	470	2.9
Egypt	600	4.1
LOWER-MIDDLE INCOME ECONOMIES		
Bolivia	630	-0.7
Philippines	730	1.3
Morocco	950	2.3
Cameroon	960	3.0
Jamaica	1,500	-1.3
Turkey	1,630	2.6
Costa Rica	1,900	1.4
Botswana	2,040	8.4
UPPER-MIDDLE INCOME ECONOMIES		
Mexico	2,490	2.8
Brazil	2,680	3.3
Gabon	3,330	0.9
Korea	5,400	7.1
HIGH-INCOME ECONOMIES		
Hong Kong	11,490	6.2
United States	21,790	1.7
Germany	22,320	2.4
Japan	25,430	4.1
Switzerland	32,680	1.4

Source: World Bank, *World Development Report, 1992*, table 1, pp. 218–219.

Table 3

Mortality Rates, Life Expectancy and Illiteracy Rates

COUNTRY	UNDER–5 MORTALITY RATES (PER 1,000 BIRTHS, 1990)		LIFE EXPECTANCY AT BIRTH (YEARS) 1980	ADULT ILLITERACY RATES	
LOW-INCOME ECONOMIES	FEMALE	MALE		FEMALE 1990	TOTAL 1990
Mozambique	194	215	47	79	67
India	121	116	59	66	52
China	29	40	70	38	27
Kenya	97	112	59	42	31
Pakistan	151	145	56	79	65
Ghana	127	144	55	49	40
Sri Lanka	21	26	71	17	12
Egypt	95	110	60	66	52
LOWER-MIDDLE INCOME ECONOMIES					
Boliva	109	127	60	29	23
Philippines	45	57	64	11	10
Morocco	84	99	62	62	51
Cameroon	117	134	57	57	46
Jamaica	16	22	73	*	*
Turkey	73	80	67	29	19
Costa Rica	18	22	75	7	7
Botswana	41	53	67	35	26
UPPER-MIDDLE INCOME ECONOMIES					
Mexico	41	51	70	15	13
Brazil	62	75	66	20	19
Gabon	148	167	53	52	39
Korea	17	24	71	*	*
HIGH-INCOME ECONOMIES					
Hong Kong	7	10	78	—	—
United States	10	13	76	*	*
Germany	8	11	76	*	*
Japan	5	7	79	*	*
Switzerland	7	9	78	*	*

Source: World Bank, *World Development Report, 1992,* tables 1 and 32, pp. 218–219; pp. 280–281.
*According to UNESCO, the illiteracy rate is less than 5 percent.

terms of human development. More than 50 per cent of the population is illiterate, as reflected in table 3.

China followed a Soviet-type strategy and had very impressive rates of economic growth in the 1950s and 1960s and truly spectacular rates of growth since the market reforms in the 1970s. China's human development performance has been equally impressive. Sri Lanka pursued a growth with equity strategy and has had modest rates of economic growth but spectacular performance on the human development indicators.

Korea followed a very interventionist export-led policy and succeeded in going from an agricultural to an industrial economy in one generation and had phenomenal success in human development. None of these countries followed the free market, free trade model being advocated today. Only Hong Kong followed the laissez-faire/free trade strategy, which worked spectacularly well there in achieving both growth and human development.

Regional results have been remarkably different. The economies of Latin America and Sub-Saharan Africa experienced disastrous performances in the 1980s. These countries have generally followed state-led import substitution industrialization strategies. The advocates of reform can point to these countries and find support for the need for reform there. The economies of South Asia, however, which have not reformed or liberalized to any great extent, grew quite rapidly in the 1980s, adding further to our confusion. The debate continues.

Conclusions

Those of us who were hopeful that governments would be able to plan and direct development efforts successfully must admit that we were wrong and naive. The failure of socialism throughout the world has led to a widespread conviction that there is no alternative to capitalism.

Efforts to direct economies and to industrialize through state-owned enterprises have failed in most places where they have been tried, with notable exceptions in East Asia. Stabilization, liberalization, market-oriented reforms, privatization and decentralization of government make sense, as long as they are not carried out as part of a crusade to dismantle the state. There remains a major role for the state to play in making markets work efficiently and equitably. Not all of the required institutions are present in developing countries. Getting the right mix of state and market is the major challenge facing developing countries today.

Although I have argued that there are no competing paradigms of development today, this is not to say that there are not alternative visions of the future. Despite the great economic success which has occurred in market economies and despite the fact that the U.S. economy has come to be seen as the model for people all over the world, surely capitalism is not the final state of societal evolution. Human beings do have the capacity to create more just, more sustainable, more humane social systems than we have yet seen.

So, how do we teach about development today? Do we accept the status quo and the argument that there is no alternative? I think not. It is important to understand what other alternatives have been tried and why they have been perceived to be failures. It is also important to engage students in thoughtful critiques and debates about the existing paradigm and strategies that are being presented today.

NOTES

James H. Weaver is Professor of Economics, The American University.

1. James Weaver and Kenneth Jameson, *Economic Development: Competing Paradigms* (Lanham, Md: University Press of America, 1981); and James H. Weaver, Steve Arnold, Paula Cruz, and Kenneth Kusterer, "Competing Paradigms of Development," *Social Education*, 1989.

2. Thomas Kuhn, *The Structure of Scientific Revolutions* (Chicago: University of Chicago Press, 1962).

3. Adam Smith, *The Wealth of Nations* (New York: Modern Library, 1937).

4. Smith, p. 674.

5. Herman Daly, "The Steady State Economy: Alternative to Growthmania," *Population and Environment*, April, 1987.

6. Clive Crook summarized the state of orthodox development economics in "A Survey of the Third World," *The Economist*, September 23, 1989. For a critique of orthodox structural adjustment, see Paul Mosely, Jane Harrigan, and John Toye, *Aid and Power: The World Bank and Policy Based Lending*, vol. 1 (New York: Routledge, 1991).

7. Hernando de Soto, *The Other Path: The Invisible Revolution in the Third World* (New York: Harper and Row, 1989).

8. World Commission on Environment and Development, *Our Common Future* (New York: Oxford University Press, 1987).

Incorporating the Humanities in Development Education

ROBERT KEESEY

Introduction

When I was asked to write this essay on the humanities and development education I welcomed the opportunity but felt more than a little trepidation.

Welcomed, because my experiences over the past seven years team-teaching what began as a fairly conventional "social science" development course in international food security, entitled World Food/World Hunger, led first to the incorporation of more humanities materials in that course; and then the class led circuitously to the development of a separate course integrating literature, film and music course from the contemporary Third World.

Welcomed, not because of some vague, idealized notion that the humanities putatively "round things out" or provide some dimension of that ambiguous concept, "culture," but because knowledge and approaches from all the disciplines—a genuine interdisciplinarity—is necessary if we are to have any chance of effectively teaching subjects so multidimensional as international food security and development.

As a broad and complex field, development studies have been victimized by the rigid disciplinary organization of the academy. Teaching macrosubjects such as development has not only been largely abandoned but is even actively discouraged by demands for disciplinary allegiance, competition for funds, and arguments ranging from the "impossible vastness of contemporary knowledge" to *ad hominum* charges of dilletantism and hubris leveled against teachers wishing to cross disciplinary boundries.

However, notwithstanding these critiques, the interdisciplinary approach needs no theoretical defense. General support of interdisciplinary teaching is already both cliche and truism throughout much of the academy. What has hardly begun, though, is the transformation of courses and curricula through the actual practice of interdisciplinary teaching. Implementing such approaches will be the primary focus of this paper.

The trepidation that I felt at accepting such a general topic as the humanities in development education stemmed largely from the ambitiousness of the topic. But also daunting was the need to avoid arid theorizing and easy generalizations while providing a solid rationale for incorporating the humanities into the study of development. For although my interests lie in concrete practice, there is no practice without underlying assumptions, rationales. The question is only whether they are explicit or implicit, conscious or unconscious, hidden or manifest.

In this essay I attempt to avoid a theory/practice dichotomy by narrating some of the problems that I and my colleague John Omohundro encountered in constructing and teaching the World Food/World Hunger course and by presenting the reasoning that led us first to incorporating more "humanities" and then to my developing a complementary course in literature, film and music from the contemporary Third World. By this combination of narrative and analysis I hope both to make a case for the utility of incorporating the humanities in development education and to provide some rationales, resources and materials for doing so.

Why an English Professor Teaches Development, and How

Like a number of people now teaching aspects of international food security who were not trained as development specialists, John and I and other faculty initiated the World Food/World Hunger course in 1986 in response to the shock of the African famines and hunger crises as these finally caught the attention of the Western news media in 1985.

The situation raised a series of troubling questions about how and why the crisis had happened in a world of "grain surpluses and butter mountains." Many in the "developed" world were shocked into remembering the forgotten knowledge of most peoples in most times, that access to food is access to life itself, and access to sufficient food is necessary for both health and any quality of life. Hence hunger represents the most fundamental of all human inequities. Without redressing such a basic inequity there is no hope of ending conflict and confrontation between haves and have-nots.

A number of us involved with teaching queried futher: Why is it that we as faculty and scholars—to say nothing of our students—knew so little about the production, distribution and consumption of food, subjects central to basic human existence, to any possibility of a sustainable environment, or any hope for long-term peace and coexistence? This question prompted at least a minor movement—involving private and government agencies and teachers across academe—to get food and hunger issues into the curriculum and thus into the public eye.

To put together our first course, we did what many of you who are reading this essay are in the process of doing. We solicited the advice and support of acquaintances who were teaching food or allied development issues. We read books and articles, with particular attention to their bibliographies. We watched every film on the subject we could get our hands on. And we fumbled our way to a syllabus and a useful course much like others being developed in the same way.

The three credit-hour, semester-length course opened with a delineation of the dimensions of the problem, the "numbers" of hunger, "who," "where," and then a week on the biology and chemistry of nutrition. It moved to various perspectives on population/consumption and demographic explanations, then a unit on the environment, and a third on seeds, genetic resources and biodiversity. We spent a week on world debt, a few weeks looking at the main development models and then did a long unit on "food and culture" that dealt with preferences, taboos and the "cultures" of agriculture. The last three weeks were spent on comparative country case studies.

And we showed films, wonderful films, one a week—and they remain central to our course. We rely largely on powerful documentaries, "visual persuasive essays," that are common to courses like ours: *Hungry for Profit*, the four-part *Politics of Food*, "Eating" from *The Heart of the Dragon* series, *Seeds of Tomorrow*, *From Sunup*, *Will the World Starve? Save the Earth, Feed the World*. We find them necessary not just because they present cogent arguments and the viewpoints of others, which they do very well, but because such films allow us to give our students glimpses of the material conditions, the faces and plants and animals and landscapes and villages and towns and clothing and houses and tools and transportation and agricultural practices, of cultures and places very different from our own.

The first few courses were good and useful. We and our students learned much and we look back at them with both a sense of pride in the temerity of the undertaking and, I believe, a certain nostalgia for lost innocence as we gradually discovered the depth and apparent intractability of the problems. With only slight alterations, the major themes outlined above still provide the basic structure of our present food/hunger course. What has changed considerably are the pedagogical approaches, causal assumptions, explanatory frameworks, materials and texts that are used to address these same themes and topics.

Reworking the Pedagogy

As we became more sophisticated, we recognized three broad interconnected deficiencies in our teaching: (1) the lack of history, of an historical approach, without which many of the forces structuring present inequities are either inexplicable or kept invisible by the more superficial explanations available in their absence; (2) not enough attention to mindsets, beliefs, assumptions, values, meanings, worldviews, to *culture*—in the anthropological conception of that term—because conditions and structures that appear natural, inevitable and necessary often turn out to be the products of culture; and (3) a shortage of materials and strategies that might facilitate bridging the perceptual gulfs between "us" and "them," because the great inequalities are probably not going to be redressed in the long-term without at least some serious understanding and real tolerance between different cultures.

1: Historicization

The first deficiency—ahistoricism—emerged early in the evolution of the course. There is much inherent "presentness" in development courses that militates against the "long view." History, as well as the other humanities, are sometimes perceived as too distant, abstract, or even "precious," to contribute much to what after all are such immediate and pressing problems as getting adequate food in people's bellies, or access to clean water and a modicum of health care, and some political and economic enfranchisement that might alleviate structural inequities and cycles of poverty. I have complete sympathy for such immediacy when focusing on famine relief and other food and medical crises, or for the daily crises faced in the field.

But most of our courses are about much more than crises and problems amenable to technological solutions. They instead try to understand why so little has been accomplished after more than three decades of proclaimed Northern resolve to eliminate hunger and promote development. Why, indeed, has the distance between haves and have-nots grown, has the environment deteriorated worldwide, and are the lives of about one thousand million people, one billion, one fifth of the world's population, dominated by a grim and tortured struggle for subsistence?

Although reducing the complexity and intellectual labor of a semester-long course to the question Why? seems a gross oversimplification, the Why?s are the essential impetus of our kind of food security course: viable solutions to contemporary inequities can be no better than the questions we raise and the problems we identify. It is virtually axiomatic to observe that if we ask the wrong questions, ascribe the wrong causes to the effects we see so clearly around us, then, barring serendipity or the intervention of deities, the best we can hope for our solutions is that they do little harm.

In attempting to understand the inadequacy of good intentions and development policies, we generally approached the question by taking the individual nation as the primary unit of analysis. While a useful and often necessary consideration, exclusive focus on the individual nation-state ironically nullifies the perspective of interdependence that many of us in development studies believe is primary. A national approach too often leads to myopic explanatory models relying on domestic structures alone. The culprits thus appear only within the boundaries of the state: undemocratic ruling oligarchies and strongmen, venal elites, and misguided policies. Such explanations are seductive: they all contain an element of truth. What is missing? The recognition that Southern dilemmas may also be the outcome of decisions made by powerful actors and forces operating elsewhere.

Ahistoricism distorts and constricts our views of the present, leading us to attribute current crises to nature—the inherent order of things—rather than to human agency. Mary Louise Pratt catches a fine example of this when she points out that twentieth-century ethnographers ascribe to the Kung, the Bushmen of the Kalahari, "natural" characteristics of "meekness, innocence, passivity, indolence,... cheerfulness, absence of greed," overlooking the possbility that such "natural" attributes might have been produced by colonial conquest and "three centuries of violence and intimidation." Indeed, prior to the eighteenth century, these same people "existed in European writings as hordes of wild, bloodthirsty marauders fiercely resisting the advancing colonists, raiding their farms at night, ... and sometimes murdering colonists or laborers" (Pratt 1986). Without a historical perspective, then, we can become trapped by the present, losing what is dynamic in the experience of the developing world and our perceptions of it.

The limitations of the nation as the unit of analysis were exacerbated by the ahistorical, synchronic methodologies that dominated the social science disciplines until recently.[1] A variety of contextualist movements have rehistoricized most of the disciplines related to the study of development, with the notable exception of economics. But my experience tells me that the actual practicing of a thoroughgoing historicity in international food security studies is still in its infancy. Hence, even when the individual nation is transcended as the unit of analysis, explanations are often in terms contemporary structures like worldwide market forces and international banking practices, as if these represented givens rather than constructs.

And it is clear that no analysis can escape history, least of all in development. There is a real need for conscious historical treatment of the development equation, so that students can surface unconscious historical assumptions.

So we must pay close attention to history. By locating the origin of European hegemony in the seventeenth century rise of science, the ideas of the Enlightenment *philosophes*, and the ensuing Industrial and Democratic Revolutions of the eighteenth century, we have privileged our cultural notions about what is good to do, over what we actually did and continue to do; we have favored the ideal over the real. We told ourselves a Eurocentric story that flattered our genius for invention and progress. It is not that the tale was false, but partial and one-sided; it ignored the degree to which the capital accumulation of Europe and European-dominated excolonies was inseparable from their command of the lands, resources and labor of the rest of the peoples of the earth. It blinded and still blinds us to our place in structural realities that keep two-thirds or more of that world in economic bondage, notwithstanding the end of colonialism and our claims to facilitating "development." It obscures the probability that Andre Gunder Frank suggested so powerfully twenty-five years ago, that European "development" is not a model that can be emulated but was, and is, the very condition that "underdeveloped" the rest (Frank 1966).

In *A Small Place*, Jamaica Kincaid's bitter essay on the historical underdevelopment of her "ex"-colonial island homeland, Antigua, the narrator catches the destructive implications of a Eurocentric history when she addresses "the tourist" who unwittingly embodies the American and European neocolonialism that has replaced the earlier British colonialism:

> You have brought your own books with you, and among them is one of those new books explaining how the West (meaning Europe and North America after its conquest and settlement by Europeans) got rich: the West got rich not from the free (free—in this case meaning got-for-nothing) and then undervalued labour, for generations, of the people like me you see walking around you in Antigua but from the ingenuity of small shopkeepers in Sheffield and Yorkshire and Lancashire, or wherever; and what a great part the invention of the wristwatch played in it, for there was nothing noble-minded men could not do when they discovered they could slap time on their wrists just like that (isn't that the last straw; for not only did we have to suffer the unspeakableness of slavery, but the satisfaction to be had from "We made you bastards rich" is taken away, too), and so you needn't let that slightly queasy feeling you have from time to time about exploitation, oppression, domination develop into full-fledged unease, discomfort; you could ruin your holiday. They are not responsible for what you have; you owe them nothing; in fact you did them a big favour, and you can provide one hundred examples. (Kincaid 1988)

And the people who go unrecognized, unwritten, rendered invisible, by particular versions of history tend to be cut out of the wealth, rewards and resources of the present.

The lesson we drew: our course required not simply greater historical content but a "World History" approach. It has become a commonplace of curriculum reform that our students should have more international and multi-cultural education because we *now* live in an interdependent "global village." However, we are probably not going to usefully think globally until we recognize that we have been *acting* globally since at least the fifteenth century, which only the study of world history, as opposed to national epics, or Western "civilization," might tell us.

We took two steps to remedy the lack of historical content. First, we simply read as much in the area of world history as we could. Given the limitations of a three credit-hour course and the number of issues to be covered, our agenda had little room to absorb new materials. Hence, much of the burden fell on us to translate and to reeducate ourselves and integrate our readings into classroom presentations. And second, we added Sydney Mintz's *Sweetness and Power: The Place of Sugar in Modern History* (Mintz 1985) to the syllabus as required reading. This book masterfully traces the historical development of a primary plantation and world trading crop with signficant relevance to the development of slavery and the course of New World history. Moreover, Mintz outlines tastes and food preferences with their ensuing profitability in Europe, and he thus synthesizes in a single readable volume many of the dimensions and issues surrounding the production, distribution and consumption of food central to international food security courses like ours. Such a work provides our students with a concrete example of a world history approach. For this coming semester we have been debating choosing from among the Smithsonian's *Seeds of Change: Five Hundred Years since Columbus* (Viola and Margolis 1991), Eric Wolf's *Europe and the People without History* (Wolf 1982) and Alfred Crosby's *Ecological Imperialism: The Biological Expansion of Europe, 900–1900*, to serve the course's world history needs.

2: The Importance of Culture

The second imperative—our emphasis on "culture"—emerged from the implications for food security courses of the contemporary nature/culture debate. In the last three decades, the nature/culture dichotomy has undergone considerable alterations. Much that was assumed to be natural is now regarded as cultural. And what is cultural, as opposed to natural, is ipso facto political: choice, not fate; desire, not necessity; what is valued, not what must be. And if something is a matter of choice, we can ask the essential political question: Who gets to choose?

The prevailing contemporary rationalist assumption that we see things through our languages or our value systems elevate culture over nature in a most basic way. Thus, it is no surprise to find that the range of the cultural has expanded while that of the natural has diminished. For example, by the mid–1970s anthropology had given up both the long-time Western assumption of, and search for, some fundamental, uniform, "human nature" underlying the flux and particularities of cultures, as well as its later ". . . hunt for universals in culture, for empirical uniformities that, in the face of the diversity of customs around the world and over time, could be found everywhere in about the same form" (Geertz 1973).

Concepts like "race" and "the primitive," which were foundational assumptions of the Western intellectual tradition of the last two centuries, once denoted "truths" about discovered significant natural characteristics and differences. We now recognize most of the "natural" differences as "cultural," and such notions as "civilization" and "the primitive" as nineteenth-century social constructions (Kuper 1988; Stocking 1987; Williams 1983).

By the late 1970s, it was difficult to find serious intellectual defenses of the long-time assumption that "masculine" and "feminine" sex roles were created by nature. Male and female are biological, natural, defined simply by different genitalia. Masculine and feminine are primarily the products of culture. And this is no minor capsizing of just the cruder forms of sociobiology prevalent until recently. As R. A. Sydie points out in her descriptively titled, *Natural Women, Cultured Men*, the social theories of Durkheim, Weber, Marx, Engels and Freud—the "fathers" of the Western sociological tradition—routinely explain the roles of women in society on the basis of biological necessity, while explaining those of men on the bases of various cultural phenomena (Sydie 1988).

Wlad Godzich has recently argued that both the modern nation state and national literary canons are rooted in mistaking the cultural for the natural. He points out that the study of national literary canons, the foundation of modern literary studies, is premised on European assumptions of two centuries ago that "nationality is a natural human attribute," and that nations could be "distinguished by some empirical features" like "language and religion," which were also seen as natural. From these assumptions it followed that "self-government by persons sharing the same nationality is the only form of legitimate government," and, among others, "the arts and most notably literature [were given] the task" of defining and perpetuating the "primary essence" of the nation state (Godzich 1991).

In response to critical contemporary questions—like why more than one billion people suffer chronic hunger in a world of plenty—we must clearly focus on cultural beliefs about who deserves what rather than "natural iron laws" curtailing supply. Totally discredited is the idea is that economic laws, like those of the natural world, rule exchange and distribution and that poverty is attributable to the failure to heed them.

The relevance of all this to international food security is illustrated well by the journey of a hero in the fight against hunger and food inequity, Francis Moore Lappé. The evolution of her perception of the underlying causes of world food inequities—and hence the problems that must be addressed—parallels this primary explanatory shift from the natural to the cultural that has taken place in many academic disciplines.

The 1975 preface to the revised edition of *Diet for a Small Planet* (first edition, 1970) recounts the first part of Lappé's journey:

> Along with many others in the late 60s, I had started out asking the question, "How close are we to the limit of the earth's capacity to provide food for all humanity?" only to be overwhelmed by the realization that I was part of a system actively *reducing* that capacity. I began with the assumption that our food problems were agricultural ones that only the food experts could solve, but came to the conclusion that feeding the earth's people is more profoundly a political and economic problem which you and I must help to solve. (Lappé 1976)

Lappé's middle books, co-authored with Joseph Collins, *Food First: Beyond the Myth of Scarcity* (1979), *World Hunger: Ten Myths* (1979) and *Twelve Myths* (1986), articulate the problem in political and economic terms.

By her 1989 *Rediscovering American Values*, she had taken her analysis to a deeper level and recognized that the political and economic structures are underpinned, created and maintained by our belief systems, our worldviews:

> As I've lived with such horrifying realities year after year, visiting the Third World myself and witnessing the misery of poverty, one question has increasingly pressed itself upon me: what could be powerful enough to allow us to tolerate, to accept, to acquiesce to, these millions of silent deaths every year? What could possibly explain our ability to condone such a status quo?
>
> I've finally come to believe that there's only one thing powerful enough. *It is the power of ideas*—the ideas we hold about ourselves and our relations to one another. It is these ideas that allow us to condone, or even support with tax dollars, that which we as individuals abhor—and somehow to tolerate the discomforting contrast. (Lappé 1989)

Alternatively, Haig Bosmajian has succinctly captured the political importance of our values and ideas: "The European invaders, having defined themselves as culturally superior to the inhabitants they found in the New World, proceeded to their 'Manifest Destiny' and subsequently to their massive killing of the 'savages'" (Bosmajian 1989).

While not at all ignoring the very real environmental and biological limitations that constrain human choices and options, we must recognize that our behavior within in these constraints is guided by the ways we see the world. From our recognition of this fact came the need to put even more emphasis on the importance of *culture* in our world food/hunger course.

3: Getting to Know "The Other"

And this need merged with the imperative for more materials and strategies to help bridge the perceptual gulfs between "us" and "them," which have long objectified "The Other." The breadth of the course and its social-scientific orientation required students to think of Southern people in groups, aggregates, societies. They were not exactly "faceless," but were collections with similar faces: victims, peasants, landowners, elites, militaries, rebels, Indians, Mestizos, slaves, tenant farmers, and on and on. We studied groups and general conditions but were seldom exposed to individuals with whom we could identify. Despite the weekly viewing of documentary films, it was difficult to move beyond "conditions" to "culture," to cross the line from "them" to people like "us" with needs and beliefs and desires and histories, to "same" as well as "different."

The breaching of this line is central to any serious empathetic response. And without a serious empathetic response, people of the South—the other—remain exotic, strange, different in kind rather than just different in circumstance. Hence, they remain at worst, objects to be either exploited or ignored, but even at best, I would argue, objects of charity. Whether on the basis of moral compunction or some form of self-interest, enlightened or otherwise, we generally *give* to the other. Only with those perceived as similar to ourselves do we *share*, rather than give, such things as food, knowledge, tools, sustenance.

For Northern students suspicious of projects to "save the world," and resistant to ex cathedra moral injunctions, empathy helps obviate the impolite question that continually lurks beneath the surface: "Why help *them* at all?" often followed by the mumbled excuse, "when so many here at home need help." More important, for those inclined to engage, empathy can lead to clearer thinking about what kinds of policies will succeed in other cultures and allow critical reflection regarding policies such as structural adjustment that force others to put into practice foreign *assumptions* and values.

I carefully use the term *empathy* here in its sense of "the intellectual identification with or vicarious experiencing of the feelings, thoughts, or attitudes of another" and not as a misused synonym for *sympathy* in its common sense of "harmony of or agreement in feeling" (Stein 1967). What we seek is cross-cultural understanding, cultural tolerance, *not* an amorphous cultural relativism. For example, one might hope to achieve some *empathy*, some cultural understanding, even for actions that are unacceptable to many of us, such as infibulation and clitoridectomy, or the ritual sacrifice of animals, while not at all having *sympathy* for these practices.

Crossing the boundary to the kind of empathy and cultural tolerance that many of us feel is necessary for sustainable long-term development policies is obviously no simple matter of pointing out their desirability. If telling people to think differently actually changed their minds, we could paste up a few homilies and be done with it. We only usefully change our inherited cultural assumptions and prejudices by encountering a wide range of others over a significant period of time.

It has impressed me for much of my academic career that there are ways of crossing cultural boundaries even if one cannot actually live in another culture. Chief among these paths to empathy is engagement of the other on both an individual and a cultural level through literature, narrative films, music, art and good ethnographies. Through them, we can vicariously experience, rather than distantly observe, the lives of individual human beings like ourselves being dramaticaly played out within the conditions, histories, possibilities and limitations of particular cultures and specific physical environments.

We tried to rectify this problem of distance between us and the other in the World Food/Hunger course by first integrating a novel, Achebe's *Things Fall Apart*; followed by a multivoiced ethnography, Else Skjønsberg's *Change in an African Village: Kefa Speaks*; and later a narrative film, Satyajit Ray's *Distant Thunder*.

Things Fall Apart has become a war-horse, *the* novel recommended for development studies courses. It is discussed here neither to rehearse its plot nor to insist upon its enormous value, but because a brief analysis of how and why we use the novel can serve as working criteria for selecting other novels and narrative films for inclusion on development syllabi.

Achebe's novel fits into a five week unit in the middle of the course. Why students get caught up in a work like *Things Fall Apart* and what additional kinds of things we would like them to experience in such a work are often quite different. One of the primary reasons for using a novel is that students identify with—empathize with—the characters. They vicariously experiece the conflicts within a particular culture, because good stories have this affective quality seldom encountered in other forms of writing or speaking. However, this often breathless involvement in the action ("how it all comes out") means that many details important to the course can be overlooked by all but the most careful students. To illuminate these, to negotiate a reading of the text, is the function of the teacher.

The two primary areas we focus on in our reading of the novel are: first, the "culture" of agriculture, the inseparability of cultural forms of food production and the structuring of that culture by those forms and their requirements; and, second, the worldviews, attitudes, belief systems, "culture" that are articulated in the text.

We begin by looking at how the cultivation needs of the yam —the particular complex carbohydrate that makes the culture portrayed in Achebe's novel possible[2]—shape the daily lives of his Ibo villagers. We note the ways in which the yam's needs structure the activities of the year: the holidays and the various periods of concentrated work and different tasks as well as the religious observances and rituals that constantly accompany these. We see these cultivation needs against a climate with very different seasons and temperatures and precipitation from our Northern temperate one. The soils and climate and geography are the environmental constraints that circumscribe a people's choice of food crops and cultivation practices.

These considerations gradually merge into cultural constructions of the yam as "wealth": as the measure of a man's status and the wives he could afford (p. 13)[3] or as venture capital at usurious rates (p. 16). Yam represents gender divisions and male dominance: "His mother and sisters worked hard enough, but they grew women's crops, like coco-yams, beans and cassava. Yam, the king of crops, was a man's crop" (p. 16); "the women planted maize, melons and beans between the yam mounds" (p. 24); "Yam stood for manliness, and he who could feed his family on yams from one harvest to another was a very great man indeed" (p. 23).

And all of these concerns help to disabuse us of our traditional notions of the "primitive" and the "civilized" which continue to inform too many contemporary views of Africa and its history. We recognize a complex political organization as the ten thousand men from the nine

villages that make up the clan of Umuofia, one of a network of Ibo
clans, are summoned to the marketplace to decide under what conditions the clan will go to war (pp. 7–8). The larger political system here
is nonurban and noncentralized. It is democratic, leaving room for
upward mobility. It seems to function as a "meritocracy" as opposed to
an "aristocracy": "among these people a man was judged according to
his worth and not according to the worth of his father". . ."Age was
respected among his people, but achievement was revered" (p. 6). The
indefensible notion still held by some that falling food productivity in
contemporary Africa is due in part to a lack of agricultural knowledge—a notion implicit in the maxim, "Give a man a fish and he will
be hungry tomorrow; teach him how to fish and he can feed himself
forever," that is still pontificated even by some development people
who should know better—is effectively countered by the large, stable,
environmentally-sound agrarian societies portrayed in the novel.

Our students are attracted to the language of the villagers, their rich
oral culture: "Among the Ibo the art of conversation is regarded very
highly, and proverbs are the palm-oil with which words are eaten"
(p. 8). When they come to realize that this kind of indirection or negotiation allows for criticism in which the criticized retains dignity,
student reaction often reflects the sentiment that this oral tradition is
much, much more "civilized" than many of the ways we talk to one
another in our culture.

All of the above segues into a discussion of the novel in terms of
manners, morals, ethics and justice; and to the clan's view of the other:
"But what is good in one place is bad in another" (p. 51); "There is no
story that is not true [somewhere]. . . The world has no end, and what
is good among one people is an abomination with another" (p. 99).

And finally we move to "things falling apart" with Christian missionaries and British colonial rule; "the Bible and the gun" penetrate
this area of Africa in the early twentieth century, bringing "civilization" and progress to this part of the Dark Continent. The novel ends
with the bitter irony of the District Commissioner contemplating the
title of the book he is going to write about "the many years in which he
had toiled to bring civilization to different parts of Africa," and the
quaint, strange and incomprehensible habits of the natives: *The Pacifi-
cation of the Primitive Tribes of the Lower Niger* (pp. 147–8).

I will give short shrift in this essay on incorporating the humanities
to our addition of Else Skjønsberg's 1989 ethnography, *Change in an*

African Village: Kefa Speaks, because ethnographies are primarily the province of Western social scientists. However, good ethnographies involve the reader with individuals from other cultures on a much more personal level than most social science analyses of larger groups and forces. The following quotation from the introduction to *Change* best exemplies how this work addresses the three needs we had in the World Food/Hunger course to historicize, emphasize the cultural, and bridge the gap between us and the other:

> It was the ambition to make the past known to the future that led the residents of Kefa village to participate in the study that comprises this book. They seemed to take it for granted that their own hand-to-mouth agriculture would soon disappear, and that a future of clean shirts and tractors lay ahead, even if it would not be their future. They wanted their grandchildren . . . to know how they, their elders, had worked and lived. . . . Kefa is a very ordinary Zambian village. Virtually every adult village resident grows his or her own food and also some for sale. . . . Like most ordinary African villages, Kefa is undergoing rapid changes. The fact is that traditional rural ways of life have little resistance to the transformations wrought by the global political economy. . . . I [a Norwegian rural sociologist] had three basic aims: first, to account objectively how villagers live and work; second, to disclose why people do what they do; and third, to describe village life within a frame of reference that is endemic to the villagers rather than to the expatriate sociologist. Of course, this latter endeavor can only meet with partial success. (Skjønsberg 1989)

This ethnography of village life in another place and time in Africa also balances, complements and reinforces Achebe's "fictional" re-creation of how it might have been. Together they illuminate the different, but not mutually exclusive, "truths" of diverse kinds of writings.

An Integrated Approach

Narrative Films in the Classroom

The inclusion of narrative films in development studies, in this instance Satyajit Ray's 1974 *Distant Thunder,* has much merit because movies do things that documentaries cannot. Documentaries usually begin with the end conditions, the results, e.g., the shanty towns, the destruction of the rainforest, or in the cases of crises and famines, the bloated bellies and the refugee camps full of skeletal figures, and then move to a series of commentators and viewpoints on the causes of and possible resolutions to the problems. Narratives move through time; they tell a story of individuals we can imagine as ourselves facing difficulty and choice.

As only good narratives can, *Distant Thunder* takes us from the ordinariness and constancy and social organization of daily life in a rural Indian village in the early 1940s to its disintegration, and to the heroism and the corruption as well as the deaths of its inhabitants along with those of millions of others from starvation and epidemics in the infamous manmade Bengal famine of 1943–44. The film gains its power from the way in which the famine almost imperceptibly seeps into the lives of ordinary people. Against a lovely, lyrically filmed agrarian landscape, the famine, the result of forces beyond both the villagers' geographical and perceptual horizons, gradually forces each person into the terrible kinds of choices that almost no one foresaw or was prepared for. The actions that hungry people are driven to under such conditions become ones we recognize that we too might choose in that situation. And the Bengali famine becomes not just one more instance in a boring historical litany of inhumanity and suffering but a powerful vicarious experience. We are transported there and forced to ask ourselves how we might choose if faced with the same conditions.

That we also catch a glimpse of the structures and institutions of village life tied to agricultural seasons, and that the protagonist is a doctor and a teacher and a religious leader in the community who is nevertheless ignorant of something so pedestrian and humble and essential as the production and distribution of food—the sine qua non of life itself—makes this film particularly useful for an international food security course.

Literature, Film and Music

Although these works were integrated into the World Food/Hunger course with real success, constraints of time limited further use of humanities materials. While we may substitute an additonal narrative film or two for some of the documentary films on the syllabus, there is just no room for more than a smattering of fiction and a good ethnography.

These time and materials constraints led me to develop a separate literature course, listed by the English Department. Offered with no prerequisites, I hoped that this class would complement the World Food/Hunger course which was offered by Anthropology and would be useful to other development studies across the campus. The course was problematically titled "Third World Literature" for want of a better alternative. After all, what sense is there in the "literature of underdevelopment" when there is no "literature of overdevelopment"? Or the "literature of the agrarian and raw-materials–exporting South" when there is no "Northern industrial literature"? And I calculated that a course with a more general title could eventually become a regular offering and from semester to semester accommodate various materials, and different emphases and themes: hopefully, in any given semester, it might co-ordinate with particular development studies and both be scheduled as a larger interdisciplinary offering.

How does one select works for such an offering? Rather than attempt to discuss individual works from what is an impossibly long list of usable choices, I will lay out the basic organizing principles of the course by quoting the introduction from the syllabus of that first course because they remain the ones I continue to select works by:

> The focus of the course will be on contemporary creative writers from within cultures often very different from our own who, by rendering so immediate and compelling the lives, conflicts, customs, and values of the peoples they creatively "re-present," help us break the barriers of our insularity and make the ways of "the other" less foreign. Throughout, we will concentrate on the similarities as well as the differences because it is only by extending familiar experiences that we incorporate, make comprehensible, what initially may seem strange and even outlandish.
>
> This semester we will read and discuss a number of writings, mostly novels, by authors who reflect particular cultural and individual responses, within specific geographic and environmental constraints, to experiences, problems and circumstances that are often common throughout much of the so-called Third World: e.g., ethnic and cultural and religious traditions and customs fractured by colonial and postcolonial geographic and political divisions, with the ones remaining often in conflict with national and international development policy demands for "modernization"; huge disparities in wealth and power between a large landless and jobless underclass and sometimes venal and often Western-educated local elites; rapidly growing landless populations either pouring into shanty-towns swelling cities that have no industrial base to employ them, or putting pressure on rapidly deteriorating

marginal lands and disappearing forests; agricultural and raw materials export economies dependent on world markets beyond their control with mounting foreign debts that hemorrhage what export earnings there are back to the financial institutions of the Industrial North; political instability with the "military" and "strongmen" often in control of politics; lower life expectancy and infant mortality rates, rapidly increasing environmental deterioration, and for large numbers an absolute and grinding poverty.

Let me emphasize here that just because these themes are overtly political, this is no call for propaganda, nor for some neo–"socialist-realism" in the service of particular ideologies. The literature here provides the reader with a wide range of vicarious experiences of events and conflicts in various places and different times within and against the conditions and realities that these themes and subjects represent. And powerful vicarious experiences of political subjects come in all kinds of literary forms, from the fantastic, and magical realism, to conventional realism: which is no more "realistic" than other literary conventions. Vicarious experiences within the framework of these common Third World issues is what makes a course such as this one valuable as a companion to development studies.

I also look for literary works that are conscious of the larger events, the history within and against which characters play their roles, the particular circumstances and culture(s) that both circumscribe and make possible the individual's choices and actions. Such works can provide the reader a significant window into other times, places and worldviews. In this way a literature course—or even a bit of literature—can help the continuing need to historicize development studies for which I argued earlier in this essay.[4]

While I remain committed to the organizing framework and thematic guidelines of this first Third World literature course, I soon realized that the course as constituted had a major flaw: I was using an increasing number of films, to the detriment of discussion of the literature in a three-credit hour course. Why did I show so many films? Because I had come to recognize that without visuals—"pictures"—it is almost impossible for students to imagine material conditions and geographies with which they have had no experience. The unfamiliar can only be imagined if there are points of reference that can be extended, built on. The "Townships" of Johannesburg have no relationship to the suburbs of Rochester. So when my students read

Mongane Serotes's novel *To Every Birth Its Blood*, a wrenching portrayal of political struggle and Township life under apartheid from Sophia-town to the Soweto uprising, they have the faint first stirrings of intellectual connection. But when students read the book in conjunction with five hours of documentary film from the 1987 Frontline *History of Apartheid*, and a screening of the narratives *Mapantsula* and *A Dry White Season*, a synergistic effect is achieved. The documentaries, the narrative films and the novel are mutually reinforcing: in tandem they provide an experience far greater than the sum of the individual parts.

My integrated film and literature course was expanded to four credit hours to allow inclusion of thirty-nine documentary and narrative films (the films are listed, each with a one-line description, in the "Literature, Film and Music" syllabus in the appendix). As I had almost no budget for the undertaking, many wonderful films, particularly those by contemporary African directors, were out of my reach. All of the narrative films that I used were on VHS and can be rented by mail quite inexpensively, as can a number of documentaries.[5] Many of the documentaries and some of the narrative films were those from PBS and other common sources often held by audio visual departments and libraries.[6]

In response to the quincentennial of 1492, I resolved that the spring semester's course would focus on literature and films from or about Central and Latin America, the Caribbean and Sub-Saharan Africa. The course was organized around the premise that many of the common social, political and economic concerns represented by these different forms of artistic expression cross diverse cultures and geopolitical boundaries and might be viewed as the legacy of the unequal and unfinished fusion of European, African and Native American cultures that began in 1492. But serendipitous circumstances led me to expand my course yet again. The result is the integrated six-credit hour course, "Literature, Film and Music from the Contemporary Third World," represented by the syllabus in the appendix. My institution agreed to fund my colleague and music mentor, Warren Wigutow, to give twelve three-hour public presentations on Tuesday evenings of films, records and commentary about contemporary Afro-based New World and African musical forms such as Reggae, Dub, Soukous, Soca, Juju, Zouk, Samba, Highlife, Cumbia, Township Jazz, Jive and Mbaqanga. An introduction to Wigutow is included in the syllabus and a complete discography for the course, which is his creation, can be found under the "Tuesday, 7–9:30" headings throughout the syllabus.

Not only do many of the contemporary popular music forms of Africa, Latin America and the Caribbean—as well as elsewhere—reflect the inheritance of the fusion of different cultures, they continue in the present to cross-pollinate as forms flow back and forth between Africa and the New World. Maybe more important, many of the lyrics of these forms have an overtly political and social content reflecting both an earlier era of forced subservience, as well as the subculture status of a number of contemporary social groups for whom music was, and is, one of the only available forms of social and political expression. It is possibly the primary form for those people sometimes intentionally and sometimes by circumstance kept illiterate. It is the most difficult of artistic expressions to censor. And for many peoples, music is a major cultural bond integral to and integrating everyday life.

Study of Southern music inevitably leads to the realization that numerous secular dances and popular forms have their genesis in the rhythms of the worship and rites of the syncretic religions: the Samba of Brazil and *Candomblé*, the Son and Salsa of Cuba and *Santería*, the popular dances of Haiti and *Voudoun*. And then there is the powerful link of Reggae and Rastafarianism. The music thus leads to a consideration of these as serious religions that are no more superstitious, magical, irrational, or primitive than any other religions including the so-called "great" ones which only warrant such an appellation on the basis of size and power and not any intrinsic theological superiority.[7]

Finally, given the powerful role of popular music in contemporary America, music might be the form most immediately conducive to bridging the gap between cultures, to extending our experiences to some understanding of those of the other. At least we found this to be so in the course: many of our students found the music the most accessible and most immediate of the humanities inputs on the syllabus. And once again, the addition of music had a synergistic effect, enlarging the overall experience beyond the impact of the constituent parts.

This essay has endeavored to present rationales and possible approaches for incorporating most of the traditional humanities in development studies—history, literature, film, music, the epistemological and ethical questions of philosophy. Noticeably absent is art—and this is only due to the lack of a qualified collaborator. Surely this is another dimension of the humanities that can enhance undergraduate instruction—another way to make development education more compelling, more immediate, more powerful.

SYLLABUS

Literature, Film and Music
from the Contemporary Third World

7286 2224–ENG–395 3RD WLD LIT, 6 hrs: M,W,2–4; T,Th2–3:15;
T,7–9:30
Fulfills General Education [CC] Cross-Cultural Perspectives
Instructors: R. Keesey and Warren Wigutow
Prerequisites: None

The purpose of this course is to help realize the General Education Cross-Cultural Requirement for courses designed to offer students a multicultural perspective.

In response to the quincentennial celebrations of the voyage of 1492 that began the European discovery, conquest and colonization of the New World, this semester's course will focus on contemporary films, literature and music from or about Central and Latin America, the Caribbean, and Sub-Saharan Africa. The course is organized around the premise that many of the common social, political and economic concerns represented across these different forms of artistic expression, as well as across diverse cultures and geopolitical boundaries, might be viewed as the legacy of the unequal, undigested and unfinished fusion of European, African and Native American cultures that began in 1492.

The "Colombian Exchange" that followed moved people, animals, plants, insects and diseases between the New World and the Old, creating in the next few centuries the worldwide redistribution of these that partially defines the emergence of the modern world, "modernity."

Also moved around were ideas, technologies, and agricultural and political and economic systems. This part of the "Europeanizing" of the earth marks the emergence of the "modern world system" which we finally come to recognize full force in the late twentieth century as the global interconnectedness and interdependence of nations, markets, information and environmental degradation.

Most important for this course, European colonization, with its forced dislocation, redistribution and domination of African and Native American cultures, left the legacy of maldistributed land, wealth, goods and political power based on assumptions about race, class, gender and religion that the contemporary cinematic, literary and musical forms we shall be studying "re-create," "re-present," and react to. Until recently, this domination also left the dispossessed a legacy of cultural invisibility, since the histories written by those on the top often ignored, denied, or suppressed others' cultural contributions. One of the purposes of this course is to explore some of these recently acknowledged contributions.

Required Texts

The following novels, collections of stories and one nonfiction work will be discussed on Tuesdays and Thursdays, 2–3:15. Readings should be completed by the first time they are listed in the calendar below.

Chinua Achebe, *Things Fall Apart*, Heinemann: 1989 (Nigeria, 1958). (A contemporary recreation of life in an Ibo village on the eve of the coming of British colonial domination.)

Ama Ata Aidoo, *No Sweetness Here*, Longman: 1988 (Ghana, 1970). (Short stories by one of Africa's leading woman writers dealing with the problems and conflicts of postcolonial Ghana.)

Pierre Clitandre, *Cathedral of the August Heat*, Readers International: 1987 (Haiti, 1982). (Twentieth-century Haitian history and a magical capturing of the religious syncretism of Voudoun by which the slumdwellers of Port au Prince make sense of their lives.)

Tsitsi Dargarembga, *Nervous Conditions*, Seal Press: 1989 (Zimbabwe, 1988). (A Black woman comes of age under the dual oppression of colonialism and gender discrimination.)

Eduardo Galeano, *Memory of Fire*: Pt. 1, *Genesis*, Pantheon: 1987 (Uruguay, 1982). (A novel of the first two hundred years of European colonization of the New World told through a collage juxtaposing significant excerpts from historical documents.)

Alma Guillermoprieto, *Samba*, Vintage: 1991 (Brazil, 1990). (The *Washington Post* called this nonfiction work "the best book ever written about the central place of music in the life of the Third World.")

Jamaica Kincaid, *A Small Place*, Virago: 1988 (Antigua, 1988). ("A passionate, savage indictment of Antigua's colonial past and the new tourism which has replaced it.")

Alberto Manguel, ed., *Other Fires: Short Fiction by Latin American Women*, Potter: 1986. (An anthology of stories by Brazilian, Argentinian, Mexican, Colombian, Cuban and Uruguayan writers.)

Mongane Serote, *To Every Birth Its Blood*, Heinemann: 1983 (South Africa, 1981). (A powerful portrayal of Black political struggle and the conditions of Township life under apartheid from Sophiatown through the Soweto uprising.)

Antonio Torres, *Blues for a Lost Childhood*, Readers International: 1989 (Brazil, 1986). ("The fascinating and convulsive history of Brazil during the past twenty-five years" as ghosts of the past visit the narrator's drink-besotted nightmare.)

Required Viewing

We will look at thirty-nine films, divided between documentaries and narrative films. These will be shown on Mondays and Wednesdays from 2:00–4:00. Most of the films are listed in the schedule below with a brief note on each.

Required Listening

Warren Wigutow will give twelve public presentations of films, records and commentary about contemporary Afro-based New World and African musical forms such as Reggae, Dub, Soukous, Soca, Juju, Zouk, Samba, Highlife, and Township Jazz and Jive. Warren is a practicing poet who has given many readings, including local ones, and is familiar with a number of Third World poets. He is also a musician, as well as being a musicologist of contemporary World Music, who for a while hosted a local Public Radio series, "Tropical Wave," where he played and discussed these African-based forms. He worked for Ras Records, the largest producer and distributor of Reggae and other forms in the U.S. In his latest incarnation he is the founder and owner of Desert Island Music in Potsdam. The music sessions are scheduled for Tuesday evenings, 7:00–9:30. Music films and a discography of the recordings that examples will be drawn from are listed in the schedule below.

Required Writing

There will be a 1750-word minimum take-home midterm examination and a 2000-word take-home final. In both you will be asked to weave the different strands of the course into coherent essays.

Tuesday, Jan. 14 (Monday schedule)
Introduction

Wednesday, Jan. 15 (as Tuesday)
Introduction
No Tuesday night Music session this first week

Thursday, Jan. 16 (as Wednesday)
From Basil Davidson's *Africa* series, Pt. 1, *Different but Equal* 55 min. (looks at some of Africa's great civilizations of the past and the

traditional European denial of these); Pt. 3, *Caravans of Gold* 55 min. (African trade with the Arab world, India and China before the coming of the Europeans)

Friday, Jan. 17 (as Thursday)
Introduction

Monday, Jan. 20
No class, Martin Luther King day

Tuesday, Jan. 21
Things Fall Apart

Tuesday, Jan. 21, 7–9:30
From Jeremy Marre's *Beats of the Heart* series, *Konkombe*, 1980 52 min. film (Nigerian music from traditional drumming to contemporary JuJu and Highlife forms). *Discography*: Sonny Okuson, "Liberation" 1984 Shanachie 43019; I. K. Dairo, "Juju Master" 1990 Original Music 9; Sunny Ade, "Return of the Juju King" 1987 Mercury 832552; Lijadu Sisters, "Double Trouble" 1984 Shanachie 43020; Dr. Sir Warrior, "Heavy on the Highlife" 1990 Original Music 12; "Fela Kuti," 1987 Celluloid vols. 1 and 2; Babatunde Olatunji, "Drums of Passion: The Beat" 1989 Rykodisc RCD 10107

Wednesday, Jan. 22
From Basil Davidson's *Africa* series, Pt. 5, *The Bible and the Gun* 55 min. (from the slave trade through the ambivalence and complicity of the missionaries with the colonizing of Africa by force); Pt. 6, *The Magnificent African Cake* 55 min. (the European scramble in the 1880s to divide among themselves the remaining noncolonial areas)

Thursday, Jan. 23
Things Fall Apart

Monday, Jan. 27
From PBS *Columbus and the Age of Discovery* series, Pt. 5, *The Sword and the Cross* 55 min. (looks at "the motivations and actions of the conquistadores and the church, and the effect on the indigenous population"); Pt. 6, *The Columbian Exchange* 55 min. (the change in the world that resulted from the interchange of plants, animals, diseases and people between the Old and New Worlds)

Tuesday, Jan. 28
Finish Achebe and begin *Memory of Fire*: Pt. 1, *Genesis*

Tuesday, Jan. 28, 7–9:30

Pt. 1, from Harry Belafonte's *Roots of Rhythm* 55 min. (the fusion of African drumming with the strings and singing styles of Spain via the Moors that underpins contemporary Latin music; also briefly looks at the *Santería* fusion of music and African religions with Catholicism). *Discography*: Roberto Torres, "Elegantemente Criollo" 1986 Guajiro Records 1043; Simon Shaheen, "The Music of Mohamed Abdel Wahab" 1990 Axiom 539865; "The Young Flamencos" 1991 Hannibal 1370; Fortaleza, "Bolivian Folkloric Music of the Andes" 1985 Flying Fish 70529; Inti-illamani, "Leyenda" 1990 CBS 45948; "Caliente-Hot," Puerto Rican and Cuban Musical Expression in New York 1977 New World Records 244; "A Carnival of Cuban Music" 1990 Rounder CD 5049; "Street Music of Panama" 1985 Original Music 8; Irakere, "Calyado Del Cerro" 1989 Vitral Records VCD 4053; Eddie Palmierri and Cal T'Jades, "Bamboleate" 1989 Charly 194; Joe Arroyo Y La Verdad, "Rebellion" 1988 World Circuit WCD 012; Cruz and Colon, "Only They Could Have Made This Record" 1977 Vaya Records 66; Silvio Rodrigues, "Los Clasicos De Cuba" 1991 Warner Bros. 26480; Reuben Blades, "Poetry" 1990 Charly 261; Tito Puente, "Mambo Diablo" 1985 Picante CD 4283

Wednesday, Jan. 29

Pontecorvo's *Burn!* 1969 112 min. (captures the impossible plight of Black slaves in a European-owned world as a British agent foments revolution on a Portuguese-controlled Caribbean island in the early 19th century)

Thursday, Jan. 30
Memory of Fire: Pt. 1, *Genesis*

Monday, Feb. 3

The Politics of Food, Pt. 1 55 min. (looks at the interconnectedness of chronic hunger, migration, environmental degradation, export crops, landholding, structural adjustment and other forces that constitute the "politics" of food); from Jeremy Marre's *Beats of the Heart* series, *Salsa* 1979 53 min. ("the interplay between Salsa and various political and cultural currents in the Latin community is explored")

Tuesday, Feb. 4
Memory of Fire: Pt. 1, *Genesis*

Tuesday, Feb. 4 7–9:30

Amelio Mendoza, Venezuelan composer and musicologist now teaching at the Crane School of Music, will present a lecture on eth-nomusicologists' reconstructions of Pre-Columbian music and on vari-ous fusions of African, Amerindian and European traditions in Latin American music

Wednesday, Feb. 5

From Jeremy Marre's *Beats of the Heart* series, *Shotguns and Accor-dions: Music of the Marijuana Growing Regions of Colombia* 1983 53 min. (the transformation of culture illustrated by the changes in a region's music by the changes in successive export crops)

Thursday, Feb. 6

Memory of Fire: Pt. 1, *Genesis*

Monday, Feb. 10

From the 1987 Frontline series, *History of Apartheid*, Pt. 1, *1830– 1948*; Pt. 2, *1948–1964*; 60 min. each

Tuesday, Feb. 11

To Every Birth Its Blood

Tuesday, Feb. 11, 7–9:30

From Jeremy Marre's *Beats of the Heart* series, *Rhythm of Resistance* 1979 48 min. (Black South African music that until relatively recently "has been ignored, suppressed or ghettoized"; much of this film was shot clandestinely). *Discography*: Soul Brothers, "Jive Explosion" 1988 Virgin 90999; "Homeland 2: A Collection of Black South African Music" 1990 Rounder 5028; "Singing in an Open Space: Zulu Rhythm and Harmony 1962–1982" Rounder CD 5027; Mahlathini and the Mahotella Queens, "The Lion Roars" 1991 Shanachie SH43081; Ladysmith Black Mambazo, "Inala"; Philip Tabane, "Unh!" 1989 ICON Records 79225–2; Dudu Pukwana, "Zila" 1990 Jika AH–UM 005; Dollar Brand (Abdullah Ibrahim), "South African Sunshine" 1985 Plane 88449; Miriam Makeba, "Sangoma" 1988 Warner Bros. 9 26573–2

Wednesday, Feb. 12

From the 1987 Frontline series, *History of Apartheid*, Pt. 3, *1965–77*; Pt. 4, *1977–86*; 60 min. each

Thursday, Feb. 13

To Every Birth Its Blood and we shall look at a Frontline update on South Africa from December 1990 (Mandela has been freed and the

ANC is now legal but violence in the townships and the provinces hampers a unified Black front) 60 min.

Monday, Feb. 17

Mapantsula 198? 102 min. (the daily life of a street hood and small-time informer in Soweto who finally cannot avoid recognizing that his apolitical stance contributes to the apartheid that is destroying his friends and his family)

Tuesday, Feb. 18
To Every Birth Its Blood

Tuesday, Feb. 18, 7–9:30

Voices of Sarafina! 1989 85 min. (a documentary in which the young South African actors in the musical *Sarafina* recount their own lives under Apartheid). *Discography*: Mahlathini and the Mahotella Queens, "Mbaganga" 1992 Polygram 511 780–2; Hugh Masekela, "Uptownship" 1989 BMG Music RCA 3070–2–N; Miriam Makeba, "Africa" 1991 BMG Music RCA 3155–2–N; Miriam Makeba, "Welela" 1989 Mercury 0501; Miriam Makeba, "Sangoma" 1988 Warner Bros. 9 26573–2

Wednesday, Feb. 19

A Dry White Season 1989 97 min. (Euzhan Palcy's "provocative anti-apartheid drama focusing on the politization of a white South African schoolteacher")

Thursday, Feb. 20
To Every Birth Its Blood

February 24–28
No classes! Spring recess

Monday, March 2

Bitter Cane 1982 Haiti Films 75 min. (a film history of external and internal exploitation of the first independent republic in Latin America)

Tuesday, March 3
Cathedral of the August Heat

Tuesday, March 3, 7–9:30

Divine Horsemen: The Living Gods of Haiti 1990 Mystic Fire Video 52 min. ("a journey into the fascinating world of the Voudoun religion of Haiti filmed by Maya Deren during 1947–51, and edited posthumously"). *Discography*: "Konbit!: Burning Rhythms of Haiti" 1989 A&M Records CD 5281; Rara Machine, "Break the Chain" 1991

Shanachie Records 64038; The Neville Brothers, "Yellow Moon" 1989
A&M Records CD 5240; Boukman Eksperyans, "Vodou Adjae" 1991
Mango 9899–2

Wednesday, March 4
Sugar Cane Alley 1984 107 min. (Palcy's reconstruction of life in a
colonial shantytown on the island of Martinique in the 1930s and a
grandmother's attempt to help her grandson escape through education)

Thursday, March 5
Cathedral of the August Heat

Monday, March 9
Black Orpheus 1959 98 min. (the Orpheus and Eurydice myth set in
a Favela of Rio de Janeiro during carnival week with a samba music
score by Antonio Carlos Jobim and Luis Bonfo; a classic!)

Tuesday, March 10
Samba

Tuesday, March 10, 7–9:30
We shall look at about 15 min. of *Carnival in Rio* (a 90 min. 1991
Brazilian videotape of the parade of samba schools in the Sambadrome
taken off the air from a New York Latin station); and from Jeremy
Marre's *Beats of the Heart* series, *The Spirit of Samba: Black Music of
Brazil* 1982 51 min. (a look at some of the political implications of the
samba schools; also ties the music to the syncretic religious traditions
of Condomble and Umbanda). *Discography*: "Afro-Brazilian Religious
Music" Lyrichord LLCT 7315; "Bahia Black: Ritual Beating System"
1992 Island Records Axiom CD 510 856–2; Escolas do 1° Grupo,
"Brazil Sambas" 1987 Atoll Music ATO 8608; Various artists, "Viva
Brazil" 1987 Musidisc MV 767; Various artists, "Brazil-Roots-Samba"
1989 Rounder CD 5045; Brazil Classics 2, "O Samba" 1989 Luaka Bop
9 26019–2; "Joag Gilberto" Verve 837 589–2; Stan Getz, "The Bossa
Nova Years" 4 discs 1989 Verve 823 611–2; Various artists, "Bossa
Nova: Trinta Anos Depois" 1988 Verve 826 870–2; Brazil Classics 3,
"Music of the Brazilian Northeast" 1991 Luaka Bop 9 26323–2

Wednesday, March 11
From *The Politics of Food*, Pt. 3, *Brazil* 55 min. (export crops displace
people who have nowhere to go except into urban slums or the rainforest); *Hail Umbanda*, U. of California 198? 48 min. (looks at some
of the practices of this large and growing, primarily urban, syncretic
religion)

Thursday, March 12
Samba

Monday, March 16
Quilombo 1985 120 min. (a celebration of the recovery of Black history in Carlos Diegues's stylized chronicle of the 17th-century "legendary South American Republic of Palmares, which was formed by runaway slaves")

Tuesday, March 17
Blues for a Lost Childhood

Tuesday, March 17, 7–9:30
Discography: "Axe Brazil: The Afro-Brazilian Music of Brazil" 1991 World Pacific CDP 7 950572; "Lambada Brazil" 1981 Polydor 841 580–2; Luiz Bonfa, "Non Stop Brazil" 1989 Chesky JD 29; "Canto Brazil: The Great Brazilian Songbook" 1990 Verve 843 115–2; Brazil Classics 1, "Belize Tropical" 1989 Fly/Sire Records 9 25805–2; Brazil Classics 2, "O Samba" 1989 Luaka Bop 9 26019–2; Brazil Classics 4, "The Best of Tom Ze" 1990 Luaka Bop 9 26396–2; Marisa Monte, "Mais" 1991 World Pacific CDP 796104–2; Caetano Veloso and Gal Costa, "Domingo" 1990 (1967) Verve 838 555–2; Maria Bethania, "Canto Do Paje" 1990 Verve 848 508–2

Wednesday, March 18
From David Suzuki's The Nature of Things, *Amazonia: The Road to the End of the Forest* 1989 94 min. (mining, ranching and the destruction of the rainforest for a few years of crops by displaced peasants from the South looking for a home)

Thursday, March 19
Blues for a Lost Childhood

Monday, March 23
L' Etat Sauvage (The Savage State) 1978 111 min. (dependency, neocolonialism, racial, tribal and sexual prejudice in this brutal depiction of a former French colony soon after independence in the 1960s)

Tuesday, March 24
No Sweetness Here

Tuesday, March 24, 7–9:30
From the *Repurcussions* series, Pt. 1, *Born Musicians: Traditional Music from the Gambia* 60 min. (explores the traditional roles of the *Griot, Jali* [minstrel] in West Africa as passed down through the generations; also a good look at instruments like the Kora). *Discography*:

"Ancient Heart: Mandinka and Fulani Music of the Gambia" 1990
Axiom 510 148–2; Africa Djole, "Live: the Concert in Berlin '78"
1986 Free Music Production FMP CD1 LC 4557; Alhaji Bai Konte,
"Kora Melodies from the Gambia" 1989 Rounder CD 5001; Jali Musa
Jawara, "Soubindoor" 1988 World Circuit WCD 008; Foday Musa
Suso, "The Dreamtime" 1990 CMP Records LC6005; Foday Musa
Suso and Mandingo, "New World Power" 1990 Axiom 539 876–2;
Foday Musa Suso and Herbie Hancock, "Jazz Africa" 1987 Verve 847
145–2; Kasse Mady, "Fode" 1989 Sterns Africa STCD 1025; Salif
Keita, "Amen" 1991 Island Records 539 910–2; Youssou N'Dour, "Nel-
son Mandela" 1986 Polydor 831 294–2; Toure Kunda, "Amadou Tilo"
1984 Celluloid CEL CD 6104; Women of Mali, "The Wassoulou
Sound" 1991 Sterns Africa STCD 1035; Alpha Blondy, "Apartheid Is
Nazism" 1988 Shanachie 43042; "Ali Farka Toure" 1988 World Cir-
cuit, Mango CCD 9826; "Giants of Danceband Highlife" 1990 Original Music OMCD 011; Koo Nimo, "Osabarima" 1990 Adasa Records
ADCD 102; "The Palm Wine Sounds of E. G. Rogie" 1989 Play CD9
LC8357

Wednesday, March 25
     From Basil Davidson's *Africa* series, Pt. 7, *The Rise of Nationalism* 55
min. (looks at the rise of African liberation movements after WWII
leading to decolonization, and the development problems of the newly
emerging states); Pt. 8, *The Legacy* 55 min. (examines the legacy of
colonialism and its continuing influence and strictures on the new
nations)

Thursday, March 26
No Sweetness Here

Monday, March 30
Chocolat 1988 105 min. (Claire Denis's cinematically beautiful
exploration of supressed sexual attraction and the unequal relations
between Blacks and Whites in French West Africa before decolonization)

Tuesday, March 31
Nervous Conditions

Tuesday, March 31, 7–9:30
     Discography: "African Sunset: A Collection of Songs, Singers and
Sounds from Zimbabwe" 1988 World Series Records ZC SLC 5000;

Sam Mangwana Franco et TP O. K. Jazz Band, "For Ever" 1989 Syllart Productions 3875–2; "Hurricane Zouk" 1987 Earthworks/Virgin 2–90882; Kassav, "Au Zenith" GD Productions 2 discs GDC 1038&1039; Les Tetes Brûlées, "Hot Heads" 1990 Shanachie 64030; Aster Aweke, "Aster" 1990 Columbia CK 46848; Samite of Uganda, "Dance My Children, Dance" 1990 Shanachie 65003; Geoffrey Oryema, "Exile" 1990 Real World Records 91629–2; Dumisani Maraire, "Chaminuka: Music of Zimbabwe" 1989 Music of the World CDC 208; Thomas Mapfumo, "The Chimurenga Singles 1976–1980" 1985 Shanachie 43066; Thomas Mapfumo, "Ndangariro" 1984 Carthage CGCD 4414; Thomas Mapfumo and the Blacks Unlimited, "Corruption" 1989 Island Records Mango CCD 9848; "Zimbabwe Frontline" 1988; Stella Chiweshe, "Ambuya?" 1990 Shanachie 65006; Bhundu Boys, "True Jit" 1988 Island Records Mango CCD 9812

Wednesday, April 1

No Easy Walk, Pt. 3: *Zimbabwe* 1987 Channel Four Production 52 min. (documentary on Zimbabwe history from colonization under Cecil Rhodes and the struggle against it with the First Chimurenga of 1896, through independence in 1980 and postcolonial problems); *Moving On: The Hunger for Land in Zimbabwe* 1982 California Newsreel 51 min. (looks at the agricultural situations of two families following independence: a Black family on poor land as a legacy of colonial displacement, and a prosperous third-generation White settler family)

Thursday, April 2

Nervous Conditions

Monday, April 6

The Battle of Algiers 1965 121 min. (shot in such a powerful documentary style that the credits have to point out that it is not one; this is Gillo Pontecorvo's anatomy of the bitter struggle against the French by Algerians from 1954 to independence in 1962—if Fanon had made a film, it might have come out like this)

Tuesday, April 7

Nervous Conditions

Tuesday, April 7, 7–9:30

No class

Wednesday, April 8

No class

Thursday, April 9
No class

Monday, April 13

The Harder They Come 1973 100 min. (despite the notorious corruption and exploitation of the business, a Jamaican "rude boy" pursues to destruction the improbable dream of the slum of escaping by making it big in music; a magnificent Reggae score underpins this "classic" that first turned many Americans on to Reggae)

Tuesday, April 14
A Small Place

Tuesday, April 14, 7–9:30

Music from the English-speaking Caribbean; we shall listen to some Calypso, Soca, Steel Band, and with Ska begin looking at the development of Reggae; we shall follow this with the film from Jeremy Marre's *Beats of the Heart* series, *Roots, Rock, Reggae*, shot in Jamaica in 1977— "a particularly fertile time in the development of reggae music" 52 min. *Discography:* Various artists, "Natty Rebel Roots" 1990 Virgin Records CDFL 9013; Various artists, "Calypso Breakaway 1927–1941" 1990 Rounder CD1054; David Rudder, "1990" 1990 Sire/Warner Bros. 9 26250–2; "Double Entendre Soca From Trinidad: Say What?" 1990 Rounder CD 5042; Joseph Spence, "Bahamian Guitarist" 1990(1972) Arhoolie Productions CD 349; The Jolly Boys, "Beer Joint and Tailoring" 1991 First Warning Records 75707–2; Various artists, "The Birth of Ska" 1989 Trojan Records CDTRL 274; Various artists, "Rastafari Elders" 1990 Ras Records 3068 CD; The Wailers, "Burnin" 1973 Island Records 7–90031–2; Lee Perry and Friends, "Give Me Power" 1988 (1970–73) Trojan Records CDTRL 254; The Abyssinians, "Arise" 1990 (1976) Blue Moon Productions BM 134; Joe Higgs with The Wailers, "Blackman Know Yourself" 1990 Shanachie 43077; U Roy, "Music Addict" 1987 Ras Records CD 3024

Wednesday, April 15

H–2 Worker 55 min. 1991 (this PBS documentary looks at the conditions of the annual migration of thousands of sugarcane workers from the Caribbean—in this case Jamaica—to Florida); from the 1985 *Frontline* series *Crisis in Central America*, we shall look at Pt. 2, *Cuba: Castro's Challenge* (a history of U.S. relations with and attitudes toward Cuba since just before the Revolution of 1959)

Thursday, April 16
A Small Place

Monday, April 20
Easter recess

Tuesday, April 21
Easter recess

Wednesday, April 22 (as Monday)
Rodrigo D: No Future 1990 92 min. (a stunning contemporary film of the casual violence and street life of disaffected teenagers in Medellin, Colombia)

Thursday, April 23 (as Tuesday)
Other Fires: Short Fiction by Latin American Women

Thursday (as Tuesday 7–9:30)
We shall explore the development of Reggae and look at the film *Bob Marley and The Wailers* 1986 Island Visual Arts 100 min., since Marley was the first Third World international music superstar, which soon made Reggae an international music form. *Discography*: Bob Marley and The Wailers, "Rebel Music" 1986 (1973–79) Island Records CD 90520–2; Various artists, "Skank: Licensed to Ska" 1989 Link Records, Skank CD 102; Linton Kwesi Johnson, "Tings an' Times" 1991 Shanachie 43084; Jean Binta Breeze, "Tracks" Shanachie 47008; Material, "The Third Power" 1991 Axiom 848417–2; Peter Tosh, "Equal Rights" 1977 Columbia CK 34670; Bunny Wailer, "Liberation" 1988 Shanachie 43059; Judy Mowatt, "Working Wonders" 1987 Shanachie 43028; Burning Spear, "Mek We Dweet" 1990 Mango 539863–2; Black Uhuru, "Brutal" 1986 Ras Records CD3015; Culture, "Three Sides to My Story" Shanachie 43088; Israel Vibration, "Praises" Ras Records CD 3045; Charlie Chaplin, "Cry Blood" 1991 Ras Records CD 3075

Monday, April 27
From the 1985 Frontline series *Crisis in Central America*, we shall look at Pt. 4, *Battle for El Salvador* 55 min. (a history of the conditions underpinning the civil war there and the U.S. support of various governments); *Maria's Story* 1990 55 min. (this PBS documentary follows a 39 year-old peasant woman, mother of three, through the 1989 campaign as she explains why she became a guerrilla)

Tuesday, April 28

Other Fires: Short Fiction by Latin American Women

Tuesday, April 28, 7–9:30

We shall finish the music sessions by looking at the spread of Afro-based Jamaican Reggae to many parts of the world, with a particular interest in its influence on contemporary African music; we shall also reprise the course with a new film, *Rhythms of the World Anthology* 1991 Island Visual Arts 57 min. (Peter Gabriel and Bobby McFerrin host an introduction to World Beat music). *Discography*: Various Dub masters, "Peeni Waali" 1992 Shanachie 5002; Various, "MNP (Peace): Reggae Round the World" 1988 Ras Records 3050; Alpha Blondy, "Apartheid Is Nazism" 1988 Shanachie 43042; Majek Fashek, "Prisoner of Conscience" 1989 Mango 539 870–2; Lucky Dube, "Prisoner" 1990 Shanachie 43073; Soul Vibrations, "Black History/Black Culture" 1991 Redwood Records RR 9104CD

Wednesday, April 29

The Time Bomb Cinema Guild 27 min. (explores the causes of the debt crisis in various Latin American countries); *Hell to Pay* Woman Make Movies 1990 52 min. (Bolivian peasant women who are not supposed to understand international finance explain quite well why they are the victims of the Latin American debt crisis)

Thursday, April 30

Other Fires: Short Fiction by Latin American Women

May 4–8

Finals week

NOTES

1. The major critical movements of the time emphasized the synchronic over the diachronic, the permanent pattern over historical change. It was some objective/authoritative critic who was to "unlock" the presumably fixed internal relationships of the "self-contained" artifact, or society, or culture, under review. This is seen in the New Criticism that dominated literature, in the structural/functionalism ruling sociology, in the "presentness" of the field-work and the structural/functional theory of anthropology, in the pure descriptivism that dominated American structural linguistics, and in the Behaviorism of psychology. Even history itself verged on the ahistorical with

its narrow emphasis on elites and ideas (Stone 1981: 5–7). And ironically, this problem was present even in the Great Books approaches to political science, philosophy and literature. These texts were often taught out of context as embodiments of "the" perennial questions, or of universal wisdom transcending time and place: Plato and Shakespeare and Machiavelli as "our contemporaries." And even when they were put in a supposedly historical context, they were often evaluated in terms of their timeless logic, consistency and coherence; that is, they were interpreted in the light of philosophers' universal criteria that often belie the historians' context in which the particular, the temporal, the contradictory, the irrational and change are often more illuminating and closer to the realities of any given epoch (Pocock 1971: 3–41; Skinner 1969).

   2. The linkage between agriculture and culture is by no means unusual. Indeed, there is a particular complex carbohydrate behind virtually every culture.

   3. All page references are to Achebe (1989 [1959]).

   4. *World Literature Today*, a literary quarterly from the University of Oklahoma Press, has been published since 1927 and is a good place to survey the field. There are a number of publishing houses that specialize in Third World literatures, and I have found catalogs from the following presses extremely useful: Readers International, P.O. Box 959, Columbia, LA 71418; The African and the Caribbean Writers Series from Heinemann, 70 Court Street, Portsmouth, NH 03801; Three Continents Press, 1636 Connecticut Ave., N.W., Washington, DC 20009, publishes a wide range of works from all over the world; The Seal Press, 3131 Western Avenue, Suite 410, Seattle, WA 98121–1028 specializes in women's voices; so does the London-based Virago Press, many of whose works are handled in the U.S. by Farrer, Strauss and Giroux, 19 Union Square West, New York, NY, 10003; The Longman African Classics (out of England) and Vintage Books of Random House (New York) also are good resources. Secondary sources are too numerous and idiosyncratic to list here.

   5. For reasonable rental by mail of VHS films seldom available in local stores, contact Home Film Festival, P.O. Box 2032, Scranton, PA 18501 (800–258–3456); Facets Video, 1517 Fullerton Avenue, Chicago, IL 60614 (800–331–6197); Evergreen Video Society, 213 W. 25th St., 2nd Floor, New York, NY 10001–4042 (800–225–7783 or 212–691–7362). Two books that I have found useful are *Foreign Films: More Than 500 Films on Video Cassette*, 1989, Cinebooks Inc., 990 Grove St., Evanston, IL 60201; John D. H. Downing, ed., *Film and Politics in the Third World*, 1987, New York, Autonomedia Inc. Invaluable is the monthly review, *Afterimage*, A Publication of the Visual Studies Workshop, 31 Prince St., Rochester, NY 14607. If you can possibly scrape up a few dollars for first-run films by African and other artists unavailable elsewhere, contact California Newsreel, 149 9th Street, San Francisco,

CA 94103 (415–621–65196); and New Yorker Films, 16 West 61st Street, New York, NY 10023, (212–247–6110, fax 212–307–7855).

6. I owe a special note of gratitude here to Edna Dana and the rest of the crew from the Instructional Media Department of St. Lawrence University, a neighboring institution, without whose unfailing kindness and guidance this course would have been unachievable. In a perfect world, these thanks would be in bold caps near on the title page rather than in a footnote.

7. For some basic music sources, see Bender 1991 (1985); Ewens 1991; Eyre 1992; Gerard and Sheller 1989; Guillermoprieto 1990; Hart and Lieberman 1991; Manuel 1988; McGowan and Pessanha 1991; National Public Radio 1992; Pareles 1992; Roberts 1972; Roberts 1985. For the religious heritage of a number of these musical forms, see Barnes 1989; Bastide 1978 (1960); Brown 1991; Davis 1985; Deren 1991 (1953); Métraux 1972 (1959); Thompson 1984.

SOURCES

Achebe, Chinua. *Things Fall Apart*. African Writers Series. London: Heinemann, 1989 (1958).

Barnes, Sandra T., ed. *Africa's Ogun: Old World and New*. Bloomington: Indiana University Press, 1989.

Bastide, Roger. *The African Religions of Brazil: Toward a Sociology of the Interpenetration of Civilizations*. Translated by Helen Sebba. Baltimore: The Johns Hopkins University Press, 1978 (1960).

Bender, Wolfgang. *Sweet Mother: Modern African Music*. Translated by Wolfgang Freis. Chicago: University of Chicago Press, 1991 (1985).

Bock, Kenneth. "Theories of Progress, Development, Evolution." In A *History of Sociological Analysis*, ed. Tom Bottomore and Robert Nisbet, 39–79. London: Heinemann, 1978.

Bosmajian, Haig A. "Defining the 'American Indian': A Case Study in the Language of Suppression." In *Exploring Language*, ed. Gary Goshgarian, 261–268. 5th ed. Glenview: Scott, Foresman, 1989.

Brown, Karen McCarthy. *Mama Lola: A Vodou Priestess in Brooklyn*. Berkeley: University of California Press, 1991.

Chen, Robert S. "The State of Hunger in 1990." In *The Hunger Report: 1990*, ed. Robert S. Chen, 1–26. Providence: Brown University Press, 1990.

Crosby, Alfred W., Jr. *The Columbian Exchange: Biological and Cultural Consequences of 1492*. Contributions in American Studies, ed. Robert H. Walker. Westport: Greenwood Press, 1972.

———. *Ecological Imperialism: The Biological Expansion of Europe 900–1900*. Cambridge: Cambridge University Press, 1986.

Davis, Wade. *The Serpent and the Rainbow*. New York: Warner Books, 1985.

Deren, Maya. *Divine Horsemen: The Living Gods of Haiti*. Kingston: McPherson, 1991 (1953).

Ewens, Graeme. *Africa O-Ye!: A Celebration of African Music*. New York: Da Capo Press, 1991.

Eyre, Banning. "African Pop in the 90's: A Musicians' Roundtable." *Afropop Worldwide 1992 Listener's Guide*, 1992, 2–9.

Frank, Andre Gunder. "The Development of Underdevelopment." *Monthy Review* 18 (1966): 17–31.

Geertz, Clifford. *The Interpretation of Cultures*. New York: Basic Books, 1973.

Gerard, Charley, and Marty Sheller. *Salsa: The Rhythm of Latin Music*. Crown Point, IN: White Cliffs Media, 1989.

Gikandi, Simon. *Reading the African Novel*. Portsmouth, NH: Heinemann Educational Books, 1987.

Godzich, Wlad. "Multinational English Stateless Literature." *ADE Bulletin* 99 (Fall 1991): 13–17.

Guillermoprieto, Alma. *Samba*. New York: Vintage Books, 1990.

Hart, Mickey, and Fredric Lieberman. *Planet Drum: A Celebration of Percussion and Rhythm*. San Francisco: Harper Collins, 1991.

Haru, Terry T. "Moral Obligation and Conceptions of World Hunger: On the Need to Justify Correct Action." *The Journal of Applied Behavioral Science* 20, 4 (1984): 363–382.

Headrick, Daniel R. *The Tools of Empire: Technology and European Imperialism in the Nineteenth Century*. New York: Oxford University Press, 1981.

Kincaid, Jamaica. *A Small Place*. London: Virago Press, 1988.

Kuper, Adam. *The Invention of Primitive Society: Transformations of an Illusion*. London: Routledge, 1988.

Lappé, Francis Moore. *Diet for a Small Planet*. Rev. ed. New York: Ballantine Books, 1976.

———. *Rediscovering American Values*. New York: Ballantine Books, 1989.

McGowan, Chris, and Ricardo Pessanha. *The Brazilian Sound*. New York: Billboard Books, 1991.

Manuel, Peter. *Popular Musics of the Non-Western World*. Oxford: Oxford University Press, 1988.

Meek, Ronald L. *Smith, Marx, and after: Ten Essays in the Development of Economic Thought*. London: Chapman and Hall, 1977.

Métraux, Alfred. *Voodoo in Haiti*. Translated by Hugo Charteris. New York: Schoken Books, 1972 (1959).

Mintz, Sidney W. *Sweetness and Power: The Place of Sugar in Modern History*. New York: Penguin Books, 1985.

National Public Radio. *Afropop Worldwide Listener's Guide*. New York: World Music Productions, 1992.

Pocock, J. G. A. *Politics, Language and Time*. Cambridge: Cambridge University Press, 1971.

Pratt, Mary Louise. "Field Work in Common Places." In *Writing Culture: The Poetics and Politics of Ethnography*, ed. James Clifford and George E. Marcus, 27–50. Berkeley: University of California Press, 1986.

Roberts, John Storm. *Black Music of Two Worlds*. Tivoli, NY: Original Music, 1972.

———. *The Latin Tinge: The Impact of Latin Music on the United States*. Tivoli, NY: Original Music, 1985.

Skinner, Quentin. "Meaning and Understanding in the History of Ideas." *History and Theory* 8 (1969): 3–53.

Skjønsberg, Else. *Change in an African Village: Kefa Speaks*. West Hartford: Kumarian Press, 1989.

Stein, Jess, ed. *The Random House Dictionary of the English Language*. Unabridged ed. New York: Random House, 1967.

Stocking, George W., Jr. *Victorian Anthropology*. New York: The Free Press, 1987.

Stone, Lawrence. *The Past and the Present*. Cambridge: Cambridge University Press, 1981.

Sydie, R. A. *Natural Women, Cultured Men: A Feminist Perspective on Sociological Theory*. Scarborough: Nelson Canada, 1988.

Thompson, Robert Farris. *Flash of the Spirit: African and Afro-American Art and Philosophy*. New York: Vintage Books, 1984.

Viola, Herman J., and Carolyn Margolis. *Seeds of Change: Five Hundred Years since Columbus*. Washington: Smithsonian Institution Press, 1991.

Williams, Raymond. *KeyWords: A Vocabulary of Culture and Society*. Rev. ed. New York: Oxford University Press, 1983.

Wolf, Eric R. *Europe and the People without History*. Berkeley: University of California Press, 1982

Reaching the Course Guide: Towards Sustainable Curriculum Development

Godfrey Roberts

Armed even with cutting-edge scholarship, sound pedagogical strategy and the best will in the world, faculty hoping to implement new courses on development may find the path to the course guide a forbidding mine field. The present essay will review the problems likely to face faculty working to develop new curricula and suggest some strategies to facilitate the difficult and complex task of creating a new course.

The statistical base of the essay is a survey of faculty participating at two institutes sponsored by Interfaith Hunger Appeal, held in 1988 at Colgate University and in 1990 at the University of Notre Dame. The objective of the survey was to determine how faculty are involved in developing innovative courses in the area of hunger, poverty and global development. The study yielded insight on both the opportunities as well as the impediments to introducing courses on these issues.

A Balance Sheet:
Faculty Strategies, Faculty Frustrations

Responses to questions concerning the sequence of events and approvals that are required to introduce a new course indicate that traditional course approval procedure remains in place in most institutions. Courses are typically first designed and promoted by one or more faculty members who sponsor the proposal through departmental review, curriculum committee approval and, usually, approval by the entire faculty. For budgetary reasons, some institutions also require approval by a dean or vice-president.[1]

The traditional route for design and final acceptance of new courses emphasizes the central role of individual faculty members. The survey made plain that it is the interest and enthusiasm of individual faculty members that result in the development and introduction of new undergraduate courses. This underscores in turn the importance of support for the work of individual faculty members.

Our survey revealed contradictions in faculty experience with interdisciplinary teaching of development issues. Many faculty reported especially keen interest, or great satisfaction, in developing interdisciplinary courses. However, the same faculty stated that it remains easier to develop and introduce courses within a specific discipline rather than within the interdisciplinary milieu—a perception that is supported by the fact that faculty are indeed much more likely to develop courses within their own specializations rather than across lines of specialization. The preponderance of strictly disciplinary teaching is particularly acute in upper-level courses, where interdisciplinary education is nearly nonexistent.

Many faculty believe that the more specialized content makes the disciplinary context necessary for upper-level teaching. But there is a countertrend in lower-level courses toward interdisciplinary courses. The majority of successful first- and second-year courses are interdisciplinary, and faculty seem to be very enthusiastic about interdisciplinary introductions to development education. But even at this level, however, faculty attempting to develop interdisciplinary curricula face formidable problems: insufficient university funding of extradisciplinary initiatives, course load (and the difficulty of obtaining teaching credit for interdisciplinary courses), departmental territoriality ("turfism"), pressures to perform in the disciplinary context and generally limited opportunities for curricular innovation in an era of shrinking instructional budgets.

More generally, development faculty cite several impediments to developing new and innovative courses. Simple availability of personnel to develop and teach new courses is often a major roadblock, especially if the proposed course would take the place of a required course in the teaching load of a faculty member. Courses designed as general education offerings face fierce competition for a limited number of slots in the general education program, which can bar access to the course guide. The growing focus on multicultural education, for example, provides a game competitor for hunger or development education in general education curricula.[2] The place of courses on hunger,

poverty and international development in general education requirements should be considered by faculty committees as a part of the
ongoing review of general educational requirements.

Time and again, undergraduate faculty return to the importance of
individual initiative in the course development process. The attention
of faculty—and faculty support organizations—is therefore best turned
towards ways of fostering this enthusiasm and creating enabling environments and skill building for faculty. Participation in conferences and
workshops seem to play an important role in the development of courses
and programs. Faculty suggest that institutions should encourage interdisciplinary or team-taught courses; they suggest as well that a special
effort should be made to integrate hunger, poverty and development
issues into new courses that are mandated to provide a global awareness
component for undergraduate general education requirements.

The conclusions one reaches in summary reflect at once considerable enthusiasm and considerable frustration. Faculty in the field of
development education remain deeply committed teachers, ready and
willing to engage students in the study of the Third World, eager to
include global poverty teaching in general education requirements and
to continue to work for interdisciplinary education. But for want of
adequate funding, release time and other incentives to develop
courses, and in the face of an academic structure often indifferent, and
occasionally hostile, to interdisciplinary teaching, the effort proceeds
only slowly, if at all.

Making Progress:
Recommendations for Program Development

The challenge outlined above is clear; but if the road to the course
guide is sometimes bumpy, sometimes circuitous, it is not impassable.
The recommendations included in the following roster may help clear
the path, at least a bit.

Disciplinary versus Interdisciplinary

In teaching about issues of hunger, poverty and international development, interdisciplinary programs and team-taught courses are especially appropriate. The cross-fertilization of ideas and teaching styles
suits well the field and the variegated subject matter, and conforms
as well to the requirements of many issue-centered general education

programs. While there are impediments to development of such courses, there are many success stories as well, particularly at the lower-division level. Here, interdisciplinary courses have been reaching a large and mostly enthusiastic audience. These students are at the stage of exploring majors and careers and constitute an important audience. Universities and colleges, therefore, as well as funding agencies, should encourage the development of interdisciplinary team-taught courses for first- and second-year students. Specialized disciplinary courses, designed for upper-division students, are important as well, but they are, in the main, major courses, supported by their institutions and in no real need of a curriculum development push.

The Small College

Small colleges with an interdisciplinary focus in their curriculum are fertile grounds for developing courses on hunger, poverty and development. Funding agencies should look at such institutions as opportunities for innovation, and programs at such institutions should be seen as a high priority for experimentation in innovative courses and programs.

Faculty in small colleges are often isolated professionally and do not have the opportunity to interact on a regular basis with faculty at research universities and others working on international development issues. Teachers at small educational institutions should make a concerted effort to participate in workshops and conferences such as the annual briefings of the Feinstein Hunger Program at Brown University and the institute series developed by Interfaith Hunger Appeal. Such faculty members might use their sabbatical years at larger institutions where they can learn more about advances in the field and participate in course development in a large institutional setting. When they return to their campus, they will find that the small college setting provides an ideal environment for innovative curriculum development. It is critical for faculty at small institutions to use the wealth of information and teaching resources available to them through various organizations described in this book and elsewhere.

Adult/Evening Degree Programs

Experimental, innovative courses on hunger, poverty and development should also be a high priority for faculty in liberal arts institutions which offer degree programs for nontraditional students. Many of the adult, minority, and urban students in these institutions have first-hand experience with problems of poverty and hunger: they constitute both a natural audience and an important resource for the development educator. Institutions offering adult and alternative degree programs should be encouraged to develop innovative experimental programs and to form consortia where they could share curriculum materials and program models. Faculty in more traditional settings might consider seeking adjunct positions in the nontraditional milieu, bringing their experience and expertise to other student bodies.

Teaching Resources

Dissemination of teaching materials such as videos, tapes and films warrant a high priority. There is already a large volume of such material available from a variety of sources.[3] Teachers looking to implement hunger/poverty courses are urged to be creative and proactive in seeking out resources: look to NGOs and PVOs, to local outreach organizations and to national awareness groups in addition to the more traditional scholarly literature. Because of the long-standing and vigorous engagement of many activist groups in the problem of hunger and development, there exists a vast nonformal, nontraditional network of educators and teaching tools. Use them!

Grants and Seed Money

Most faculty cite time and cost as major impediments to developing new courses. In this context, short-term seed money from funding agencies is especially important. A small grant can initiate significant curriculum development by providing released time or resource acquisition. Faculty must take the initiative to seek out external funds. Federal, state and local government programs offer possible funding streams for curriculum development. The nonprofit sector is richer still, with organizations ranging from the national to the community offering small grants. It is the initiative of faculty, and their creative identification of possible sources, that will increase the pool of funds in this area.

Faculty Linkages

Faculty who participate in workshops and conferences find it particularly important to construct and sustain a network with other educators as well as with funding agencies. Support for these linkages should be a high priority for funding agencies and activist faculty. Faculty should also establish linkages with students and student organizations. For example, at Rutgers University, I serve as the advisor to the Rutgers Hunger Project, a student group which does a variety of programming on campus and in the community. Such programs offer excellent opportunities for faculty and students to work together on local and global development issues within and among institutions, building the constituency for development education in the process.

The Sciences

The "hard" sciences are a fertile but often neglected area for innovative teaching about global development. Science courses for students not majoring in the sciences are an especially good place in the curriculum for such outreach; large lecture courses, often taken by students outside the major in fulfillment of science requirements, offer the means of reaching substantial numbers of students. Issues such as genetics and biotechnology and food production, food and population policy, the biology of hunger and malnutrition and the ethical issues surrounding these problems could be included in such science courses. Faculty in disciplines more traditionally associated with development education—anthropology, political science, etc.—should lobby colleagues in the hard sciences for a scientific curriculum that includes a global perspective.

Upper- and Lower-Level Courses

Educational institutions must come to terms with the curricular aspects of the distinction between upper- and lower-division courses and their respective roles in undergraduate education. This is particularly important regarding issues such as hunger, poverty and development, which are too often left out of the lower-level general education requirement of undergraduate degree programs. There is national concern that the study of multicultural issues be required in undergraduate education. And in an increasingly interdependent world, problems of global hunger and poverty deserve high curricular priority. These issues should be kept on the front burner in discussions of multicultural and general education: it is up to development education faculty to keep them there by taking a high profile both in campus debates and in closed-door meetings of curriculum committees. We must not lose sight of the fact that these issues are a key way of exposing our students to their ethical and social responsibility as global citizens.

Issues of Women, Children and Development

Courses and programs which focus on problems of poverty and hunger among women and children should also be a high priority. Unfortunately, this seems to be a largely neglected issue and could earn special focus in areas such as Women's Studies. The biology and science courses I teach address issues of women and children and development, above all in areas like population policy, food policy, hunger and malnutrition. My experience has been that students begin to appreciate and understand development issues in a powerful and personal way when exposed to the tragedy of the large proportion of the world's women and children who are denied access to the most basic of human rights—freedom from hunger. Data on indicators such as infant mortality, differential life expectancies, total fertility rates, birth and death rates, literacy levels, access to contraceptives, etc., can be used creatively to discuss these issues in a variety of disciplinary contexts.

Playing the Game

Finally, it is important that faculty wishing to implement new courses recognize frankly that as academics they operate in a political milieu and must plan a strategy accordingly. The broader a constituency a course can appeal to, within a department and throughout a college or university, the better its chances for acceptance. Network throughout your institution; make a conscious effort to understand the life and culture of other, allied departments; learn who the faculty are in other departments working in development-related issues, and cultivate them as allies in an interdisciplinary proposal—or at least sensitize them to a forthcoming course proposal so as to obviate a later clash. Turf battles are more often than not a function of misunderstanding or unfounded suspicion, easily defused in advance with a friendly caucus. Faculty must take care not to step on colleague's toes. They must be careful, for example, not to implement courses likely to draw students from preexisting courses either within or outside their department; these are the factors that generate the most stubborn resistance in the approval process and the bitterest kinds of turf fights.

Moreover, faculty committed to development education must energize themselves to zealous participation in faculty committees at the departmental and campuswide level. It is in these dreary forums that the shape of the course guide is hammered out, and engagement at this level, though sometimes punishing, is essential. Faculty must take the initiative in committee work to make development education, and even interdisciplinary courses, part of the departmental requirements for majors and part of overall general education requirements for undergraduates. With evolution toward these objectives in the undergraduate curriculum, faculty can influence broad-based, sustainable course development at their institutions.

Conclusion and Summary

Teaching about global development has been most successful when individual faculty members have taken the initiative to develop innovative programs and courses.

Since individual faculty initiatives have been so successful, institutions and funding agencies should encourage and fund such innovation.

While disciplinary courses in development issues within departments are common, faculty are interested and enthusiastic to develop interdisciplinary courses. Faculty should work through committees and interested campus administrators to overcome barriers to the introduction of interdisciplinary courses. Faculty committees, deans and presidents should endeavor to remove these barriers and encourage teams of faculty to develop interdisciplinary courses on global development issues.

Interdisciplinary first- and second-year courses should be the highest priority of faculty looking to develop new courses.

Continued linkages between faculty at various institutions, and between faculty and private agencies, has proved to be valuable and should be supported.

In the final analysis, it is the individual faculty member who has the greatest impact on successful course design and implementation. With the help of supportive institutional structures and agencies from outside the academy, we must share ideas and develop a network of committed global development educators.

NOTES

1. While this procedure varies considerably from institution to institution, courses are uniformly subject to review and approval at the departmental and university level—with important results for the politics of course development, to be reviewed below.

2. One means of neutralizing this competition, and turning it to the benefit of both multicultural and development education, would be to search for

commonalities between them. See remarks by W. Savitt in *Hunger TeachNet*, volume 3:4 (October 1991).

3. See Robert Keesey's contribution to the current volume. Pat Kutzner's *World Hunger: A Reference* (ABC-Clio, 1992) also contains a large and useful annotated list of visual and computer teaching tools. Faculty interested in further resources, particularly those used in the nonformal education sector, are encouraged to seek information on the NCODE resources clearinghouse of the American Forum of Global Education, 45 John Street, New York, NY, telephone (212) 732–8606.

Student Activism and Pedagogy: A Reciprocal Relationship in Development Studies

Kathleen Maas Weigert

Introduction

What do those who teach in the area of development studies have to offer students who want both knowledge about and action opportunities in the area of global poverty and hunger? What do students' desires for activism in global poverty and hunger have to offer their teachers? In attempting to answer these questions I want to present a thesis: To the extent that the official teachers and the official students are both really "students" as well as "teachers," the formula both for advancing knowledge about world hunger and poverty, and for taking action to eradicate world hunger and poverty will be stronger. The argument has three basic elements: a sympathetic appraisal of alternative pedagogies; a particular conceptualization of activism; and a focus on curricular and cocurricular links with activism.

Models of Education

Many of us who received our higher education in the seventies or before did not have much formal training in teaching. Some of us have been fortunate enough to have a colleague or two who cajoled or inspired us to think about what "education" entails and what it means to "teach." Others of us have been in programs or departments where teaching really is a goal (see, for example, Weigert 1984). Some of us have stumbled onto some creative ideas while others have been pushed into thinking about these topics by students who simply would not let us continue in the old ways. Whatever the source of our reflection, we have come to understand that teaching is not exclusively lecturing, and that learning is demonstrated by more than regurgitating information on a machine-readable examination. While lectures and machine-readable exams may have a part to play, teaching and learning must be much more. But what do we mean, then, by "teaching" and "learning"? I want to mention the contributions of three pivotal influences on my own thinking about these processes.

First is Brazilian educator Paulo Freire. In his classic work, *Pedagogy of the Oppressed*, Freire (1970) presents two models of education: the banking model and the problem-posing model.

The banking model relies heavily on a sharp distinction between teacher and student that is built on clear role differentiation and classroom hierarchy (see especially chapter 2 for an elaboration of the model). Baldly stated, this model holds that teachers "teach" and students do not; students "learn" and teachers do not. This model, given the type of educational system in which many of us operate, has an implicit corollary: the process occurs in an "appropriate" place—the classroom.

Freire's alternative, problem-posing model relies on a "teacher-as-student" and "student-as-teacher" conception of the pedagogical process, in which both participants in the educational relationship teach—and learn. While its detractors may argue that such a model undermines authority and creates confusion, advocates of this view counter that it leads to the acceptance of responsibility by each member for contributing where possible and for learning from others. The authority that comes from the formal educator's training and professional development will remain present and available as a key resource for the education of others. In short, this model affirms that teachers can learn and students can teach and that the process is important—is, indeed, central to education. The problem-posing model allows for creative responses to the activism of students, a point which I address in the next section.

Another contributor to my thinking is David Orr (1990) who recently addressed the issue, "What is education for?" An environmental educator, he is deeply concerned about the uses we make of the knowledge we have. In presenting various myths about the foundations of modern education, Orr suggests we need to rethink education and he offers six principles for doing that. I refer here to two of his principles: first, *"knowledge carries with it the responsibility to see that it is well used in the world"*; and, second, *"we cannot say that we know something until we understand the effects of this knowledge on real people and their communities"* (Orr 1990 p. 54; emphasis in original). Implicit in these principles is the idea that the link between the classroom and the larger society is built into education. Unless we acknowledge and address that linkage, we fail in our role as educators. As with Freire's ideas, Orr's insights offer creative possibilities for those interested in the activism-academy relationship.

Finally, there is an area of pedagogy that continues to inform my thinking, namely, experiential education. I return to it in more detail later in this essay. Here I want to cite only one of the definitions of such education because it helps provide an orientation from which we can build on students' interests in the "real world." Experiential education "refers to learning activities that engage the learner directly in the phenomena being studied" (Kendall et al. 1986: 1; see also Dewey 1963; Henry 1989; and Weil and McGill 1989). One implication of this definition is that we can extend the classroom beyond four walls.

How can these ideas help us think about student activism?

Student Activism

For some, the very word "activism" congers up images of flower children, mass demonstrations, and the sixties. For others, the word suggests hollow exhibitionism or knee-jerk reactions. For still others, it bespeaks a phase that young people (must) go through. Although there may be some truth in each of these images, there is another way of conceptualizing activism, a way that allows us to recognize and harness its potential educational value. I have in mind here three elements: action, risk taking, and interdependence. Each of these three components merits further examination, for in them we find the crucial ideas implicit in the term "activism" that we educators can affirm and build on. For people trained to be "value free," this passage of my essay may present some difficulty, but I would ask them to hold their objections in abeyance until they have examined the argument which follows (see also Weigert 1991).

Action

The root meaning of activism is action. We are talking about people being involved in some activity. How many of us, educators and citizens in general, decry the apathy of others? We ask, "Why don't people get involved?" To be sure, we do not all agree on the "how" of people getting involved, but at least some of us feel that getting involved is, on the whole, better than *not* getting involved, if we are to bring about positive change in our society and world. The 1991 data on incoming first-year students that was collected by the American Council on Education and the University of California at Los Angeles, under the directorship of Alexander Astin, provide evidence to suggest that there are, relatively speaking, small percentages of college-bound students who believe individuals can effect change. On the item, "Realistically, an individual can do little to bring about changes in our society," 28 percent of the women and 35 percent of the men checked the responses, "strongly agree" or "agree somewhat" (see Anonymous 1992). Some may argue that such a perspective is indeed realistic. Others surmise that such an attitude almost certainly provides a strong disincentive—if not an outright barrier—to student involvement in society's challenges.

To the extent that activism is a means of getting involved in positive ways in society and society's problems, we educators can support it. When our students want to be activists, our first response can rightly be supportive: to affirm their energy, to applaud their willingness to get involved. We can, and I argue we must, however, be sure that the action they want to undertake is not the opposite of "reflection" but the opposite of "apathy."[1] We can encourage student activism to the extent that it is rooted in knowledge (theoretical and practical), respectful of the rights of others, and indicative of an understanding of alternative positions and possibilities. Then we can rightfully say that if our knowledge about development is going to move beyond the ivory tower, we need such activists: energetic, reflective, involved.

Risk Taking

Activists surely are risk takers. They are willing to push boundaries, to challenge people and structures, in order to effect some change. Their ways of so doing may not always be the ways we would choose. But what needs to be emphasized here is the importance to our society of people who are willing to get involved to bring about positive social change. Student activists are part of this group. Development studies needs such risk takers.

If we agree to that idea in principle, we necessarily run up against the issue of the means activists choose to effect their ends. Those of us interested in issues of development are perforce interested in models of social change. One important issue in social change concerns the means used to bring it about. Many of our students will seek to use nonviolent means of involvement, for example, petition drives for better legislation or peaceful demonstrations for pricking the conscience of the community to the plight of the poor (see, for example, Lofland et al. 1990; and Weigert 1989: 42–45). What if, however, some of our students decide that the best (or at least one) way to bring about long-lasting social change is to use violence?

The history of our nation—and of our world—is replete with examples of the use of violence to achieve social, political or economic goals. Some uses of violence are state-sanctioned (e.g., war and riot control); others are not. Some individuals approve the use of violence in a variety of contexts; others do not. What is our obligation as educators when it comes to this issue? I would argue that the education we offer our students must include the story of violence and nonviolence in social change: the purported advantages and disadvantages, the uses by officials as well as by citizens and the implications for uses by either or both. One long-standing model in the area of war and revolution, for example, allows for a "just revolution" in recognition of the fact that "an oppressive government may lose its claim to legitimacy" (National Conference of Catholic Bishops 1983: para. 89). If we do not discuss this story we mask part of our collective experience and deny our students the opportunity to reflect with others on the uses of nonviolence and violence to achieve social change.

Interdependence

Finally, a key element in activism is the recognition of a fundamental social reality: interdependence. The word activism often connotes a group or groups of people working together. Some coordination of efforts, some sense of common goals, some willingness to forgo personal glory for the greater social good—such ideas seem integral to activism. In social traditions (like the Western tradition) that heavily stress individualism (see Bellah et al. 1985), activism reminds us of the fact and the importance of being interdependent.

There is a second element of interdependence, namely, that activist groups see themselves linked with people they will in all likelihood never meet, and see these distant lives somehow, nevertheless, intertwined with their own. Thus, we have groups working to relieve hunger or to ensure the protection of human rights of people they

simply have read about or seen pictures of but have never met person-
ally. Both of these aspects of interdependence are crucial in development studies and ones that we educators can affirm.

Taken together, it seems to me, these three elements—action, risk
taking, interdependence—are "values" that most educators can applaud
and that as such can be useful in advancing educational goals.

Curricular and Cocurricular Links with Activism

If the reader is willing to agree that the problem-posing model of
education has some merit and that educators can encourage activism
(as conceptualized above) as a potentially fruitful extension of what is
done in the classroom, it still remains to be shown how student
activism can be linked to the classroom in ways that advance knowledge about world hunger and poverty.

Two important ways in which both undergraduates and teachers/
researchers can benefit from student impulses toward activism are
experiential learning opportunities in the curriculum itself and student
involvement in cocurricular opportunities. The range of possibilities is
enormous; I shall simply highlight some of them.

As noted above, experiential education "refers to learning activities
that engage the learner directly in the phenomena being studied"
(Kendall et al. 1986: 1). It should be emphasized, especially for those
new to this pedagogy, that there are excellent resources available to
assist faculty in learning the theory and practice of experiential education.[2] The challenge of experiential learning is to provide an opportunity that is well integrated with the course of study: it should be a solid
experience that provides adequate preparation and follow up, has on-
site supervision appropriate to the level of the assignment and includes
specific assignments for reflection and evaluation (oral and/or written
projects or reports).

Such opportunities can range from those requiring significant periods of time, say a semester or a year-long cross-cultural study program,
to much briefer experiences. One of the exemplars in the former area is
the required Study Service Term at Goshen College in Indiana,
wherein students live, study and serve in a developing country (see
Kendall and Associates 1990, 2: 314–316). Another is provided by the
Center for Global Education at Augsburg College in Minneapolis,
which offers semester-length programs in Cuernavaca, Mexico (see

Center for Global Education). Many of our colleges/universities have study-abroad programs or can make such programs available to our students through other colleges/universities. A not-for-profit organization created "to foster service-learning and to develop and share domestic and international service-learning opportunities" is The Partnership for Service-Learning, which offers college/university students the chance to combine service and learning in a variety of countries, including several in the developing world (see The Partnership for Service-Learning).

The possibilities for shorter-term projects are almost endless, from simulation games and role playing to oral interviews and field trips. The simulation, "A Visit with a Local Peacemaker," has proved particularly effective in my Introduction to Peace Studies course. Here the students sign up to meet in small groups (while I limit each group to five, it could probably work with as many as ten) with one of a number of people in our local community who integrate into their daily lives the active concern for making the world more peaceful and more just. The assignment calls for discussing a range of topics from definitions of peace to the appraisal of the link between the "peacemaker's" efforts and the global society. Another involves two brief experiences in local soup kitchens.

Carefully planned, these shorter-term projects can enhance the students' understanding of the key issues and dilemmas involved. At the same time, these kind of activities can sharpen the focus on the issues. How so? Because the students bring back to the class questions that arose from the project, and as these questions are further explored we have the opportunity to examine the issues in new and/or different ways, to clarify confusing ideas, to challenge a regnant hypothesis. In short, knowledge about hunger and poverty can be advanced as a result of this kind of assignment.

We can also steer our students toward cocurricular options. At the University of Notre Dame, where I teach, on a campus of 7,500 undergraduates, we have a half-dozen student groups that are working, in one way or another, on issues of development. One of the oldest, the World Hunger Coalition, promotes a weekly fast during the semester to raise awareness about hunger and money for relief projects around the world. In a recent semester, 650 students gave up their Wednesday lunch, generating over 7,000 dollars for projects in Argentina and Bangladesh. Oftentimes, students will spontaneously bring up such experiences in our classroom discussions or we can build in the occasion to examine such involvement. In either case, we have an opportunity to raise anew such issues as What does my experiencing "hunger" have to do with the lives of those for whom it is not an exercise? What is the relationship between relief and development? What about the role of international agencies and governments?

In both cases—the experiential learning opportunities incorporated into the class or course of study and involvement in cocurricular activities—we have vehicles for encouraging the kind of activism that can contribute to the advancement of knowledge about issues and attitudes in development studies.

Conclusion

What is it that we want our students to leave with when they have completed a course with us? Surely, we want them to have new knowledge. If we want that knowledge to be more than academic (in the pejorative sense of the term), we probably also want them to be newly (or renewedly) motivated to contribute to the building of a more just, more humane world. The title of a new book by Nan Unkelsbay (1992) suggests this orientation: *World Food and You.* We want our students to understand somehow, that they are not only part of the problem but also part of the solution in development.

It is my contention that we can contribute to both these goals—greater knowledge and informed action—if we enlarge our understanding of pedagogy to include more than the lecture/machine-readable exam model; if we affirm an educationally rich conceptualization of activism; and if we make concrete links between what we do (and how we do it) in the classroom and experiences of students in the "real world." While this perspective is not a panacea for development studies, it can, I submit, make for more involved, interactive student-teachers and teacher-students, and, ultimately, for more engaged citizens.

NOTES

1. I note here that Freire (1970: 76) himself spoke of activism in this sense, action that excluded reflection.

2. See, for example, Bing 1990; Honnet and Poulsen 1989; Kendall et al. 1986; Kendall and Associates 1990; and National Society for Experiential Education 1992.

SOURCES

Anonymous. 1992 "Fact File: This Year's College Freshmen: Attitudes and Characteristics." *The Chronicle of Higher Education* (January 22, 1992): A 34.

Bellah, Robert, et al. *Habits of the Heart: Individualism and Commitment in American Life.* New York: Harper and Row, 1985.

Bing, Anthony G. "Peace Studies as Experiential Education." *The Annals of The American Academy of Political and Social Science* 504 (July 1989): 48–60.

Center for Global Education. *Crossing Borders, Challenging Boundaries: A Guide to the Pedagogy and Philosophy of the Center for Global Education.* Minneapolis, MN: Center for Global Education, Augsburg College, 1988.

Dewey, John. *Experience and Education* (1938). New York: Collier Books Edition, 1963.

Freire, Paulo. *Pedagogy of the Oppressed.* New York: The Seabury Press, 1970.

Henry, Jane. "Meaning and Practice in Experiential Learning." In Susan Warner Weil and Ian McGill, eds., *Making Sense of Experiential Learning: Diversity in Theory and Practice*, 25–37. Philadelphia, PA: The Society for Research into Higher Education and Open University Press, 1989.

Honnet, Ellen Porter, and Susan J. Poulsen. "Principles of Good Practice for Combining Service and Learning." In *Wingspread Special Report.* Racine, WI: The Johnson Foundation, October 1989.

Kendall, Jane C., and Associates. *Combining Service and Learning.* Volumes 1, 2, 3. Raleigh, NC: National Society for Internships and Experiential Education, 1990.

Kendall, Jane C., et al. *Strengthening Experiential Education within Your Institution.* Raleigh, NC: National Society for Internships and Experiential Education, 1986.

Lofland, John, Mary Anna Colwell, and Victoria Johnson. "Change-Theories and Movement Structure." In Sam Marullo and John Lofland, eds., *Peace Action in the Eighties: Social Science Perspectives*, 87–105. New Brunswick, NJ: Rutgers University Press, 1990.

National Conference of Catholic Bishops. *The Challenge of Peace: God's Promise and Our Response, A Pastoral Letter on War and Peace.*Washington, DC: United States Catholic Conference, 1983.

National Society for Experiential Education (NSEE). *Experiential Education.*(*Experiential Education* is the newsletter of the NSEE, previously known as the National Society for Internships and Experiential Education. The newsletter is very helpful and appears five times yearly. For information, contact NSEE at 3509 Haworth Drive, Suite 207, Raleigh, NC 27609–7229; telephone 919–787–3263).

Orr, David "What Is Education For? Six Myths about the Foundations of Modern Education, and Six New Principles to Replace Them."*In Context* 27 (1990): 52–55.

The Partnership for Service-Learning. *The Mission Statement.* New York: The Partnership for Service-Learning, no date. (Contact the Partnership for Service-Learning at 815 Second Avenue, Suite 315, New York, NY 10017; telephone 212–986–0989).

Unklesbay, Nan. *World Food and You.* New York: Food Products Press, 1992.

Weigert, Kathleen Maas. "Sermonizing on the Great Books." *The Educational Forum* 48 (Winter, 1984): 155–164.

———. "Peace Studies as Education for Nonviolent Social Change." *The Annals of The American Academy of Political and Social Science* 504 (July 1, 1989): 37–47.

———. "Experiential Learning: Contributions to the Development of Values." Paper presented at the International Symposium on Value Development and the University Classroom, Fu Jen University, Taiwan, October 21–23, 1991.

Weil, Susan Warner, and Ian McGill. "A Framework for Making Sense of Experiential Learning." In Susan Warner Weil and Ian McGill, eds., *Making Sense of Experiential Learning: Diversity in Theory and Practice,* 3–24. Philadelphia, PA: The Society for Research into Higher Education and Open University Press, 1989.

Development Education and Mass Media

James K. Gentry
and
Lillian Rae Dunlap

"Hell."

That's what a number of London schoolchildren said when asked how they perceived the Third World. And not one of the schoolchildren could envision a Third World person.

This incident—reported by John Pilger in *New Statesman and Society*—illustrates how poor coverage of development issues by Western media generates dramatically distorted views of the South. The intermittent and crisis-oriented coverage of the less-developed world is no accident. It is a direct reflection of "news" as it is taught in many introductory journalism classes and, more insidiously, as it is reinforced in most Western newsrooms.

In fact, news about development in the Third World seldom receives attention in Western media. "Development news," is, indeed, unlikely to be considered news at all: stories about education, agricultural breakthroughs, economic recovery, decreases in infant mortality or the use of new technologies appear rarely in the popular press. Instead, news gathered in the Third World and reported in the West is more likely to be about disasters, unrest and wars. One unsurprising result of this systematic, long-term crisis orientation of the media is the enormously negative perception of the South in the popular consciousness of the North, reflected in Pilger's report.

This essay looks at how Western journalists define news; examines complaints from the developing world; suggests ways to improve Western understanding of development issues; and, finally, considers classroom approaches to the problem of development and the media.

"News"—What Is It?

The problem begins with journalists' definition of news. Generations of journalists have used similar criteria in calculating the "news value" of each day's happenings, deciding which issues and events to report and which to ignore. While these criteria have been broadened somewhat in recent years, they still limit the scope and sophistication of reporting on the developing world. To understand better how these criteria shape the news, this essay will review traditional news values and then evaluate some new approaches.

Many journalists begin to decide what is news by looking at a story's "audience," and certain types of stories appeal to certain audiences more than others. In recent years, news media organizations have conducted enough research to know a good bit about their audiences. But that precipitates a crucial question: should news decision makers give audiences what they want, or what they need to be informed citizens in a complex society?

If the answer is that journalists should give audiences what they need, then development issues clearly belong on the media agenda. But American news consumers are seeking different kinds of media gratification, and news decision makers, concerned to improve profitability, have decided to err on the side of "wants." This approach encourages newspapers to emphasize color, short stories and visual appeal at the expense of in-depth reporting.

After considering the audience, editors assess impact, or consequence—how many people an event or issue will affect and to what extent. The editor might ask, How much of the audience will be affected? How direct is the effect? and How immediate is the effect? Events affecting a large percentage of a target audience (for example, residents of a particular city) would receive much more coverage than events affecting a limited area or a group of people outside the target audience.

Proximity constitutes a further editorial consideration: the closer to home an event occurs, the greater the audience's interest in knowing about it. Such reasoning means that events in the Sudan, no matter how compelling, are too far removed for the editor of the Reno (Nevada) *Gazette-Journal* to give the story much attention or "play." Obviously, local news is not always the most important news. But local news tends to have the greatest potential impact.

The notion of proximity also leads to the localizing of regional, national or international stories. A plane crash in Detroit, for example, becomes important in Salina, Kansas, only because a Salina resident is killed in the accident. Or the impact of AIDS on San Francisco might be the starting point for a piece about AIDS in another city.

Timeliness, too, drives editors' news decisions. Today's news is stale tomorrow. For years the competition among media organizations fired the urge to print or broadcast a story first. But lately many print editors have decided that because broadcast journalists can always get news to the audience first, newspapers and magazines should emphasize the "why," "how" and "what it means" of a news story.

Timeliness as a news criteria becomes especially questionable when considering that some information has been around for years before reporters find out about it. Yet editors will argue that it becomes timely when they find it. Conversely, much damage is done when media report incomplete or misleading stories in an effort to scoop the competition.

Editors also operate on the assumption that some people are more newsworthy than others: the bigger the name, the bigger the news. Journalists generally assume that, simply due to prominence, public officials and celebrities are more newsworthy than "ordinary" people like store clerks, apartment managers or retirees.

Another news value is novelty. The unusual, the bizarre, the first, the last, the once-in-a-lifetime seem to have an irresistible appeal for both journalists and audiences. These have been staples for decades, along with freak occurrences and pseudoscientific phenomena. Undeniably, novelty provides diversion and captures the imagination. However, what is considered unusual by audiences in one culture might well be accepted practice by people in another. A reliance on novelty, then, can be dangerously misleading, prompting news decision makers to reinforce unwittingly Northern cultural myopia.

Conflict, whether physical, social or political, is yet another long-time news staple. Murders and manhunts. Gorbachev and Yeltsin. Democrats and Republicans. Exciting, yes. But casting too many stories as tales of conflict often leads Western reporting to ignore context or explanation.

In the fall of 1992, two international trouble spots reflected how these news values affect news decisions. When war broke out in the republics of the former Yugoslavia, the news value of conflict drew reporters immediately. After all, wars provide good footage of bombs exploding and people suffering. In addition, it required little effort for many European news agencies to get their crews on site since the events were in their backyard. Even U.S. media gave prominent attention to the conflict in its early days. But as the days turned into months, interest by U.S. media waned, even after reports of egregious atrocities.

At about the same time the world's attention turned to the starving in Somalia. UN attention shifted Somalia from the media back burner where it had been just another simmering story of starving people of color, like Bangladesh or Ethiopia. As the U.S. administration began to discuss action in Somalia, conditions in the Horn of Africa moved up the news agenda. And when U.S. troops swarmed ashore in Somalia, the by-now infamous media legion was there to greet them.

What had been a distant tragedy, a conflict of sorts but not on the level of the civil war in the Balkans, suddenly became a truly local story as American soldiers from Philadelphia, Atlanta and Los Angeles faced danger in a faraway country. Prior to that, the suffering was simply an ongoing story in a land that most Americans could not even find on a map. And ongoing stories without proximity, prominence or the other news values are, unfortunately, the least compelling for many editors. Hence the enduring dearth of development news and the continuing negative press of the South.

New Approaches to News

In recent years, some journalists have insisted on expanding the traditional criteria for news to provide a broader and richer picture of issues and events. For example, many editors are putting greater emphasis on what some call "human" news, or news about emerging social issues. A related approach examines the effect of social changes, of new or proposed laws or court decisions, on the daily lives of audience members. These stories require explanation and should tell people how they, as well as society at large, will be affected. Such approaches require more time to report, more space to tell, and somewhat more sophisticated analysis and writing. And time, space and sophistication all cost money.

Many veteran journalists and academics, however, fear a counter-trend: that market research will lead to greater use of short stories, lightweight reporting and eyecatching graphics, and will not improve the overall quality of the news product. These strategies of appealing to audience wants might sacrifice analysis, context and the type of reporting that could provide adequate and accurate news of developing nations to a variety of Northern audiences.

Limits on Quality

Media decision makers are limited in other ways as well. Sociologist Herbert Gans observed in his groundbreaking 1979 book, *Deciding What's News*, that the foremost "enduring value" of American news is that it places its own nation above all else. This ethnocentrism is most easily observed in the reporting of foreign news, where U.S. journalists judge other countries by the extent to which they live up to or imitate U.S. practices and values. Ethnocentricsm is reinforced by occasional headlines in *USA Today* and other papers that use the word "we" when referring to trends in the United States.

Beyond the limits that these values impose are the economic realities that affect how media deal with development issues. For example, Gannett Corporation owns several newspapers and is one of the most popular stocks on the New York Stock Exchange. Gannett newspapers have won a number of Pulitzer Prizes, but the company is much better known for its nearly unbroken string of increasing quarterly profits.

Following the lead of Gannett's *USA Today*—which now has an international edition—local Gannett papers are characterized by short stories, color, snappy graphics and better-than-average profit margins. They do not take risks and they seldom devote space to anything remotely resembling development news. Moreover, even well-heeled organizations like Times Mirror Co. and the Tribune Co. have cut back on their international bureaus in recent years.

As for broadcasting, coverage of development issues is limited on the three major television networks—they too have closed a number of international bureaus. In general, however, time devoted to international reporting has increased on television in the 1990s, particularly through Cable News Network's "International Hour" and "World News Report," which features the reports of international journalists. Time limitations, however, still preclude many development news stories.

Network and local evening television news programs are usually each thirty minutes long including commercials. News stories must be catchy and short. When a network covers a story about a developing country, the issue must be shoehorned into television format (an average of ninety seconds with strong visuals). The result? Stories which are short on background and analysis, long on emotion and (often catastrophic) pictures.

The overall effect of these limitations is that precious little development news of substance makes it into daily news reportage. And the international news that does get into print or on the air tends to be stereotypical, superficial, without context and refracted through an American cultural filter.

Developing Nations' Perspective

Developing countries complain they are left out of the world's conversation because their side of the story is told by outsiders. Third World scholars say that information regarded as news by the world traditionally has been reported by four transnational wire services: Associated Press (U.S.), Reuters (U.K.), Agence France Presse (France) and United Press International (U.S.). Thus, when news is reported about a Third World country, it is likely to be edited by someone in New York, London or Paris before we read it in our local papers.

During the 1970s and 1980s, the former Communist Bloc countries backed the Third World in calling for a New World Information Order (NWICO). People in developing countries argued for more news that originated in developing countries and for the ability to force Western media to print retractions when their stories were inaccurate. This last point was very important to developing countries since a negative image in the Western press could discourage foreign investment or block funding from multilateral organizations.

No new world information order was ever adopted, but the United Nations Educational, Scientific and Cultural Organization (UNESCO) held discussions about it and formed a commission in 1976 to look at world information and news flow. The result was the 1980 book *Many Voices, One World*. In it the commission warned the West about disqualifying news from the Second (socialist) and Third (developing) Worlds, but it also cautioned the Second and Third Worlds about government controlled news and the restriction of journalists. The commission said that promoting national development was not a sufficient reason to restrict access to information or to jail journalists—common tactics in many developing nations.

U.S. representatives to UNESCO viewed Third World press systems as government owned and/or operated controlled propaganda machines that prevented journalists from finding or publishing the truth. The governments of developing nations, however, often defend the restriction of a free press, arguing that such tactics were used by the West itself during times of development and crisis. The U.S. withdrew from UNESCO in 1984 and has not returned. Among other things, the Americans charge the developing world with promoting a new order that guaranteed government control of news and journalists. While UNESCO has ended its discussions of the NWICO, Third World journalists and scholars continue to call for a new order that more highly values news produced by Southern journalists.

Clearly the developing and the developed worlds define news differently and prioritize news values to reflect their unique histories and cultures. Well-informed consumers of news, however, need both perspectives. Just as some people see the glass as half empty when others see it as half full, Western correspondents may report a country as nearly primitive while nationals might describe it as almost developed!

The Bad News Habit

Third World leaders admit that crises happen but deny that crises are the only available stories. Such leaders accuse Western scholars and journalists of using Western news values that highlight disaster and chaos at the expense of development news—news that is more process than event oriented. Unlike most Western news, the aim of development news is not to tell what happened at a particular moment or on a given day, but what is happening over a period of time.

Indian scholar Narinder Aggarwala goes further to argue that the goal of journalists ought extend beyond simple description of development. He challenges Third World journalists to critically examine, evaluate and report (1) the relevance of a development project to the local needs of people; (2) the difference between its impact on people as claimed and its actual impact on the country; (3) the difference between a planned program and its actual implementation.[1]

Western scholars have been slow to embrace the idea of "development news." First, many in the West perceive development news as government "say-so" news or only good news and not a critical evaluation of development efforts. Second, examinations of Third World newspapers and radio and television newscasts show very little development news as described by Aggarwala. Instead, the news of Third World print and broadcast media tended to be just as event and crisis oriented as First World journalism.

Christine Ogan (1984) concluded from her study of Third World newspapers that development news is more likely to come from local sources than from the transnational wire services. She urges Third World journalists to stop waiting for the wires to report development news.[2]

Third World countries have responded to the lack of development news by establishing Third World news services. For many countries, the news services offer a chance to get news about developing countries directly from developing countries. Critics say, however, that government-owned news agencies contribute most of the news available from many of the news services. Subscribers complain about poorly written and unusable copy. Despite the difficulties, these services greatly increase the amount of Third World–generated news.

Third World television services exchange television news packages. Asiavision and Arabvision are two such services. Subscriber nations receive stories contributed by Third World journalists. The stories are often used by the member countries, but Western services complain that most of the contributing networks are government owned. They say too that the news stories are often of poor quality and lack essential elements of good reporting.

Part of the problem is training. Most Third World journalists receive training on the job. Others attend poorly equipped universities or polytechnical institutions; only a small percentage train in local journalism departments, elsewhere in the Third World or in Western universities.

The clash of news values sometimes makes Western training a handicap for many non-Western journalists—especially if Western news values are incompatible with the home government's political goals. The training also can be unrealistic, as students are often taught on equipment not available in their own countries.

Occasionally Western-trained journalists do not return to their Third World homes or resign their posts out of frustration. In most cases however, journalists choose to work within the country's guidelines "for the good of national development." As citizens first, they forgo many privileges taken for granted by Western journalists. It is not true, however, that Third World journalists are not committed to press freedom, balance, fairness and accuracy—history has shown that many risk their lives to report the truth fairly and accurately.

Freedom and Ownership

Developing world leaders say that government participation in media ownership does not always prohibit journalists from reporting the truth. In many countries, the government is the only institution that can afford to operate the media or is the only institution trusted by an ethnically diverse population to treat people fairly. In other countries, there would be no press without government advertising or subsidy. Moreover, many Southern observers question the U.S. logic of turning the press over to private corporations and calling it "free."

Broadcasting traditionally has been more restricted than the print media in the Third World. In many instances, Third World governments inherited broadcasting from their former colonial rulers and chose to retain control after independence. The models of press ownership that have evolved now include (1) government ownership and control of all media; (2) government control of all media; (3) government corporation control of broadcasting and private control of print; (4) private ownership of broadcasting and print.

Bear in mind that control of the press can be more powerful than guns in many Third World countries. Consider that a typical Third World coup attempt almost always begins with the takeover of the country's radio and/or television station. It is not uncommon then to find Third World stations guarded by soldiers twenty-four hours a day. The guards are there to protect the government and the image of the nation in the eyes of the world. Western journalists report many difficulties in gathering news in developing countries: they are denied visas, given little or no access to government information, and can be jailed or fined for reporting on sensitive issues. People in the South, in contrast, accuse Western journalists of routinely ignoring available resources. Western journalists, they maintain, often overlook information about development while pursuing "real news" in the Western sense—political scandal and corruption in government. This lack of attention to development issues, which points out cultural variations in news values, can even limit the impact of political stories by failing to provide adequate context.

Classroom Approaches

Rather than viewing deficiencies in development reporting as problems to be overcome, an educator can decide that this flawed and incomplete reporting provides an excellent opportunity to help students apply their critical thinking skills to the media. In other words, the incomplete or misleading reporting should not be seen as an impediment to learning but, rather, as a starting point for development education efforts.

For example, an educator might first acquaint students with traditional news models and values. The instructor can do this by drawing on the material in the section above, "News: What Is It?" or by inviting a colleague from the journalism department to come tell the class about how news stories are developed. The class could examine the daily newspaper to see how these models and values are reflected.

Once the Western journalistic model and its limitations are understood, the class then should gather examples of development-related reporting. The conscientious student of development must look further than the local newspaper to find reliable information about development. Newspapers that regularly include substantive pieces about Third World development are the *Christian Science Monitor*, which is perhaps the best source of international news in context, the *Miami Herald*, the *New York Times*, *Newsday* and the *Los Angeles Times*. International newspapers like the *International Herald Tribune*, some major British papers and others also could provide material for analysis. Less in-depth reporting can be found in many Associated Press wire stories. Many libraries also carry newspapers from other parts of the world. They should be examined frequently for development-related pieces.

Magazines are perhaps the best source for development news because they give journalists more space and time to provide background and context. The most popular news magazines often include in-depth articles on developing nations, as do magazines such as the *New Internationalist*, the *Economist* and the *Nation*. Add to this list magazines produced in the countries of interest, such as *West Africa Magazine*, *New African* and *Africa Now*.

Once the stories are collected, analysis can begin with a simple examination of what they emphasize. Do the articles focus on the "who" or the "what"? Do they focus on novelty or conflict? Do they actually help the reader understand the issues being examined?

The analysis might also consider the cultural filters employed by the reporter and the editors. For example, Does the story evaluate a development in Africa or Asia according to American cultural values? Does it praise or criticize development projects? Does it provide context or background information? Notice if there is some comparison with neighboring countries in terms of development. Check for praise and/or criticism of the nongovernment players.

Look for evidence of developing world input into the stories. Sometimes there will be references to alternative and Third World news sources such as the Pan African News Agency (PANA), Caribbean

News Agency (CANA), Arabvision, Asiavision, Asian News Network (ANN), Non-Aligned News Agency Pool (NANAP), InterPress Service (IPS) or DepthNews.

Students can identify the language that creates a positive or negative impression of the person, country or problem under discussion. For example, critics long have contended that reporters use the word "arrived" when a government figure reaches a travel destination but use the words "showed up" or "surfaced" when referring to a member of a dissident group.

Students also should analyze the sources in a story. Does the story rely on government officials, on U.S. diplomatic officials in the country being written about, on man-on-the-street interviews, on academics, or on a combination of these sources? Generally, the number and diversity of sources determine the thoroughness of a news story.

Is it a one-source story? Are the sources identified? Unidentified sources sometimes are often suggested by who the likely winners and losers will be from conflicts mentioned in a story.

Critics speculate that many reporters, when sent on an assignment out of town or out of the country, talk to the cab driver on the way from the airport, the bartender at the reporter's hotel and a local government official (the U.S. consulate when overseas) and that's the extent of their "reporting." Does the story seem to rely only on these types of sources?

Stories about hunger in the Third World have the power to promote empathy or action. Well-written stories, such as Troth Well's "Raw Food, People, Plants and Politics," in the November 1991 issue of *New Internationalist* magazine, succeed because they rely on the following techniques:

1. humanize the people in the story;
2. provide background and historical context for the story;
3. use examples and make comparisons;
4. use statistics for perspective;
5. identify the key players in world hunger, and who has what to gain if the situation is not remedied;
6. present several perspectives on the issue;
7. report the limitations of any program put in place.

The ambitious instructor and class especially might enjoy and learn a great deal from a research project based on content analysis. The project could compare coverage of hunger in the *New York Times* with coverage in an international publication. Or the class could examine how coverage of development issues by *Time* or *Newsweek* has changed in the past ten or twenty years. In any case, students can evaluate coverage on sheer quantity, measured in words or column inches, and qualitatively, using some variation of the criteria mentioned above as well as noting the kinds of imagery used to describe persons and events in the South.

Often U.S. correspondents from foreign publications are based in Washington, D.C., or New York City and can be reached for comments. A speaker phone can connect the whole class for an interview with an expert on development.

Regional magazines published by Western companies provide a different perspective because the reporters and editors are often non-Westerners and they usually live in the regions about which they report. Examples are *Asiaweek*, *Far Eastern Economic Review* or *Asian Wall Street Journal*. Even the Latin American editions of *Time* and *Newsweek* tend to be more instructive than the U.S. edition reporting on Latin American development issues.

Scholarly academic journals carry good analytical pieces that can be used in classroom discussion. Consult journals such as *Third Channel*, *Gazette*, *Media Asia*, *Media Development* and *Comparative Political Studies*.

Universities also may have access by satellite to television news reports from other countries. If your college or university does, use the newscasts to stimulate discussions. For those who speak foreign languages, many news programs can be heard on shortwave radio. Immigrants, foreign service officers, international students and those who travel to developing countries also can be good alternative sources of news and may be able to critique Western coverage of the Third World. Finally CNN's International Hour and World News Report usually mention the items being discussed in foreign countries even when the reports do not include analysis.

Why Should We Care?

Our world is increasingly interdependent—the well being of the United States is tied directly to the progress of other nations.

U.S. economists used to say that when the U.S. economy got a cold, the rest of the world got pneumonia. Now, if nations do not preserve the rainforests, educate citizens about the danger of AIDS or control water pollution, the world is at risk. As consumers of news, citizens of the West can no longer be satisfied with the "who," "what," "when," and "where" of international news; we also must ask "why" and "how." We must heed the advice of Aggarwala to examine development reports critically—that includes reports about hunger. Like Third World debt and other development problems, Africa's recurring famines and extreme poverty have political causes rooted in the West. Currently, those root causes are not regarded as news—only an event like starvation is news.

Journalist John Pilger asks, "How many of us were aware during 1985—the year of the Ethiopian famine and of Live Aid—that the hungriest countries of Africa sent twice as much to the West as we sent them: billions of dollars in interest payments alone?" The answer has to be, "Not many of us," but we all need to know.

NOTES

1. Narinder Aggarwala (1978), "A Third World Perspective on the News," reprinted from Freedom at Issues, May–June, 1978, in L. John Maring, ed. (1990), *Current Issues in International Communication.* (New York: Longman), 355–362.

2. Christine Ogan and Jo Ellen Fair (1984), "A Little Good News: The Treatment of Development News in Selected Third World Newspapers," *Gazette* 33, 173–191.

PART 2

Annotated Syllabi

INTRODUCTION

PETER CENEDELLA

When we speak of development, we are speaking neither of any one particular discipline nor of a single perspective or set of analytical tools. As critical thinkers whose task it is to ask questions, to analyze, and ultimately to teach, we must acknowledge that development is primarily a dynamic process; increasingly there seems to be consensus in the field that attempts to define development in static terms, to "solve" the problems associated with it, only stunt the teaching of development. The courses presented below share this rejection of stasis; their authors reveal time and again that for them, development education is a constantly shifting series of questions. As Edward Weisband says, "the quality of . . . discourse is not to be measured by the answers any one theory provides, but rather . . . by the richness of the questions the theories provoke."

It was not always so. The collapse of formal colonialism in the 1950s and 1960s lifted the curtain on the problem of underdevelopment, which in turn emerged as a subject of scholarly attention in the North. Development studies in the 1960s focused on the search for the Right Answer to the problems of lesser developing countries (LDCs) and was fueled by both geopolitical imperatives and the urgency of crisis abroad. Although practitioners in the field spanned the ideological spectrum, their approaches shared an unspoken but fundamental assumption that the First World was in a position to diagnose the Third World's ills and prescribe the cure. The American academy was thus colored by, and lent intellectual support to, the Cold War ideological battles for Southern resources, human and physical.

Today a survey of the field loosely conceived of as Development Education yields a different view. The infusion of Southern perspectives into the Northern academy has led to a virtual paradigm shift in the way we research and teach development. Consider, for example, women and development; grassroots or bottom-up development; traditional agriculture; sustainable development; indigenous peoples (or "Fourth-World" peoples): all these areas of inquiry represent the entrance into the academy of people and perspectives previously absent. In the process, something exciting seems to have happened, and each of the annotated syllabi in this part bear this out: researchers and educators have increasingly become students as well. Sociologist Mary J. Osirim uses women-in-development perspectives as a unit and a recurring theme in her Sociology of Africa course; Edward Weisband calls for humility and moral centeredness in addressing issues of political economy; Kareen B. Sturgeon maintains her ability to critique her own assumptions by keeping an upside-down map on her office wall; William F. Fisher's course, Anthropological Perspectives on Development, unflinchingly grapples with the discipline's colonial legacy and considers the possibility of a "new" anthropology (using readings from Huizer and Manheim's *The Politics of Anthropology: From Colonialism and Sexism toward a View from Below*).

At the inception of development education, such multilayered inquiry and nuanced self-criticism were unheard of: today they inform not just what we teach, but how we teach. These syllabi are offered as representatives of development education at its multidisciplinary best: a pedagogy of inclusion and of exploration. The work of the educators in this section reflects these encouraging tendencies.

It is also a pedagogy which seeks, not the Right Answer, but good answers, which can only be arrived at through self-critical reflection. A main purpose of the essays and annotations that accompany these syllabi is to trace the processes of critical thought and intellectual development which led the author toward the course as configured.

A second goal is to provide an anatomy of the courses themselves, with description of the course's internal logic: its pacing, its objectives, the use of resources and assignments—in short, the nuts and bolts of the pedagogical approach, with some explication of its basis.

Finally, the authors offer evaluations of their courses: what worked and why, what has changed or might yet, how the course and in particular its target audience—the students—contributed to the evolution of the course and the author's intellectual development.

Readers are warned that not all of the annotation essays are strictly bound to this tripartite scheme. Osirim traces her sociology course from its educational goals and its institutional beginnings, detailing her use of the case-method approach from its conceptual basis through its advantages and pitfalls, ultimately offering her own and her students' critiques.

Fisher integrates his annotation into the syllabus itself as a way of emphasizing teaching objectives and how carefully chosen and wide-ranging readings can help meet those objectives.

Riddell draws on statistical and anecdotal evidence to argue that geography is a rich and important discipline with a key contribution to make to development studies—a contribution which he illustrates by describing the development of his course.

Sturgeon focuses on her own intellectual and personal growth, and how—as a teacher assigned the familiar and unpopular role of teaching an intro-level course for nonmajors—that growth has been reflected in her classroom, semester by semester. Her essay also suggests the need for a fuller integration of the "hard" and the social sciences.

Manrique's rigorous annotation provides a detailed walk-through of his Development Economics course, affording us a welcome look at the anatomy of a staple development education offering as taught from a multidisciplinary perspective, yet firmly lodged in the traditional discipline of economics. Its explication of assignments, resources, and use of computer interactives, as well as quotidian impediments and classroom victories extends its usefulness to teachers in virtually any department.

Bailey and Busch provide a useful service by discussing the institutional impediments to inclusive international curricula and effective negotiation. Women in development (WID) has become a staple at many an institution in the last decade—a testament to the very changes in the development education field discussed above. Rather than highlighting a well-established WID course at an internationalized and inclusive campus, this annotation offers inspiration for teachers trying to implement development education in a less than supportive administrative atmosphere.

Finally, Weisband rounds out the section with his innovative approach to political economy. This selection is noteworthy for the syllabus itself, which, in Weisband's words, represents an "open letter" to students. Because one of the central objectives of presenting syllabi for the perusal of fellow educators is to call attention to the role the syllabus itself can play, it is appropriate to close with this highly democratic and inclusive approach to the syllabus: Weisband truly shares his intellectual and ethical processes with his students, as well as his enthusiasm for the subject. All of this augurs well for class rapport and the individual student's sense of empowerment in the class. The syllabus is often the first real engagement of the student, and this syllabus sets the tone for an inclusive pedagogical process.

Global Education and the Teaching of African Development

MARY J. OSIRIM

Goals and Objectives

This course was designed, under the auspices of a Pew Faculty Fellowship in International Affairs, with two specific goals in mind: First, to introduce students to the major theoretical paradigms in the sociology of development, and, second, to place students in the roles of policymakers regarding modern issues of development in two African states that shared a British colonial legacy—Nigeria and Zimbabwe. Although this course was taught as an advanced-level seminar, the first few weeks were devoted to providing a theoretical foundation for analysis. Using the familiar lecture and readings format, students were instructed in the major schools of thought in the sociology of development: the modernization, psycho-cultural, classical Marxist, dependency and world systems approaches.

The remainder of the course was devoted to active learning, fostered through student-led class discussions and use of the case method. During the second week, students were asked to sign up as discussion leaders for one week of assigned readings. Discussion leaders would summarize the week's readings, comparing the key issues raised with other works explored in class, critiquing the material and providing questions for discussion. Such tasks enable the participants to improve their analytical skills and engage in close, critical reading, and empowers them by shifting the role of "authority figure" away from the

The author would like to extend a special thanks to the Pew Faculty Fellowship Program in International Affairs, without whose support the development of this course and this essay would not have been possible.

135

instructor. Students can further expand their specialized knowledge in some area of African development.

Another vehicle for enhancing student participation was the introduction of the case method which casts students as decision makers, asking them to distinguish among the many facts presented and to suggest a course of action based on central issues raised in the case (Christensen and Hansen, 1987). Students were assigned to teams engaged in conflict resolution and other imperatives inherent in the case. This fostered collaborative learning, as did role-playing exercises where the participants would assume the positions of government officials and leaders of nongovernmental organizations. Because roles were selected randomly, students became acquainted with varying points of view. This approach proved very effective in providing students with a better contextual understanding of issues of Third World policy and planning and international negotiations.

This advanced-level seminar was designed for sociology majors and Africana Studies minors/concentrators. Africana Studies is a new, interdisciplinary program at Bryn Mawr that combines the study of the peoples and cultures of Africa and those of the African diaspora with the study of development and inclusion in the global economy. Preference for enrollment was given to students in these fields, with others accepted provided they had completed at least one course in either sociology or economics; knowledge of basic sociology and economics was prerequisite for this advanced course. This selection procedure, combined with a limited enrollment of fifteen students, created an atmosphere where students could interact with a small group sharing similar interests.

The Course at Work:
Teaching African Development

The course began with an overview of sociological explanations of how and why development occurs (originating from the social change literature in the discipline first embodied in Comte's work, *The System of Positive Polity* [Comte, 1966]). Students were then presented with the modernization approach in the study of development which argues that changes in the norms and values of a society over time lead to transitions in certain key components of that society which result in its emergence as a modern nation (Moore, 1960).

Thus in week two of the class, we explored Parsons and Bales's argument that a social shift from the extended to the nuclear family was a precursor to development. Further, the linkage of such shifts to the division of labor in modern capitalism were examined, drawing on Durkheim's *The Division of Labor in Society* (1964). Authority, compliance and sense of identity, it is argued, were no longer derived from one's extended family and clan but rather from a more impersonal state, society and workplace where self-worth often stemmed from individual achievement.

Modernization theory also led us to explore those other macrostructures of society that according to scholars in this tradition required change, such as the polity and the economy. Participatory democracy, as defined by the electoral process and the right to vote, the establishment of a legal system, the separation of home from work and the emergence of industrialization were also viewed as essential components in the drive towards modernity.

Through both lectures and discussions, we engaged in serious critiques of this perspective. Students were quick to note that what these theorists were really presenting was the process of Westernization. In their critiques, students cited the dangers of applying such approaches to analyses of Third World nations. At this point, students were given a teaching case, "The Offended Colonel" (discussed below) to prepare for the next class meeting.

Our attention then shifted to a more microlevel analysis of development, as demonstrated in psycho-cultural theory. In this approach, becoming modern was regarded as the result of individual attitudes and behavior, and consequently Weber's example of the diligent, rational Protestant entrepreneur was viewed as essential for development. We explored how Weberian theory led to the creation of the psycho-cultural perspective.

Through lectures, students were introduced to such models as those developed by Schumpeter and McClelland, which specified the essential values and traits that Third World entrepreneurs must possess to spearhead development in their societies: creativeness and goal orientation. Students encountered a more recent version of this perspective in their reading of Inkeles's *Becoming Modern*. In both my lecture and our discussion of the reading, we critically discussed the inherent ethnocentrism and absence of structural analysis found in this perspective.

"The Offended Colonel" was an excellent vehicle for problem-based learning, where students learn abstract and difficult ideas by working through the resolution of a particular problem (Wilkerson, 1989). The case focuses on the classroom dynamics between a visiting

professor and students, where a student is insulted by a statement made
by the instructor. This placed my class in the role of having to decide
what the professor should do, enabling easy student identification with
characters and conflicts. This case forced my students to explore the
uses of the case method, as well as to confront the impact of gender differences in perceptions and performance in the classroom. Issues of
teaching and personal style as well as faculty members' and students'
expectations for a course were also discussed. This session provided a
firm foundation on which we would embark on our case discussions in
the following week.

The study of African political economy is clearly integral to the
course, but again it was theory which set the stage. We investigated
conflict approaches in the sociology of development, exemplified by
classical Marxism, dependency and world systems theories. Students
were first familiarized with Marx's modes of production analysis, and
then the contrasting positions of Marx and Lenin (Lenin, 1969). The
relationship between the development of dependency theory and the
works of earlier Marxists and neo-Marxists was explored through
Baran's contributions on unequal exchange between First and Third
World societies (Baran, 1968). Drawing on the works of the Latin
Americanists on this topic, students were introduced to the contributions of such scholars as Frank and Cardoso and began to explore the
application of dependency theory to Africa through the work of
McGowan and Evans (Frank, 1969; Cardoso, 1979).

Further connections were made between dependency theory and
the emergence of world systems analysis as put forth by Wallerstein.
Historical and contemporary examples of unequal exchange in international trade and development were traced through the emergence of
the world capitalist system, beginning in Western Europe in the six-
teenth century. We examined the concepts of metropole, periphery
and semiperiphery, and the position of each in the global system, with
an eye towards applying such models to various sub-Saharan African
nations today. How does the status of these nations in the world economy affect their prospects for development? In other words, How does
a nation's position in the periphery affect its possibilities for improving
the quality of life for its population?

This conclusion of my lectures on theories in the sociology of development marked a turning point in this course in terms of content
and pedagogy. The course would henceforth examine some of the
major empirical issues in African development against this theoretical

backdrop. These issues included political change focusing on racial/ethnic and/or religious cleavages in Nigeria and Zimbabwe; political economy and the call for a new international economic order; and socioeconomic change centered on the labor market and education for development. Throughout the course, the status and roles of women in development and the position of the African poor remained major themes.

This substantive shift was accompanied by a pedagogical one, as the lecture format was replaced by discussion. The next four weeks of the class were devoted to an investigation of political transitions in the emergence of Zimbabwe and Nigeria as modern nation states. This section began with a brief discussion of British colonialism in these societies and covered topics such as social and political development in northern Nigeria under the auspices of indirect rule in that area. Also considered was the relationship between colonialism and the emergence of a gender-based division of labor and how this affected the balance of power between women and men.

In discussing the cases, "Rhodesia Becomes Zimbabwe" and "The Lancaster House Constitutional Conference on Rhodesia," students were introduced to Zimbabwe's struggle for independence through role playing and team problem solving. Through random selection, participants were assigned to the roles of members of the Carter administration, the Ian Smith regime and the presidents of the Front Line states. The following week, the Lancaster House Conference was recreated in the classroom with the students as members of the British and Rhodesian governments and members of the Patriotic Front. In both cases, my role was that of facilitator—asking questions, writing their responses on the blackboard and seeking clarification of their ideas before considering the next question. In addition to what they taught concerning Zimbabwe's history, these exercises were valuable for what they demonstrated about the negotiation processes and the bargaining and jockeying for position that political leaders engaged in. Students realized that Western powers played a major role in establishing terms of the negotiations that still affect Zimbabweans, such as U.S. efforts to provide funding for land transfers from whites to indigenous Africans.

Unfortunately, the cases fell far short of providing a Zimbabwean perspective on the negotiations—they provided very little information on the roles of the leaders of the Front Line states or the political philosophies and actions of the Patriotic Front, Muzorewa or his supporters. Reflecting on these discussions, students noted and objected to the strong Western bias of the cases and some remarked that they actually enjoyed reading and analyzing the cases precisely for this reason. It was clear that the students were excited and challenged by their roles as policy makers and expanded their skills of argumentation and analysis through the case method. Further, these activities enabled them to become immersed in a range of political perspectives often quite different from their own, enhancing their international understanding and appreciation of diversity.

During the two weeks that followed, the seminar focused on the role of the state in African development. In particular, What were the roles of race/ethnicity, class and gender in the making of the modern state in Nigeria and Zimbabwe? How could we understand the many military coups in Nigeria and the transitions to democracy that followed, particularly the shift from a military government under Obasanjo to civilian rule under Shagari, as well as more current developments? Further, we investigated the role of patron-client relations in charting a course for both local and national politics in Nigeria.

In exploring economic development in these two nations, we emphasized contemporary shifts in the national and global economies. We examined the Nigerian oil boom in the 1970s and the attempts to control the economy through the passage of indigenization decrees, followed by the decline in the oil market and the debt crisis in the 1980s. The responses of the civilian and military governments to these crises at the time were considered through an analysis of the austerity measures and the structural adjustment program enacted in 1986. Zimbabwe's early attempts to foster the development of a socialist economy immediately after independence and the increases in Gross National Product and employment during this period were also studied. Unfortunately, Zimbabwe's "success story" did not last—by the end of the decade, major increases in unemployment and declines in output were threatening economic security. Our attention then shifted to the establishment of Zimbabwe's structural adjustment program in 1990–1991 and the initial and potential impact of such policies on the most vulnerable in the population, especially women and children. Similar attention was paid to the devastating blow that Nigeria's attempts at stabilization have dealt to the rural and urban poor.

Our discussion of African political economy was not limited to the role of internal actors in the current economic crisis, but also considered the roles of foreign governments and the international lending community. Through the use of cases, for example, we were able to study the call for a new international economic order by the Third World community and the responses of Western powers to this proposal. In their case memos, students were asked to choose any one section of the Declaration on the Establishment of a New International Economic Order or The Programme of Action and apply this to an analysis of development problems or policy in either Nigeria or Zimbabwe. They were then asked to consider how the enactment of this particular policy might affect the nation's position in the world order.

Students were further exposed to the roles of domestic and international actors in economic development policy through the case on Nigeria's negotiations with the IMF. This case involved Nigeria's several attempts to obtain an IMF loan once the economic crisis hit in the early 1980s. Participants presented the positions, throughout the negotiations, of the Nigerian heads of state; the IMF and The World Bank; and the London and Paris Clubs. This case discussion enabled students to trace Nigeria's history of monoproduct dependence, and explored the stumbling blocks of the negotiations—trade liberalization, the removal of petroleum subsidies and devaluation of the naira. What consequences would the enactment of such policies to gain an IMF loan have on Nigeria's polity and economy? What did such policies mean for political stability? In this process, students also familiarized themselves with the personal politics of Nigeria's leaders and the responses of various segments of the Nigerian population.

The final three weeks of the course were spent exploring major issues in social development, particularly the position of women and men in the labor market and the prospects of education and training for alleviating poverty and fostering development. The position of women in formal and informal income-generating activities was studied. Special attention was given to diversity in the experiences of Hausa Moslem women in northern Nigeria and Yoruba and Ibo women in the south, as well as of Shona and Ndebele women in Zimbabwe. Issues of identity and empowerment for women were considered in the public and private spheres as well as the existence of and/or access to governmental and nongovernmental support services in these areas to assist women in their varied roles and responsibilities. Students were further able to examine the impact of gender, race, class and culture in the formation of and support for grassroots development projects in Africa through the discussion of the case, "In the Shadow of the City." This case, which focused on the improvement of housing, employment and health in a poor neighborhood of Addis Ababa, Ethiopia, exposed students to the complexity of decision making in these areas when foreign donors are the major sources of financial support and local planners and leaders are responsible for the implementation of a development project. Through role playing, students came face to face with the discrimination suffered by an Ethiopian woman in her attempts to negotiate with several aid groups and their British representative. Students formulated solutions to surmount the impasse that had emerged in the negotiations and explored the daily concerns of development planners in Africa.

Finally, in our concluding discussion, we addressed the major problem areas in African development and attempted to formulate policies to improve them. At the macrolevel, the creation of regional organizations to facilitate production and promote fair trade were seen as the very minimum requirements for self-sustaining development.

Planning and Evaluation in Global Education

The case method can be quite challenging for the instructor as well as for the students. Participants were given two questions on the case to address in a case memo of two or three pages due the day before each case discussion. One of these questions was usually directly related to the case and the other usually required some critical thinking of issues beyond the parameters of the case. The second question often provided students with the opportunity to apply a theory in the sociology of development to an analysis of a problem and/or to incorporate information from other assigned readings into their response. Questions for the cases included these:

1. Does any theoretical perspective within the sociology of development enable us to account for the role of external actors in Zimbabwe's struggle for independence? ("Rhodesia Becomes Zimbabwe")

2. If given the opportunity to rewrite one of these cases in light of what you have been reading about Zimbabwe, which case would you rewrite and how? ("The Lancaster House Constitutional Conference on Rhodesia")

3. Explore the historical development of the Nigerian economy. What explanations can you offer for the economic crisis of the 1980s? Assume the role of one of Nigeria's heads of state from 1979–1986 and discuss how you attempted to resolve the crisis. ("Nigeria's Negotiations with the IMF")

Case teaching requires careful preparation. The instructor should develop four or five questions for the discussion. It is essential that an opening question encourage students to participate, and not intimidate them. While all students are expected to contribute to the discussion, some are likely to hesitate to join in for myriad reasons ranging from shyness to low self-esteem often resulting from cultural, racial or gender differences and/or discrimination. Reticent students are more likely to join the discussion early in the period with questions that seek information such as the description of actors and their positions, rather than "why" questions seeking explanations that require additional reasoning. Questions of the latter type should be withheld until the case discussion is well under way. Case method teaching might also involve students presenting their positions as part of a team; e.g., what should the transition to an independent Zimbabwe entail according to members of the Patriotic Front, in contrast to the position of the Smith government?

Throughout the case discussion, the instructor assists in affirming and reinforcing students' positions by writing them on the board. Before the class, the instructor should have devised a rough board plan—what issues will be addressed and what are the categories in which these responses will fit? What column headings should be used and where will these appear on the board? Of course, the final board content and design will not be exactly what was anticipated; but, rather, the plan provides a useful outline in case there is a lag in the discussion, and can function as a reminder of some issues the faculty member might want to see addressed. During the last 10–15 minutes of the discussion, the instructor (or a student) can summarize the major findings/decisions by reviewing the board work. Depending on the nature of the case, an instructor might also take a vote on the various policies and programs outlined on the board that were presented as solutions to the dilemma posed in the case. At the end of these discussions, I also found it beneficial to debrief the case for at least 10 minutes. How useful was the case discussion in addressing and clarifying certain problems in African development? What were the advantages and/or shortcomings of the particular case content in decision making about political, economic and social policy in African societies?

In addition to their oral and written work on cases, seminar participants were also expected to write a final research paper. Immediately before spring break, students were asked to submit a prospectus for these papers. Two major criteria had to be met in these projects: (1)

the research had to involve a two-nation comparison on some issue in sub-Saharan African development and could include the societies studied in this class; and (2) the student had to recommend policies to alleviate the development problems investigated. The two- to five-page written proposals were expected to include a statement of the problem to be studied and reviews of at least three relevant articles pertaining to the topic. As part of the prospectus, students were also asked to submit a preliminary bibliography.

During the last four class meetings, members of the seminar were required to give a five- to ten-minute presentation of their projects. These sessions enabled other students to comment on and contribute to the research process—suggestions were frequently made regarding appropriate books, articles and reports to consult and where to find them. Topics of these final papers included "The Ivory Trade, International Agreements and the Impact on the Economies of Zimbabwe and Kenya"; "Women and the Liberation Struggles in Mozambique and Zimbabwe"; and "The Impact of AIDS on the Economies of Uganda and Kenya."

Students were required to complete a final take-home examination, where they answered two essay questions. The first part of the exam focused on questions about social, political and economic development, while the last part engaged participants in the analysis of case material. In this second section, students had the choice of further exploring the case on Zimbabwe's struggle for independence or to analyze a case on Singapore's choice to pursue an export-oriented development strategy. Assuming no background on East Asian development models, the latter case tested their skills in interpreting issues they had frequently encountered in our discussions of African planning and development.

The Teaching of African Development: Reflections on the Course

The evaluation process has led me to consider some changes for the next time I teach this seminar. While I would continue to present students with a theoretical foundation in the study of African development, I would attempt to integrate this better with the study of development problems through the discussion of assigned readings and cases. Students did have the opportunity to apply the theories in the sociology of development to an analysis of problems in their case memos, but encouraging the greater use of such applications in their discussions and critiques of weekly readings would provide more coherence and depth in their arguments.

The history of Nigeria and Zimbabwe deserves more attention. Students generally enter this course without significant background in African history. Greater knowledge of events, such as Zimbabwe's liberation struggle and Nigeria's quest for independence, would enrich student understanding of the opportunities and obstacles contributing to stability and change in Africa today.

Readings on gender and development need to be better integrated throughout the course. Although gender issues were often discussed, the assignment of the majority of these readings at the end of the seminar reinforced the marginalization of gender studies common in scholarship and teaching on development.

Although I did use one film on Kenyan women traders this semester, I hope to increase the use of audio-visual materials. The inclusion of more films and videos would introduce students to the African landscape and give indigenous Africans a voice, as well as contribute to the teaching of African history through such films as Mazrui's *The Africans*.

While the case discussions were a major success in this class, one major problem lies in their inherent Western bias. Through the choices of what actors and situations to include and the perspectives presented on an issue, readers are continually reminded of the First World's role in international affairs (especially the U.S.'s position) as told from its viewpoint. For this class, there is a definite need to write some cases on Nigerian and Zimbabwean development from an African perspective, possibly including the actual words of indigenous Africans from my interviews over the past decade with such populations as market traders. This would provide an excellent context within which students could offer meaningful proposals to improve the quality of life of the African people and to contribute to global understanding, security and peace.

SYLLABUS

Sociology 311:
Stability and Change in Africa:
Nigeria and Zimbabwe

Thursdays 11:00–1:00 PM   Mary J. Osirim
Office: Thomas 125   526–5393

The international debt crisis and the recession of the 1980s dealt a very severe blow to the majority of sub-Saharan African nations. During this period, issues of monoproduct dependence, corruption, control of the economy by the state and in some cases by transnational corporations, as well as the role of the informal sector in development became hotly debated issues among scholars and policy makers in Africa and the West. Many nations still faced political instability, military coups and one-party rule that became increasingly threatened by weak economies. Poverty and unemployment continued to rise, especially among the most vulnerable populations—women and children. For some, the solutions to these problems would emerge from an examination of the internal structural conditions in these nations that gave rise to the current dilemma. In this course however, students will explore and attempt to offer solutions to these problems by studying both the internal and the external conditions responsible for the crisis in modern African development. Thus, the relations and interactions of sub-Saharan nations within the modern world system are important considerations in any analysis of the current situation.

As an advanced-level seminar in Sociology and Africana Studies, this course explores such issues through an examination of theories, case studies and other empirical works in the sociology of development. During the first few weeks of the course, students are introduced to some of the major paradigms in the study of social change and development, namely, the modernization, psycho-cultural, dependency and world systems perspectives, drawing on the works of Marx, Weber, Parsons, Evans and Wallerstein. We will then apply these approaches to the study of transition and stability in the state and socioeconomic order in Nigeria and Zimbabwe. In addition to reading some recent texts in these areas, students will explore problems of contemporary development using the case study method. "The purpose of a case study is to place participants in the role of decision-makers, asking them to distinguish pertinent from peripheral facts, to identify central alternatives among several issues competing for attention and to formulate strategies and policy recommendations" (McDade, "An Introduction to the Case Study Method: Preparation, Analysis and Participation"). Assuming the roles of government officials and grassroots organizers among others, students will have the opportunity to examine different perspectives and to make policy recommendations focusing on several issues including: (1) the mediation of Western powers during Zimbabwe's liberation struggle; (2) Nigeria's transitions to democracy after several periods of military rule; (3) the international debt crisis and the adoption of structural adjustment programs in these nations; and (4) the role of women in development, given the legacy of customary law and colonialism in these societies.

Using the cases and other assigned readings, this course will also explore stratification based on gender, race/ethnicity and social class. Employment prospects in the formal and informal sectors of the economy, and educational challenges in the 1990s. Although this course will emphasize modern development in these nations, readings and discussions will consider historical conditions as a backdrop for the current situation, as well as the issues of poverty and inequality more generally throughout sub-Saharan Africa.

In analyzing the problems of contemporary African development, students will engage in "hands-on" problem solving involving active class participation. This course will adopt a seminar format, with students engaging in weekly discussions of the readings and cases, while taking turns as discussion leaders. Students will submit case memos on four of the five cases assigned in this class. These short papers will enable the participants to determine the central issues of a case, identify the objectives and goals that a policy maker may want to achieve, given the evidence presented and the student's knowledge of development theories and empirical research. The student can further assess the consequences of such actions on various segments of the indigenous populations, such as different class, gender and/or ethnic groups. Participants will design their final research papers in consultation with the instructor based on the analysis of a development problem confronting two nations in sub-Saharan Africa. Knowledge of development theory and current policy debates on the chosen topic should be demonstrated in these final papers. In preparation for this assignment, students will submit a prospectus and preliminary bibliography. Finally, students will receive a final take-home examination.

Books Available for Purchase

Biersteker, Thomas. *Multinationals, the State and Control of the Nigerian Economy.*
Iliffe, John. *The African Poor.*
Nafziger, E. Wayne. *Inequality in Africa.*
Onimode, Bade, ed. *The IMF, the World Bank and African Debt.*
Sylvester, Christine. *Zimbabwe: The Terrain of Contradictory Development.*

Cases Available for Purchase

Biersteker, Thomas. "Reaching Agreement with the IMF: The Nigerian Negotiations."
McCleary, Rachel. "The New International Economic Order."
Reed, James, et. al. "In the Shadow of the City."
Stedman, Stephen. "The Lancaster House Constitutional Conference on Rhodesia."
Treverton, Gregory, et.al. "Rhodesia Becomes Zimbabwe."

Course Requirements

Four Case Memos	30%
Presentation/Participation	25%
Final Exam	20%
Final Paper	25%

***Case Memos are due in my office on the Wednesday before discussion of the case by 4:00 p.m.

Week of January 23rd
Introduction to the Sociology of African Development

Week of January 30th
Theoretical Frameworks in the Sociology of Development
I. *The Modernization Approach*
Parsons, T. *Societies: Evolutionary and Comparative Perspectives.*

Week of February 6th
II. *The Psycho-Cultural Approach*
Weber, M. *The Protestant Ethic and the Spirit of Capitalism.*
Inkeles, A. *Becoming Modern*, chapters 1, 2, 18–21.
***Practice Case: "The Offended Colonel."

III. *Conflict Theory: Classical Marxism, World Systems Analysis and the New Dependency Theory*

Tucker, R. *The Marx-Engels Reader*, Capital, vol. 1 and 3. Skim (pay particular attention to the theory of surplus value and the division of labor in volume 1 and to the section on "Classes" in volume 3).

Mc Gowan, P,. et al. "Economic Dependency in Black Africa," *International Organization*, vol. 6, 1978.

Biersteker, T. *Multinationals, the State and the Control of the Nigerian Economy*, chapter 1.

Evans, P. "The Emergence of a New Comparative Political Economy," *Theory and Society*, vol. 17, 1988.

Recommended Reading: Wallerstein, I. *The Modern World System*.

The Historical Background: The Pre-Colonial and Colonial Periods in Nigeria and Zimbabwe

Laitin, D. "Hegemony and Religious Conflict: British Imperial Control and Political Cleavages in Yorubaland," in Evans, ed., *Bringing the State Back In*.

Iliffe, J. *The African Poor*, chapters 3, 4, 6, and 9.

Nafziger, E.*Inequality in Africa*, chapter 5

Afonja, S. "Changing Modes of Production and the Sexual Division of Labor Among the Yoruba," *Signs*, vol. 7, no.2, 1981.

***Case Discussion: "Rhodesia Becomes Zimbabwe."

Zimbabwe Struggles for Independence

Sylvester, C. Zimbabwe: *The Terrain of Contradictory Development*, chapters 1 and 2.

Weiss, R. *Women of Zimbabwe*. Selections.

***Case Discussion: "The Lancaster House Constitutional Conference on Rhodesia."

Making Sense of the State in Africa

Falola, T., et al. *The Rise and Fall of Nigeria's Second Republic, 1979–1984*, chapters 2–4.

Sylvester, C. chapter 3.

Elaigwu, J., et al. "Federalism and the Politics of Compromise," in Rothchild, et al., *State vs. Ethnic Claims: African Policy Dilemmas*.

Prospectus for Final Paper Due on March 5th!

Week of March 19th

Stratification and Contemporary African Politics: Gender, Class and Ethnicity

Lemarchand, R. "The State and Society in Africa. . . ," in Rothschild, et al., ed., *State vs. Ethnic Claims*.

Sylvester, C. chapter 5.

Nafziger, E. chapters 8, 12, and 13.

Okonjo, K. "Women's Political Participation in Nigeria," in Steady, ed. *The Black Woman Cross-Culturally*.

Week of March 26

The New International Economic Order and the Crisis of the 1980s

Payer, C. "Causes of the Debt Crisis," in Onimode, B., ed. *The IMF, the World Bank and African Debt*.

Campbell, B. "Indebtedness in Africa. . . ," in Onimode.

Nafziger, E. chapters 6 and 7.

***Case Discussion: "The New International Economic Order."

Week of April 2nd

Attempts to Control the Economy from Within: Indigenization and "Growth vs. Equity"

Biersteker, T. chapters 2–6.

Sylvester, C. chapter 4.

Nafziger, E. chapters 1 and 6.

Week of April 9th

External vs. Internal Actors: Austerity and Structural Adjustment

Green, R. "The Broken Pot: The Social Fabric, Economic Disaster, and Adjustment in Africa," in Onimode, ed., *The IMF, the World Bank and African Debt*.

Elson, D. "The Impact of Structural Adjustment on Women: Concepts and Issues," in Onimode.

Bonat, Z., et al. "The World Bank, IMF and Nigeria's Agricultural and Rural Economy," in Onimode.

***Case Discussion: "Reaching Agreement with the IMF."

Week of April 16th

Education, Poverty and Inequality in Contemporary Africa

Iliffe, J. chapters 10 and 13.

Nafziger, E. chapters 3, 4, 10, and 11.

Zvobgo, R. "Education and the Challenge of Independence," in Mandaza, ed. *Zimbabwe: The Political Economy of Transition, 1980–86*.

***Case Discussion: "In the Shadow of the City."

Week of April 23rd
Gender and Work in Nigeria and Zimbabwe
Read at least four of the following articles:

Nafziger, E. chapter 9.

Sudarkasa, N. "Female Employment and Family Organization in West Africa," in Steady.

Schildkrout, E. "Dependence and Autonomy: The Economic Activities of Secluded Hausa Women in Kano, Nigeria," in Bay, ed. *Women and Work in Africa*.

Lewis, B. "Fertility and Employment. . . " in Bay.

Fapohunda, E. "The Child-Care Dilemma of Working Mothers in African Cities. . . " in Bay.

Raftopoulos, B. "Human Resources, Development and the Problem of Labor Utilisation," in Mandaza.

Kazembe, J. "The Women Question," in Mandaza.

Week of April 30th
Conclusion: The Current Crisis
Nafziger, E. chapter 14.

Sylvester, C. chapter 7.

Onimode, B. chapter 12.

April 30th
Final Papers Due and Take-Home Final Examination Distributed

Issues in Development: An Anthropological Perspective

WILLIAM F. FISHER

Course Abstract

The purpose of this course is to review and evaluate the issues of international development from an anthropological perspective. This is a complex undertaking, and students are expected to do a considerable amount of reading on a wide variety of substantive topics. The course is designed to enable students to understand the difficulties inherent in attempts to analyze and direct social and economic change.

The first part of the course establishes the framework within which to consider contemporary development by evaluating the world market system and the historical impact of imperialism, the market economy and Christianity on traditional institutions and values. The course also examines the contributions of neoclassical and Marxist orientations to the anthropological analysis of non-Western socioeconomic systems, and analyzes anthropology's connection to European traditions and colonialism.

The second part of the course considers factors contributing to the transformation or tenacity of traditional institutions and values, different responses to economic and ideological domination, and the impact of urbanization, ethnicity, and the changing role of women. The course evaluates the social costs paid for economic "progress" and examines the social and political processes fostering and hindering economic development in traditional societies.

The third part of the course considers alternate ways of evaluating the development of the Third World, including grassroots or local-level strategies for social and economic change which have emerged in the Third World in the postcolonial era.

Lastly, the course considers how successful anthropologists have been in development agencies and projects, why anthropologists' experience and appropriate knowledge are not more widely used in development efforts, and what anthropologists might do to make what they know more useful.

The course depends heavily on class presentations and active participation. Students are responsible for leading weekly discussions. The role of the student facilitators is to ask pivotal questions based on the readings, to play devil's advocate and otherwise to provoke their classmates into discussion and debate.

Part 1 (Weeks 1–5):
Conceptual Framework
The Political Economy of Rural Development

Week 1: Introduction: Anthropology, Development, Culture

Teaching Objectives

This week provides an introduction to the course. The lecture and discussion focus on drawing out the various meanings commonly attached to the term "development." Next, questions are raised about the current state of the world's poor (What is the state of underdevelopment and development? Who are the poorest of the poor?) and the actions designed to improve their welfare (When and why did development become a priority of Western planners and economists? Why do we assume that everyone wants "it"? What is the ideology of development?). The nature of an anthropological perspective on international development—with its emphasis on incorporating local and regional perspectives, its stress on processes that go beyond the boundaries of the nation state, and its concern with culture—is outlined. This week sets up a variety of broad questions which recur throughout the course: What is culture? What do anthropology and culture have to do with development? How are the goals and methodologies of anthropology and development compatible and how are they incompatible? What is poverty? What causes it? What is to be done?

Readings

Abdallah, Soedjatmoko and Wallerstein are used to provoke the students' thinking about what development is or should be. Three anthropologists—Bennett, Horowitz and Huizer—address the connections between the fields of anthropology and development. Two other contemporary anthropologists, Sider and Mintz, address the issue of culture from an analytic perspective. C. van Nieuwenhuijze lays out the various ways these two concepts—culture and development—are seen to interact with or impinge upon each other.

Abdallah, Ismail Sabri. 1984. "Development Then and Now," *SID:Prospectus 1984*.

Bennett, John W. 1988. "Anthropology and Development: The Ambiguous Engagement," in Bennett and Bowens, eds. *Production and Autonomy: Anthropological Studies and Critiques of Development*. University Press of America.

Horowitz, Michael M. 1988. "Anthropology and the New Development Agenda," in *Development Anthropology Network: Bulletin of the Institute for Development Anthropology* 6.1:1–4.

Huizer, Gerrit. 1979. "Anthropology and Politics: From Naivete toward Liberation?" in Gerrit Huizer and Bruce Mannheim, eds. *The Politics of Anthropology: From Colonialism and Sexism toward a View from Below*. The Hague: Mouton.

Mintz, Sidney. 1974. "Afro-Caribbeana: An Introduction." *Caribbean Transformations*. Columbia University Press. C.A.O. van Nieuwenhuijze. 1988. "Culture and Development: False Dilemmas and Real Issues," *International Social Science Journal* 40(118).

Sider, Gerald. 1986. "Anthropology and History, Culture and Class," *Culture and Class in Anthropology and History*. Cambridge University Press.

Soedjatmoko. 1984. "The Human and Cultural Dimensions of Development," *SID: Prospectus 1984*.

Wallerstein, I. 1984. "The Development of the Concept of Development," in *The Modern World System*. New York: Academic Press, pp. 173–185.

Week 2: Theoretical Paradigms

Teaching Objectives

This week's readings review the major paradigms of Western development theory since the 1950s. Students are expected to be able to identify the major figures and models, their units of analysis, and their principle points of agreement and disagreement. Students are asked to compare various perspectives on development and underdevelopment and their causes. Participants should understand why unilineal models of development were rejected by many First and Third World theorists. The goal of this review is to get the students to begin to examine their own assumptions and positions critically in light of the issues raised by the various theorists.

Readings

Dillard, Dudley. 1972. "Capitalism," in Charles Wilber, ed. *The Political Economy of Development and Underdevelopment*. New York: Random House.

Frank, Andre Gunder. 1966. "The Development of Underdevelopment," reprinted in Charles Wilber, ed. *The Political Economy of Development and Underdevelopment*. New York: Random House, pp. 109–120.

Rostow, Walter. 1965. *The Stages of Economic Growth*. Cambridge, pp. 4–16.

Ruccio, David F., and Lawrence H. Simon. 1988. "Radical Theories of Development," in Charles Wilber, ed. *The Political Economy of Development and Underdevelopment*. New York: Random House.

Wilber, Charles, and Kenneth Jameson. 1988. "Paradigms of Economic Development and Beyond," in Charles Wilber, ed. *The Political Economy of Development and Underdevelopment*. New York: Random House, pp. 3–27.

Suggested Readings

Nash, Manning. 1984. *Unfinished Agenda: The Dynamics of Modernization in Developing Nations*. Boulder: Westview Press, pp. 1–20.

Roxborough, Ian. 1979. *Theories of Underdevelopment*. MacMillan.

Week 3: Historical Framework:
The Making of the Third World

Teaching Objectives

This week continues the focus on theory, but it weaves in many of the themes introduced in the first week by raising the anthropological critique of development paradigms. The objective is to make students aware of the need to take a historical view of the evolution of the world system and of what is now referred to as the Third World; to consider ways in which anthropological criticisms have challenged the Eurocentric bias of earlier models of global development and integration; and to learn about the relationship of local cultures and so-called indigenous peoples to the "march of progress." Students should be able to discuss the importance of the global system of economic and social relationships to the present state of poverty in many countries in the world.

Readings

Wolf, Eric R. 1982. *Europe and the People without History*. Berkeley: University of California, pp. 1–125, 385–end.

Worsley, Peter. 1984. "The Creation of the Third World," in *The Three Worlds: Culture and World Development*. Chicago: University of Chicago Press, pp. 1–59.

Suggested Readings

Achebe, Chinua. 1959. *Things Fall Apart*. New York: Fawcett Crest.
Critchfield. 1983. *Villages*. Garden City: Anchor.

Week 4: From Paradigms to Policies:
North-South Relations, the Politics of Aid

Teaching Objectives

This week moves from the concern with development paradigms to a reflection on policies. The objective is to get students to examine how assumptions about the nature of change, and the constraints of the current world system, affect the options of actors. The discussion focuses on the motives of First World states (What are the politics of aid?) and options open to Third World states.

Readings

Gendzier, Irene L. 1985. *Managing Political Change: Social Scientists and the Third World*. Westview Press, pp. 1–47.
Hancock, Graham. 1989. *The Lords of Poverty*. Little Brown.
Hellinger, Stephen et al. 1988. *Aid for Just Development*. Lynne Reinner.
UNDP. 1990. *Antalya Statement on Change: Threat or Opportunity for Human Progress*. UNDP Development Study Programme.
World Bank. 1990. *Social Indicators of Development*.

Suggested Readings

Klitgaard, Robert. 1990. *Tropical Gangsters: One Man's Experience with Development and Decadence in Deepest Africa*. Basic Books.
Morrison, Elizabeth, and Randall B. Purcell, eds. 1988. *Players and Issues in US Foreign Aid*. Kumarian Press.

Week 5: Putting Theory into Practice:
Analyzing and Assessing Development:
Categories, Statistics, Assumptions, etc.

Teaching Objectives

This week examines the implications of development ideology for the practice of development. The objective is to show that development cannot be apolitical, that there is no practice without theory (or development without ideology). Class discussion examines the policies and practices of contemporary development rhetoric to determine whether there has been a significant change from past practice or merely a change in rhetoric. Students are encouraged to examine their ideas of successful development. How is development success measured? What has been achieved in the past forty years? What has worked? What has not? What are the most persistent economic and social problems?

Readings

Chambers, Robert. 1983. *Rural Development: Putting the Last First*. London: Longman.

Frank, Leonard. 1986. "The Development Game," Granta 20:229–243.

Hill, Polly. 1986. *Development Economics on Trial: The Anthropological Case for a Prosecution*. Cambridge: University Press, pp. 1–80.

Wood, Geoff. 1985. "The Politics of Development Policy Labelling," *Development and Change* 16:347–373.

Suggested Readings

Campbell, J. Gabriel. 1979.*The Use and Misuse of Social Science Research in Nepal*. Kirtipur: CNAS. Excerpts.

Robins, Edward. 1986. "Problems and Perspectives in Development Anthropology: The Short Term Assignment," in Edward C. Green, ed. 1986. *Practicing Development Anthropology*. Boulder: Westview Press.

Part 2 (Weeks 6–10)
Issues and Cases:
Processes and Obstacles

Week 6: The Green Revolution

Teaching Objectives

Students are asked to assess the "success" of the Green Revolution and are thus encouraged to identify the motives, assumptions, and objectives of various actors responsible for the introduction of high-yield varieties of grains. What do each of these groups of actors see as the objectives of development? How is change to be instigated? How does a policy emerge from theoretical assumptions and support foreign policy objectives? The objective of the class discussion is to encourage students to recognize how far-ranging and varied the impact of these technical inputs were. By examining the many unintended and unanticipated results of the Green Revolution, students recognize the problems inherent in projecting the "success" of development initiatives.

The processes leading to the implementation of high-yield varieties of grain in India can be discussed as a case during the first hour of the class.

Readings

Attwood, Donald. 1988. "Poverty, Inequality and Economic Growth in Rural India," in Donald W. Attwood, Thomas C. Bruneau and John Galaty, eds. 1988. *Power and Poverty: Development and Development Projects in the Third World*. Boulder: Westview.

Baker. 1984. "Frogs and Farmers: The Green Revolution in India and Its Murky Past," in Tim Bayliss-Smith and Sudhir Wanmali, eds. *Understanding Green Revolutions: Agrarian Change and Development Planning in South Asia.* Cambridge: Cambridge University Press.

Chambers, Robert. 1984. "Beyond the Green Revolution: A Selective Essay" in Tim Bayliss-Smith and Sudhir Wanmali, eds. *Understanding Green Revolutions: Agrarian Change and Development Planning in South Asia.* Cambridge: Cambridge University Press.

Spitz, Pierre. "The Green Revolution Re-examined in India," in Bernhard Glaeser, ed. 1987. *The Green Revolution Revisited: Critique and Alternatives.* London: Allen and Unwin.

Dhanagare, D. N. 1988. "The Green Revolution and Social Inequalities in Rural India," *The Bulletin of Concerned Asian Scholars* 20.2.

Week 7: Peasant Resistance

Teaching Objectives

There are two basic objectives to this week: First, through the use of a case study of the impact of the Green Revolution in one particular location students are encouraged to focus on local-level dynamics (How does technical change disrupt local social relationships? What means do the disadvantaged have to resist change? How effective are these weapons? What are the implications for development practitioners?). Second, students are asked to focus on the theoretical implications for the analysis of change (In what ways may studies of local resistance and the formation of counterhegemonies be integrated into models of development? What is cultural hegemony?).

Reading

Scott, James C. 1985. *Weapons of the Weak: Everyday Forms of Peasant Resistance.* New Haven: Yale.

Week 8: Culture and Conformity:
Indigenous Interpretations of Capitalist Modernization

Teaching Objectives

This week has two main objectives. First, it follows upon the previous week's discussion and furthers our consideration of the ways in which studies of local resistance and the formation of counterhegemonies may be integrated into models of development. The situation of Bolivian miners serves as a case study in social alienation and the power of culture as resistance to exploitation. Secondly, students are asked to consider the implications of Taussig's argument that we need to question how our own categories affect our analysis of development.

To what degree can or need we break away from our Eurocentric categories of analysis?

Readings

Taussig, M. 1980. *The Devil and Commodity Fetishism in South America*. Chapel
Hill: University of North Carolina Press.

Nash, June. 1979. *We Eat the Mines and the Mines Eat Us*. New York: Columbia University Press.

Week 9: Natural Resources, Culture and Development:
The Question of Sustainability

Teaching Objectives

This week has two main objectives: First, to illustrate how analytic
and conceptual categories affect the way various actors perceive nature
and the relationship between people and nature, the problems of environmental degradation and the appropriate solutions; and second, the
critical importance of seeing environmental problems and solutions
within a wider social, economic and political context. In the face of
conflicting local and international interests, what is a sustainable
exploitation of the environment?

Readings

Hecht, Susanna, and Alexander Cockburn. 1990. *The Fate of the Forest:
Developers, Destroyers and Defenders of the Amazon*. New York: Harper
Collins.

Murray, Gerald F. 1987. "The Domestication of Wood in Haiti: A Case Study
in Applied Evolution," in Robert M. Wulff, and Shirley J. Fiske. 1987.
Anthropological Praxis: Translating Knowledge into Action. Boulder: Westview.

Suggested Reading

Gregersen, Hans and Stephen McGaughey. 1987. "Social Forestry and Sustainable Development," in Douglas D. Southgate and John F. Disinger.
Sustainable Resource Development in the Third World. Boulder: Westview.

Hansen, David, and J. Mark Erbaugh. 1987. "The Social Dimension of Nat-
ural Resource Management," in Douglas D. Southgate and John F.
Disinger. *Sustainable Resource Development in the Third World*. Boulder:
Westview.

Hueting, Roefire. 1989. "Correcting National Income Accounting for Environmental Losses." Yusuf Ahmed et al. *Environmental Accounting for
Sustainable Development*.

Shiva, Vandana. 1988. *Staying Alive: Women, Ecology and Survival in India*.
London: Zed Books.

Week 10: "Tribals" and Development

Teaching Objectives

To examine and dispel our assumptions of what "tribals" are like. To clarify the processes that so often make tribal people the victims of progress. To recognize that the problem is one of conflict between those whose power is recognized as legitimate (the state, multinationals, etc.) or semilegitimate (settlers, peasants) and those whose rights are not recognized. To recognize the complex connections between cultural clashes and conflicts over resources.

Readings

Bodley, John H., ed. 1988. *Tribal Peoples and Development Issues: A Global Overview*. Palo Alto: Mayfield, pp. 135–298.

Davis, S. H. 1979. "The Social Responsibility of Anthropological Science in the Context of Contemporary Brazil," in Gerrit Huizer and Bruce Mannheim, eds. *The Politics of Anthropology: From Colonialism and Sexism toward a View from Below*. The Hague: Mouton.

Dorfman, Ariel. 1988. "Wandering on the Boundaries of Development," in Annis and Hakim, eds. *Direct to the Poor*. Boulder: Lynne Reinner.

Suggested Readings

Cultural Survival Quarterly. 13.1 1989. "Brazil: Who Pays for Development?"

Fernades, Walter, and E. G. Thukral, eds. 1989. *Development, Displacement and Rehabilitation*. New Delhi: Indian Social Institute.

Part 3 (Weeks 11–14)
Transforming Development:
Development Alternatives or Alternatives to Development

Economic development is the process whereby the structure of our culture changes in ways that improve the quality of peoples' lives by providing them, through wealth creation, with the opportunity to participate in the ownership of an expanding capital base. Under this definition, job creation without ownership is not enough, economic growth that leaves a segment of our population in permanent poverty is unacceptable. (Jill Shellow, ed. 1985. *Grant Seekers Funding Sourcebook*)

Week 11: Socialist Alternatives

Teaching Objectives

This week's readings examine alternative models of development. Most of the class time is devoted to Nyerere's development strategy and Hyden's critique of it; we thus examine both the empirical conditions of Tanzania's socioeconomy and the theoretical explanations that describe various aspects of it as precapitalist, capitalist and socialist. Issues to be raised include Hyden's notion of an "uncaptured peasantry," the causes of underdevelopment in Tanzania, the appropriation of indigenous traditions to achieve national development objectives, and the means by which a peasantry may be motivated or "captured."

Readings

Bhatt, V. V. "Development Problem, Strategy, and Technology Choice: Sarvodaya and Socialist Approaches in India," *Economic Development and Cultural Change* 31.1 (October 1982).

Croll, Elisabeth J. 1981. "Women in Rural Production and Reproduction in the Soviet Union, China, Cuba and Tanzania: Socialist Development Experiences," *Signs* 7.2.

Hyden, Goren. 1980. *Beyond Ujamaa in Tanzania: Underdevelopment and an Uncaptured Peasantry.* Berkeley: University of California Press, pp. 9–37, 96–128, 209–262.

Suggested Readings

Chan, A. et al. 1984. *Chen Village.* Berkeley: University of California Press.

Week 12: Women and Development

Teaching Objectives

This week raises a variety of central issues related to gender and development: To what degree is an emphasis on gender necessary and justified in anthropology and development? Is it analytically productive to isolate women conceptually from the rest of the poor? To what degree are their experiences similar and to what degree do they vary according to class, ethnicity or religious background? To what extent have strategies designed to achieve overall economic growth and increase agricultural and industrial productivity proved inimical to women? Why? How do changes in the larger world economic system impinge upon gender relations at the local level? Is modern capitalism a liberating force for women or does it undermine their position relative to men? How do special targets for women further marginalize them and prevent their full participation in development projects?

Readings

Beneria, L., and G. Sen. "Accumulate Reproduction and Women's Roles in Economic Development: Boserup Revisited," *Signs* 7.2 (1981).

Borque and Warren. 1987. "Technology, Gender and Development," *Daedalus* 116.4.

Leacock, Eleanor, and Helen Safa. 1985. "Postscript," in *Women's Work*. New York: Bergin and Garvey.

Mies, Maria et al. 1988. *Women: The Last Colony*. Atlantic Highlands, NJ: Zed Books.

Suggested Readings

Leacock, Eleanor. 1979. "Women, Development and Anthropological Facts and Fictions," in Gerrit Huizer and Bruce Mannheim, eds. *The Politics of Anthropology: From Colonialism and Sexism toward a View from Below*. The Hague: Mouton.

Rogers, Barbara. 1980. *The Domestication of Women*. New York: St. Martin's Press, pp.49–120.

Week 13: Development from Below:
Grassroots Alternatives in South Asia

Teaching Objectives

This week students are asked to examine critically the prospects for community participation and grassroots alternatives. What is a community? What are community issues? How and by whom can they be identified? What are the costs and problems of participation? What kinds of grassroots projects are sustainable? Can they be taken to scale?

Readings

Annis, Sheldon. 1988. "Can Small-Scale Development Be Large-Scale Policy?" in Annis and Hakim, eds. *Direct to the Poor*. Boulder: Lynne Rienner.

Dhungel, Dipak P. 1986. "The People's Movement and Experiment in Nepal," *Community Development Journal* 21.3 (July 1986): 217–225.

Goulet, Denis. 1988. "Development Strategy in Sri Lanka and a People's Alternative," in Donald W. Attwood, Thomas C. Bruneau and John Galaty, eds. 1988. *Power and Poverty: Development and Development Projects in the Third World*. Boulder: Westview.

Shiva, Vandana. 1986. "Ecology Movements in India. *Alternatives*. 11:255–273.

Suggested Readings

Annis, Sheldon, and Peter Hakim. 1988. *Direct to the Poor: Grassroots Development in Latin America*. Boulder: Lynne Rienner.

Cultural Survival Quarterly. 1987. Volume 11.1. "Grassroots Development."

Week 14: Anthropology and Development Reconsidered:
The Anthropology of Development and Development Anthropology

Teaching Objectives

The final session (1) reviews the theoretical and methodological contributions that anthropology has made or could make to the practice and study of development, and (2) considers the ways in which anthropology can learn from and be enriched by development studies.

Readings

Bowen, John R. 1988. "Power and Meaning in Economic Change: What Does Anthropology Learn from Development Studies?" in Bennett and Bowen, eds. *Production and Autonomy: Anthropological Studies and Critiques of Development*. University Press of America.

Escobar, Arturo. 1991. "Anthropology and the Development Encounter: The Making and Marketing of Development Anthropology," *American Ethnologist*. 18.4 (November 1991).

Kottak, Conrad. 1991. "When People Don't Come First: Some Sociological Lessons from Completed Projects," in Michael Cernea, ed. *Putting People First: Sociological Variables in Rural Development*. Oxford: Oxford University Press.

Korten, David. 1984. "People-Centered Development: Towards a Framework," in Korten and Klauss. *People-Centered Development*. Kumarian Press.

Rew, A. 1985. "The Organizational Connection: Multidisciplinary Practice and Anthropological Theory," in Ralph Grillo and Alan Rew, eds. *Social Anthropology and Development Policy*. New York: Tavistock.

Robins, Edward. 1986. "The Strategy of Development and the Role of the Anthropologist," in Edward C. Green, ed. 1986. *Practicing Development Anthropology*. Boulder: Westview Press.

Suggested Readings

Green, Edward C. 1986. "Themes in the Practice of Development Anthropology," in Edward C. Green, ed. 1986. *Practicing Development Anthropology*. Boulder: Westview Press.

Robertson, A. F. 1984. *People and the State: An Anthropology of Planned Development*. Cambridge.

Sacherer, Janice. 1986. "Applied Anthropology and the Development Bureaucracy: Lessons from Nepal," in Edward C. Green, ed. 1986. *Practicing Development Anthropology*. Boulder: Westview Press.

Grillo, R. 1985. "Applied Anthropology in the 1980s: Retrospect and Prospect," in Ralph Grillo and Alan Rew, eds. 1985. *Social Anthropology and Development Policy*. New York: Tavistock.

The Political Economy of World Geography

TOM RIDDELL

In 1988, the National Assessment of Educational Progress tested three thousand high school seniors around the United States on their skills and knowledge in world geography—map reading, climate, trade, population growth and the environment. The average score was 57 percent. Later, then-Secretary of Education Lauro Cavazos bemoaned that "the results show a disturbing gap in our knowledge of geography. Many of our young people do not know as much as they really should know" (*Washington Post* 1990). Newspaper accounts throughout the 1980s frequently reported on the growing geographical illiteracy of U.S. students. In response, Congress created a National Geography Awareness Week, the Senate held hearings on geography education, and the National Geographic Society developed a campaign to resurrect geography education in grade schools and high schools throughout the United States.

The *Christian Science Monitor* highlighted another aspect of this problem in a December 1987 article: higher education in the United States had by and large abandoned geography programs. While leading universities in Europe and Asia have strong geography departments, very few U.S. universities and colleges do. Only about 15 percent of the institutions listed in the 1991 edition of the *Peterson's Guide to Four-Year Colleges* offer undergraduate majors in geography.

This is particularly problematic when one considers that geography is more than simply maps and locations. The *Christian Science Monitor* made a forceful case for greater emphasis on geography in higher education:

A previous version of this article was presented to a Union for Radical Political Economists session at the Allied Social Science Associations Meetings, New Orleans, LA, January 2–5, 1992.

Geography is not just the ability to recite continents, countries, and capitals. It is the search to understand the "why of where," to explore the complexity of languages, cultures, economies, histories, and ecologies that lies behind places on a map—places that make up the world we live in and pass on to our children. The two great themes of geography are the relationship between nature and society, and . . . between location and society. These themes capture the essence of today's great challenges, such as resource management and regional development in the Third World; regional conflicts fed by longstanding economic, religious, or territorial differences; and individual and institutional responses to both environmental and technological hazards."(Christian Science Monitor News Service 1987)

The Genesis of the Course

In January 1990 the Five College Program in Peace and World Security Studies (PAWSS) sponsored a faculty workshop entitled Peace and the Environment: Making the Connections in the Classroom. Its major theme was the threat posed to world security by problems of development and the environment: regional, ethnic and religious conflict over resources, forms of government and culture, as well as the potential ravages of the greenhouse effect, the depletion of the ozone layer and acid rain. The workshop not only presented the work of leading scholars on these issues, but included sessions on incorporating them into college curricula (*PAWSS Perspectives* 1990). All this inspired me to accelerate a long-term interest in creating a course on the political economy of world geography.

Curriculum development grants from PAWSS and the Fund for the Development of a More Inclusive and Multicultural Curriculum at Smith College supported summer work on developing the course, the purchase of relevant books for the library, and the acquisition of videos, computer simulations and other supplementary materials.

The course required the approval of both the Economics Department and the College's Committee on Academic Policy. The department was cooperative and recognized the potential student interest in the course. In the college committee, there was some concern about the interdisciplinary nature of the course and my "competence" to teach "scientific" material. There was also some resistance to the catalogue description of the course—". . . developing a basic understanding of world geography, global interdependence, and the political economy of the world system for responsible citizenship in the twenty-first century." Most of the criticism, quite frankly, revolved around turf battles and political differences. However, these objections reflected a minority position and the course was approved. I have taught the course, The Political Economy of World Geography, in the spring semesters of both 1991 and 1992 (see Syllabus).

Course Objectives and Themes

The course had three main objectives. The first was simply to expose students to world geography: what the countries of the world are, where they are, and what their distinguishing economic, social, cultural and political characteristics are. The second was to identify the accelerating development of a globalized economy—the internationalization of production, trade and finance. And the third was to focus on the transnational environmental threats that have accompanied the emergence of a worldwide economy. I believe that these were also the reasons why seventy students (more than twice the enrollment I expected) have selected the course each time I have offered it. They recognized the importance of the material as well as the knowledge and skills that they could develop in studying world geography from an economic perspective.

The primary text for the course was Anthony R. de Souza's *A Geography of World Economy*. De Souza notes that "economic geography is concerned with the distribution of economic activity, the use of the world's resources, and the spatial organization and expansion of the world economy" (de Souza 1990:12). In establishing the framework for his presentation, he emphasizes a variety of perspectives for understanding the world, reviewing conservative, liberal and radical interpretations throughout. It is an excellent textbook, with balanced treatment of the material and good graphics.

At the outset of the course, I outlined several themes that I hoped to develop during the semester. These themes together reinforced a focus on the threats to global security from international economic factors and attendant environmental and development problems. We live in a world that has seen an increasing internationalization of capital and labor. Within certain social and cultural constraints, resources, goods and services are mobile all over the globe. Indeed, as a result of advances in transportation and communications technologies, we increasingly live in a "global village." There is a complex symbiotic relationship between nature and society—mutual dependence, yet conflict. A sophisticated web of economic interdependence has developed among nation states and peoples, and within that system there is a clear hierarchy of power and development. Students discover how the components of a simple cotton shirt, for example, follow an intricate geographic journey in their construction, assembly and consumption—and some participants in the process gain more than others (Reagon 1985).

While economics focuses on the material aspects of human life, nature and culture are also fundamental themes of this course. Such nonmaterial subjects as religion and spirituality are not irrelevant to developing a fuller understanding of international economic relationships and events. It is important to recognize and value cultural perspectives and their diversity; combatting ethnocentrism contributes to creating the conditions that encourage global awareness, security, development and peace. The ethical dimensions of the global interactions of people, nations, corporations and institutions are appropriate for consideration in the study of economics. Learning about the world requires the development of empathy for others. In a fundamental sense, we are connected; as we learn more about the world, we should grow to appreciate such interdependence. Lastly, the pursuit of knowledge about a rapidly changing world full of challenges should encourage critical and anticipatory thinking—identifying problems, understanding them and searching for creative solutions.

The bulk of the course explored the fundamentals of economic geography—the distribution of the world's resources, the identification of the relevant economic actors and institutions, and the logic of locating economic activity. The conclusion focused on global environmental threats and the concept of sustainable development—improving the global distribution of income, resources and wealth, and developing economic activity that is less environmentally destructive. We also examined alternative policy proposals for pursuing sustainable development (World Commission on Environment and Development 1987; Brown 1991a and 1991b).

Approaches to the Material

I endeavored to incorporate active student participation in the course as often as possible and in different ways (a challenge given the size of the class). As part of the introduction to the subject matter, along with reading in the main text (de Souza), I included several recent magazine and newspaper articles that identified global economic, cultural, political, environmental, population and social problems. As an exercise, I posed several different questions about the assigned reading, and in class I broke the students into groups of four or five where they discussed their responses and then reported back to the whole class. This process actually occupied two classes, but it prompted active student discussion about the material. I used this technique frequently to maintain interest, intensity and participation.

In such a course, current events can provide pedagogical opportunities. During 1991, the Persian Gulf War engendered a lively discussion about resources, development, economic disparity, interdependence and global hierarchy—not simply about the war, the technology of the weapons or the rhetoric of George Bush and Saddam Hussein. In 1992, we spent a considerable amount of class time anticipating the U.N. Conference on the Environment and Development in June in Rio de Janeiro; in 1993, we can analyze the results of the Earth Summit.

In addition to de Souza's texts, students read a collection of photocopied readings and two other books—Lester Brown et al., *The State of the World 1991* (in 1992 I substituted Brown et al., *Saving the Planet* because I thought it would be more general and would have more "staying power"), and Scientific American's *Managing Planet Earth*. I developed ten sets of review questions throughout the semester to keep the students focused on fundamental concepts and issues presented in the readings.

For change of pace, we watched eight videos during the semester on a variety of issues: global environmental threats; health, housing, and water problems in poor countries; and the work of exemplary individuals dedicated to making the world a better place (Bill Moyers's interviews with Jessica Tuchman Mathews and Chinua Achebe). We also spent two classes watching *Local Hero* (1983), a great movie about global corporate location decisions and their impacts. In 1992, I added *Salaam Bombay!*—a classic about urban life in "the informal sector" (what de Souza calls the "proto-proletariat") in the Third World. To break up the length of each class (80 minutes twice weekly), I played a piece of music each day with some relevant theme, including, for example, Nanci Griffith's "From a Distance"; Sam Cooke's "Wonderful World" ("don't know much about geography. . ."); Bob Marley and the Wailers' "So Much Trouble in the World"; and Bruce Cockburn's "If a Tree Falls (in the forest)."

A number of maps were placed in the classroom to literally surround the students with the world. Several maps from the World Bank focused on population growth, social statistics and economic progress. A Peter's projection map served to correct the severe distortions of the "traditional" Mercator projection maps. And the new Robinson projection map from the National Geographic Society offers a compromise representing as accurately as possible both the relative size of countries and their shapes. I look forward to updated maps to reflect the changing political geography of the world.

As a supplement to the course, we used PC Globe (1990, also soon to be updated), a computerized atlas software program (I'm also investigating World Atlas). Students were asked to explore the world (in color) on maps and in data. There were two specific assignments. The first was straightforward—using PC Globe to select the country in the world that you'd most like to go to (to work or travel), print a map of it and explain (in a page) why you want to go there and what the economic implications of that choice would be. Students selected over forty different countries each year; Australia was in first place both years. In 1991 one person wanted to go to Iraq to examine the war damage; and in 1992 several wanted to visit newly independent republics in the former Soviet Union. The other task was to make up an assignment using PC Globe, and then to do it. Some of these were pretty imaginative—an analysis of the location of Euro Disney, a global treasure hunt taking two different directions and solved by the intersection of those paths; several games mimicking Jeopardy! Trivial Pursuit, Where in the World Is Carmen San Diego? and College Bowl; and a proposal to the creators of PC Globe to include world music in their package. Some were "how-to" manuals—forming an MNC, developing an elementary school lesson on world geography, eliminating world hunger. In the spring of 1992 I added an option of using the more sophisticated International Futures 1990 (IFs90): A Global Computer Simulation, developed by Barry Hughes at the University of Denver (Hughes 1991). Two projects that resulted concerned changing parameters to relieve suffering in Africa and the relationship between literacy and development.

Conclusion

Because of the immediate relevance of course themes, students were genuinely engaged by the material. Its key issues will persist into the twenty-first century, giving the course purpose as well as an inherent logic. I will teach the course every year now instead of in alternate years as originally planned—time will tell if the demand remains as high as it was in the spring semesters of 1991 and 1992 for increasing literacy in world geography.

Syllabus
Economics 202
The Political Economy of World Geography

Spring 1992
Tom Riddell
138 Elm Street
x3618

Objectives of the Course

We live in an increasingly internationalized economy. Production, trade and finance are organized and operate on a global logic. People, communities and nation states are interdependent in terms of access to resources, goods and services. Relative economic welfare is also determined in these interrelationships.

This course will explore the theme of economic interdependence on a worldwide basis. What is the logic and the historical background for the emergence of the global economy? What are the components of the global system? What are the consequences of this organization of economic activity?

The approach we will take is that of economic geography, which is concerned with the location of economic activity (resources, production, markets) and its spatial organization and expansion. We will pay attention to where things are located on the earth. And we will also be particularly concerned with the interaction between economic activity and the earth's environment.

Work for the Course

I expect everyone to do the required reading and to be prepared to discuss it in class. Given the nature of the topics in the course, you'll get a lot more out of it if you read a newspaper or magazine on a regular basis. Pick one—the *Globe*, the *Times*, the *Wall Street Journal*, the *Daily Hampshire Gazette*, *Business Week*, *Fortune*, whatever. The world is a very fascinating place, read about it!

There will be an in-class, mid-term exam on March 12th. This exam will count for 30 percent of your grade.

There is a computer software program, PC Globe, available in the computer lab in the Jahnige Social Science Research Center. To get access to it, enter "Economics" and then "PC Globe." PC Globe is a computerized atlas with maps, graphics, facts, figures, and even sound effects on 177 countries. Your assignment is to use the software program (explore the world!) and to make up an assignment for future students in this class. Then, of course, you'll do the assignment yourself! You may work on this in groups if you'd like. This assignment is due April 9th and will count for 30 percent of your grade. Make sure you emphasize economic concepts, variables and issues in your project.

You might want to combine using PC Globe along with reading the paper, e.g., following events, trends, etc., and how they have geographical dimensions. Or you might want to attend the upcoming lecture series by the Five-College Peace and World Security Studies program on the Gulf War a year later and incorporate these into your project.

There will be a take-home, final exam due May 8th. It will count for 40 percent of your grade.

Texts

Available in the Smith bookstore and hopefully on reserve at Neilson Library:

Anthony R. de Souza, *A Geography of World Economy*, Merrill Publishing Company, 1990.

Scientific American, Managing Planet Earth, W. H. Freeman and Company, 1990.

Lester R. Brown et al., *Saving the Planet*, W. W. Norton, 1991.

There is also a packet of photocopied materials for the course available at Paradise Copies, 30 Crafts Avenue, Northampton.

Recommended Books:

World Commission on Environment and Development, *Our Common Future*, Oxford University Press, 1987.

Ward L. Kaiser, *A New View of the World*, Friendship Press, 1987.

Course Outline

January 28, 30

Introduction: Understanding a Troubled World
Packet of photocopies, "Introduction."

February 4, 6

The Approach of Economic Geography
de Souza, chapter 1.
Scientific American, chapter 1.
World Commission, Introduction (skim) and chapter 1 (on reserve).

February 11, 13, 18

Viewing the World

de Souza, chapter 2.

Packet, "Viewing the World."

Ward Kaiser, all (on reserve).

PC Globe. (For those of you who like to read instructions, they should be
available in Jahnige.)

February 20, 25

The World Economy

de Souza, chapter 12.

Packet, "The World Economy."

World Commission, chapter 3.

Bruce Marshall (ed.), "Globe Inc," in *The Real World*, Houghton Mifflin, 1991
(on reserve).

February 27, March 3

World Population(s)

de Souza, chapter 3.

Scientific American, chapter 6.

Terry G. Jordan and Lester Rowntree, *The Human Mosaic: A Thematic Introduction to Cultural Geography*, Harper & Row, 1990, chapter 1 and pho-
tos after pages 32 and 444 (on reserve).

March 5

World Resources

de Souza, chapter 4.

March 10

Locating Economic Activity

de Souza, chapter 5.

March 12

Mid-Term Exam

March 24, 26

Urbanization around the World

de Souza, chapters 6, 8 and 9.

March 31, April 2

The Economic Geography of Industrial Production

de Souza, chapters 10 and 11.

April 7, 9

Development, Underdevelopment and Military Impacts in the
Third World

de Souza, chapter 13.
World Bank, *The Development Data Book* (on reserve).
Packet, "Military Impacts in the Third World."
Ruth Leger Sivard, *World Military and Social Expenditures, 1991* (14th ed.),
World Priorities, Inc., 1991, browse, especially pp. 16–42 (on reserve).

April 9
PC Globe Assignment Due

April 14, 16, 21
Global Economic Activity and the Environment
Scientific American, chapters 2, 3, 4, 9, 10, 11 and epilogue.
Packet, "Global Economic Activity and the Environment."

April 23, 28, 30
Reshaping the Global Economy
Brown et al., *Saving the Planet*, all.
World Commission, chapters 2, 10, 11, and 12.

May 8
Final Exam Due

Videos and Films

January 28—Bill Moyers's "A World of Ideas" (Jessica Tuchman Mathews),
28 minutes
February 13—"Stopping the Coming Ice Age" (Larry Ephron), 45
February 27—"Rivers of Life" (World Bank), 10
March 5—"A Plague upon the Land" (World Bank), 24
March 24—"The Neighborhood of Coehlos" (World Bank), 28
March 31 & April 2—"Local Hero," 111
April 9—Bill Moyers (Chinua Acehebe), 28
April 14 & 16—*Salaam Bombay*, 114
April 23—"The Greenhouse Crisis" (Union of Concerned Scientists), 11
April 28—"Changing Tides along the Mediterranean" (Legacy, International), 23.

SOURCES

Brown, Lester et al. *State of the World 1991* (A Worldwatch Institute Report on Progress toward a Sustainable Society). New York: W. W. Norton, 1991.

Brown, Lester et al. *Saving the Planet: How to Shape an Environmentally Sustainable Global Economy.* New York: W. W. Norton, 1991.

Christian Science Monitor News Service. "Geography Education Declining," *Daily Hampshire Gazette*, Northampton, MA, December 3, 1987.

de Souza, Anthony R. *A Geography of World Economy.* Columbus: Merrill Publishing Company, 1990.

"Geography Enters the Liberal Arts," *Garnet Letter.* Swarthmore: Swarthmore College, March 1989.

Hughes, Barry B. *International Futures 1990 (IFs90): A Global Computer Simulation.* Denver: Graduate School of International Studies, University of Denver, 1991.

PAWSS Perspectives, "Peace and the Environment: Making the Connections in the Classroom," volume 1, number 1, April 1990.

Peterson's Guide to Four-Year Colleges, 1991. Princeton: Peterson's Guides, 1990.

Reagon, Bernice Johnson. "Are My Hands Clean?" Songtalk Publishing Co., 1985.

Scientific American. *Managing Planet Earth.* New York: W. H. Freeman and Company, 1990.

Washington Post. "Test of Geography Knowledge Stumps U.S. Students," *Daily Hampshire Gazette*, Northampton, MA, February 8, 1990.

World Commission on Environment and Development. *Our Common Future.* New York: Oxford University Press, 1987.

The World in the Classroom: Environment Education in a Liberal Arts Context

Kareen B. Sturgeon

> What we do in the classroom is not an isolated moment sep-
> arate from the "real" world. It is entirely connected to the
> real word, and is the real world. . .[1]

On one wall of my office at Linfield College I have mounted a colorful map of the New World. It's an upside-down map, geographically
correct but with South America at the top and North America at the
bottom; ". . .only the perspective has been changed," says the caption.[2]
In many ways the map serves as a metaphor for the Environmental
Science course syllabus I discuss in this essay. Certainly, the syllabus
has changed since I first designed the course twelve years ago. But the
changes that link the transformation of the course and my thinking
about it to global development are not as apparent in the syllabus as
one might imagine. Like the geographic facts of the upside-down map,
the "facts" of earlier and later syllabi are much the same; I still give
exams and require the students to do group projects and keep a journal.
What has changed is my perspective—my understanding of the relationship between education and global transformation and, therefore,
of my role as a teacher. In this essay I discuss the course goals, objectives and assignments shown in the syllabus in the context of these
changing perspectives about the relationship of education to global
development.

An earlier version of this article, with a different focus, appeared in *Environmental
Ethics* 13 (1991):165–173. Both essays are based on a paper delivered at the Interna-
tional Development Ethics Association Second International Conference held at the
Autonomous University of the Yucatan, Merida, Mexico, 3–8 July 1989.

Environmental Science:
Initial Goals and Objectives

In 1981, when I began teaching Environmental Science, the field was just beginning to develop. It had first shown up in college curricula in the early 1970s (often, as it is taught at Linfield, as a science-based course for nonscience majors) in response to an increasing public awareness of the detrimental effects of human activities on the environment. Focusing on interrelations among population growth, resource consumption and environmental quality, the field emphasized the ways in which science could help us solve an increasing number of unprecedented and seemingly intractable global problems. As an evolutionary biologist and botanist, I knew little about the field, so I selected a textbook and wrote lectures based on it. Like the text, the course structure focused on healthy ecosystems, how human activities disrupt them, and the potential biological consequences of these activities for life on earth.

Each year that I taught the course, global environmental problems intensified and accelerated. The pronounced increase in world population was accompanied by a rise in poverty, hunger, pollution and resource depletion. Simultaneously, cause and effect seemed to blur: Was population pressure the cause of our world problems, as I had previously assumed, or was it an effect of widespread poverty? Or were our world problems a function of something more fundamental yet? Each year, I became more and more concerned with the urgency of teaching students to care about their world and of convincing them to do something to help resolve the problems. The students, however, became increasingly immobilized by the overwhelming magnitude of the problems and the realization that solutions would require international cooperation. For some students, the response was denial. For others, despair. They looked to me, a scientist—the expert—for answers, and, because I had none, I began to think of ways I could get out of teaching the course.

The Role of Science in
Solving Global Environmental Problems

One of the most troublesome questions I was to raise in the class in the early 1980s was What is the role of *science* in helping us to solve our world problems? No matter which problem I selected for study—

overpopulation, hunger, deforestation, extinction, the threat of nuclear war—the answer returned loudly and clearly: very little. Scientists could help us understand our world; they could document the extent of our impact on it. But they were seemingly as powerless as anybody else to come up with workable solutions. In fact, scientific solutions—technological solutions—seemed to be a large part of the problem. Was more research needed to reduce the high levels of uncertainty inherent in scientific analyses of complex global systems? If so, how much more? Was more evidence—more information—what students needed to be convinced that they should care about the planet and change their behavior? I was becoming increasingly skeptical . . . and anxious. The more I lectured on the research being done to reduce levels of scientific uncertainty (for example, about the effect of increasing atmospheric levels of carbon dioxide on global climate), the more convinced the students were that something was being done. They need not do anything, because experts were working on the problem and would probably soon come up with a technological solution. Telling them about environmental problems and the current scientific research only seemed to contribute to their passivity.

What then was it going to take to get us to alter our present path toward self-destruction? Was there any hope for change? As these questions began to surface, I realized that the apparent lack of interest regarding global issues and the self-interest that characterized so many of my students were but reflections of my own sense of powerlessness. Did that matter? Should I be concerned with whether I motivated students to act? Is motivating students an aim of education, or is education only to inform? Assuming that motivation is a legitimate educational goal, how should it be done? Did I have a right to tell students what needs to happen? Was I imposing my values on the students? I feared I was beginning to sound like a preacher.

I had doubts about my competency to deal with complex environmental issues, and I harbored considerable resentment about my having to teach such an interdisciplinary subject—one that went way beyond my area of expertise. I even began to question whether I was teaching science any longer! This was one of the only science courses these nonscience majors would take at Linfield. Was I doing what was expected of me? I decided I ought to learn more about the history and philosophy of science. I was curious to know if science was defined simply by its methodology or if there was more to it than the so-called hypothetico-deductive method that I had been using as the conceptual framework for Environmental Science. Without reference to its methodology, I, a scientist, could not define science. In fact, I could not even distinguish a scientific way of knowing from other forms of inquiry anymore.

This astonishing revelation prompted me to audit a course on the philosophy of science and read what the authorities had to say. Within the class, I read the canonical texts—Popper, Kuhn, Toulmin and others; simultaneously, I ventured for the first time into the writings of feminist historians and philosophers of science who seemed to be asking ever more probing questions. For example, Sandra Harding (116) asks whether the applications of science that harm the environment, support militarism, degrade human labor and are used to control women, the poor and others are just misuses of science, or whether what we call bad or misused science is, in fact, science-as-usual? Was it possible that science, to which I had committed my professional life, was not value neutral and dispassionately objective after all? I began to sense the truly systemic nature of what I had thought was simply an "environmental" crisis. I learned from the philosophers that the questions I had been asking remained unanswered; it was not that I simply had not read the right books. And I learned that the history of science was being rewritten; our endangered planet was forcing us to look at the dark side of science.

The Teacher and the Course Transformed

As question upon question left me confused and insecure, my teaching was being transformed. From an original unquestioned assumption that to teach was to lecture and that "content," as usually defined, "counted," I annually discarded more topics and restructured the course to include projects that actively involved the students. Ultimately I abandoned the lecture format almost completely in favor of a dialectical approach.

One example will illustrate the dramatic results I experienced. Instead of giving my standard lecture on the nitrogen cycle, which regularly generated little interest or understanding, I walked into class one day and said, "OK, tell me what *you* know about nitrogen." To my astonishment, as a group, they already knew a lot about nitrogen. One student knew that nitrogen was part of the air we breathe; another shared how his family alternated planting clover with other crops to restore nitrogen to the soil on his family farm. Others knew that legumes, such as peas and beans, were important components of a properly balanced diet, and still others recalled that proteins, which contain nitrogen, made for strong bodies and sharp minds. Working together, we combined these bits and pieces of information and constructed the nitrogen cycle. Moreover, students seemed genuinely interested in knowing more; for example, one student (a nonscientist no less) wanted to know how nitrogen-fixing bacteria in the root nodules of legumes break the triple bond in atmospheric nitrogen! This remarkably sophisticated question led to a discussion about the enzyme nitrogenase that catalyzes the reaction and is produced by the bacteria. From there, the discussion seemed to flow naturally to other questions about soil fertility and soil bacteria, about the deleterious effects of pesticides and herbicides on soil microorganisms, even about the philosophical implications of our destroying humus—the rich, dark layer of decaying organic material upon which our soil fertility depends (and whose etymology is identical with human, humane, and humble).

It was another year and a new group of students before I mustered the courage to allow the questioning to proceed one step further—to moral issues. By then I understood that from so seemingly mundane a question as "What do you know about nitrogen?" moral questions would emerge spontaneously. Do we have a right to poison the bacteria on whose activities our lives depend? Do we have a right to engineer their genes? Do bacteria have intrinsic worth quite beyond their value to human beings? I began to trust my intuition that not only are moral questions valid in a science class but also that their absence—their compartmentalization to humanities classes—lay at the very root of our world problems.

I became increasingly dissatisfied with textbooks—with their litanies of dreary facts, statistics, and predictions, and with their relegation of politics, economics, and ethics to one chapter at the end of the book, if treated at all. I began to supplement the text with poems and essays that had been central to the development of my own personal worldview. At first, I did not discuss them openly, considering such emotional stuff inappropriate for the science classroom. But students indicated that they appreciated my openness, and they reciprocated by sharing some of their own thoughts. Gradually, I was coming to understand that I did not have to teach students to care about the world; they already cared very deeply. I began to realize that my task as an educator was to create the environment in which their feelings could be drawn out, expressed freely. I no longer carried the burden of the expert—of feeling compelled to fill up the students with volumes of current, state-of-the-art information and to know the answers to all of their questions. Rather, I was satisfied that I had encouraged the students to think and question and that I was learning and growing along with them. I could be comfortable with not having resolved every issue at the end of the semester.

I turned part of the course over to the students to pursue topics of their own choosing. The feedback was so enthusiastic that eventually I gave each group of 6–8 students an entire class period—which they used fully—to deliver their presentations. In one student's evaluation of the assignment, she wrote,

> I enjoyed this assignment both in researching a topic and listening to how others presented their topics . . . I'm not a science person, and having other non-science people explain things like hazardous chemicals, power-producing garbage dumps, and ozone depletion, is great—it puts the technical information into more digestible language. This was far more interesting than straight lecture, and the class discussion was wonderful.

Another wrote:

> I thought that an hour was going to be too much time, and we would run out of things to say. But as every group proved, they could have used another 15 minutes or so. I really enjoyed the group projects, it gave a nice break to lectures. It gave me the opportunity to learn about things I would have probably never had the chance to. I was even able to help my roommate do a paper on the yew tree! I feel I learned a lot from all of this, but especially from my own group. I am really excited about the things that I have learned and will definitely keep track of what's going on with taxol in the future.

The old course was transformed. Transdisciplinary in form, it treated science in the context of the economic, political and social environments in which it was embedded. In the process science became less authoritarian, losing its dominant position in some abstract hierarchy of value, and now took its place alongside other ways of knowing in the search for truth. I sensed that the rigid walls between the disciplines were beginning to break down. As a result, the class, as a whole, seemed to take on a new personality.

The World in the Classroom

In 1988, I spent the spring semester as Visiting Scholar at the University of Costa Rica. As a biologist, I had long felt it was important that, one day, I should make a trip to the tropics to see the forests that had become the focus of so much attention from scientists. During my stay, however, I found myself curiously uneasy about entering into discussions with Costa Ricans about their environmental problems. I knew from teaching Environmental Science that my own lifestyle and that of other North Americans were heavily implicated in contributing to their difficulties. If I discussed their problems without acknowledging my part in creating them, I would be justifiably open to criticism. On the other hand, when I did acknowledge my role in their problems, I understood equally well their distrust of my patronizing concern. I found myself in a classic bind. In the context of my Environmental Science class, I had understood intellectually that, as a citizen of one of the most developed countries in the world, I was a "bad guy"; but in Costa Rica, I really felt like one. Grazing on once-forested land were the cattle soon to be hamburgers in some fast-food restaurant in my home town. There, in the midst of poverty, were the multinational corporations loading bananas onto boats destined for my favorite fruit and vegetable market. But more than anything, it was the logging trucks that hit home. How could I, who make my home in the richly forested region of the Pacific Northwest, preach to anyone about deforestation when, in my own backyard, the last remnants of the vast coniferous rainforests that once stretched unbroken from Alaska to California were being harvested?

Herein lay a way out of the dilemma. I realized that I felt empathy, not sympathy, for the Costa Ricans and their history of deforestation. Upon my return to Oregon, I began to educate myself about the fate of Oregon's rainforests. I learned that the United States was managing the natural resources of the Pacific Northwest with what one author (Williams, 49) called "a Third World mentality," more accurately described as a colonial mentality. Just as we, in the United States, treat the Third World as a colony from which to extract precious resources with little regard for the ecological, social, economic and political consequences of our actions, so have we, in the Northwest, become an internal colony, permitting, for example, the extraction and shipment of raw logs to Japan rather than milling them in Oregon and developing our own wood products industries. My commitment quickly led to action. I wrote an editorial for the *Oregonian* newspaper making the connection between deforestation in the tropics and in the Pacific Northwest. For me, the Third World–First World dichotomy was collapsing. In a very concrete sense, I understood that we are all part of one ecosystem: what we do to others in that ecosystem, we do to ourselves. I had begun to internalize the aphorism, "Act locally, think globally"!

As I gained a sense of empowerment, the effect on my class was dramatic. We started every day with two student summaries of newspaper articles on the environment. These minipresentations linked the students' daily lives to the larger world and gave them an opportunity to share their interests and opinions with their classmates. Over the course of the semester, the class began to understand how particular issues developed over time, who the key players were, what agencies and organizations were involved, what rules and regulations were invoked, and how the events were interpreted by different constituencies and by the media. Leaving behind the more-or-less routine mixes of objective and short essay questions that typified my exams, I introduced take-home components whereby students could write, on a subject of their own choosing, a letter to the editor or an opinion editorial much like the newspaper articles they had been sharing with one another daily. Exams felt less like exams and more like training for "real" life.

We went on a field trip up into the Coast Ranges that frame the rich, agricultural valley in which the college is situated. There we visited a tree farm where Douglas firs are grown as a crop, and students learned what it means to intensively manage forest lands for timber production. I asked them to give four hours of community service or to participate in a campus or community event in order to link their classroom activities to the larger society in a more concrete way. They helped plant flowers in preparation for the spring campus open house; they helped with the clean-up of the creek that runs through campus. They went to talks about the Pacific Northwest salmon fisheries and old growth forests. The assignment got them out into the local community: planting trees with citizen-minded locals; attending, along with county commissioners, lawyers, company executives and other concerned citizens, controversial public hearings concerning the local landfill; and participating in the beach clean-up that occurs, every year, along Oregon's coastline. They discovered parts of Oregon they had not known before; they met new people, formed opinions, took themselves seriously, dared to speak up. In the words of one student, "We learned so much during our visit to the landfill that, even though I was nervous to talk in front of the class, I wanted to share what I had learned. It was a good experience for me."

The Classroom in the World

Just as I found that the world was in my classroom, I continue to be reminded that the classroom is also in the world. What I do in my classroom at Linfield College is, to some extent, constrained by institutional structures and by student and faculty expectations of what constitutes education.

For example, one semester I experimented with having no graded assignments. I made daily participation and timely completion of assignments the only requirements for a grade at the end of the semester (the college requires that we assign A–F grades in regular classes). The student response was enthusiastic; in their evaluations of the course (which are done prior to my assigning grades and are seen by me only after I have assigned grades), students claimed they had never learned more. Fifty out of fifty-five students in the class earned As.

While some faculty encouraged this approach to grading, others questioned its appropriateness. One faculty member wrote in a memo to me,

> I do have a lot of sympathy with the desire to experiment with new methods. After all, that is the way that we continue to grow. But the grading issue is an incredibly complex thing, and I am not sure that we can allow people to experiment too much with grades. . . [N]o class is an island by itself. All classes fit together to make up the continent that is a college education. When you give all As you make it harder for me to maintain a traditional grading system in my classes.

Faculty had just recently voted down a request by one member to allow written evaluations in place of grades under certain circumstances; thus, I decided that, in the context of Linfield College, my grading experiment had been premature.

Respecting the will of the larger community, I chose to pursue a middle ground, providing several opportunities for students to earn letter grades in traditional ways along with other opportunities to complete assignments without being graded. I made participation a crucial component of the course, particularly by requiring it, for example, during student presentations. And although material covered during those presentations is not included on exams, students are required to include entries in their journals describing what they found most interesting about each one.

In selecting reading and viewing materials, I am also faced with increasing restraints. I have alternatively required a text, not required one, supplemented or replaced texts with other readings, and placed several texts on reserve in the library and recommended their use. My current approach is to order a text and use it sparingly for required readings, while encouraging students to use it as a resource for their own projects. The real world of copyright laws, prohibitive costs of film/video rental or purchase, and ethical considerations associated with the excessive use of duplicated materials (for example, when one is discussing deforestation!) add further complexities to this already complicated issue. More and more, I rely on the newspaper and television to provide timely, lively, ongoing dialogue about local, national, and international environmental issues.

Class size and classroom structure continue to make it difficult, although not impossible, to encourage and maintain class discussions. The two lecture halls at Linfield large enough to hold 50–60 students are amphitheaterlike structures with seats bolted to the floor and arranged in rows facing the front of the room; under these conditions it is difficult for students to maintain eye contact with—or to hear—anyone other than the teacher at the head of the class. Group presentations and class discussions of current events in the newspaper provide one means for students to share the podium with me. I also use the journal assignment to counter these structural impediments to dialogue. Through the journals, I learn how students are reacting to the class, and I provide personal feedback to them. Often, with the student's permission (and always anonymously), I read entries aloud to the class. In this manner some students who would normally remain silent in a large classroom are heard, and others are privy to writings that would otherwise be seen only by me. Nevertheless, the difficulties of sustaining discussions and keeping students actively involved in classrooms designed as lecture halls are sufficiently great that I have decided to split this class into two sections of 25–30 students in the coming year which will enable me to use another, less structured classroom.

Outlook

Probably the most fascinating aspect of this process of growth/development/transformation has been that it is on-going, never finished. At the same time as I continue to harbor doubts about the success of my various endeavors, I discover new ways to improve the class and accomplish my goals. Insights gained in Environmental Science inform my thinking about other classes that I teach. As I continue to question, the circle widens, and distinctions between First and Third Worlds, student and teacher, majors' courses and nonmajors' courses, and science and other ways of knowing dissolve. The liberating results are perhaps best expressed in the words of a senior on the last day of class this spring:

> Well, this is my last entry. It has been interesting to write down my thoughts about the environment. I have never really thought through my feelings or opinions until this class. I was somehow hoping that it would answer some of my questions. Instead the class just caused me to ask more, but I guess that's what a liberal arts education is all about.

SYLLABUS

Environmental Science—Biological
GEC 182
Spring 1992

Instructor: Kareen Sturgeon, Ph.D.
            Associate Professor, Biology
   Office: Murdock 206
            472–4121, extension 466
    Hours: Tuesday and Thursday 3:30–5, or by appointment
     Text: Miller, G. T., Jr. 1992. *Living in the Environment: An
            Introduction to Environmental Science*, 7th edition.
            Wadsworth Publishing Co., Menlo Park, California.

Course Description

Science is a way of knowing—it is one among several ways whereby
humans come to understand themselves and their world. Environmental Science deals with those scientific concepts and principles that
define our relationship to our environment. The science of ecology,
which is the study of interrelations among living organisms and their
environment, is central to this understanding.

Course Objectives

1. To introduce you to the science of ecology and to the structure
   and function of natural, healthy ecosystems.
2. To investigate the ways by which humans are having an
   impact on natural ecosystems and to evaluate the consequences of our actions.
3. To help you appreciate the interrelatedness of environmental
   problems and the systemic nature of the environmental crisis.
4. To provide a framework within which each of you may develop
   your own worldview—a deeply felt perspective that will serve
   as a foundation for making informed decisions about the environment.

My personal opinion is that the survival of the human species
depends upon our willingness to modify traditional attitudes about our
relationship to nature *and* to make the necessary changes in our behavior. I encourage discussion and debate on these topics in class, and I
anticipate and welcome a variety of perspectives and opinions!

Course requirements

Newspaper Article

We will begin each day with a brief (5-minute) student presentation to the class on an article, editorial, letter to the editor, etc., on the environment from the *News-Register* or the *Oregonian*. Each presentation should include the type of piece (editorial, news story, etc.), the author's name and perspective (if known), the section and page of the paper where the article was found, a brief summary of the main points or point of view, the people and agencies mentioned, and any new terms (define them if you can). Make an effort to link the article to a previous presentation (if applicable), and tell us what you think about the topic. The purpose of this assignment is to develop skills in reading and analyzing media coverage of environmental issues.

Community Service/Activity

You are required to contribute four hours of your time to any one of several activities pertaining to the environment that will be taking place in the local community and at Linfield throughout the semester. This may include attending meetings of Linfield Students for Environmental Awareness (LSEA) or the Yamhill Environmental Alliance (YEA) and/or participating in LSEA- or YEA-sponsored activities; attending a talk, presentation, conference, or going on a field trip. The purpose of this assignment is to provide an opportunity for you to "act locally" while "thinking globally." Summarize what you did in a one- to two-page typewritten journal entry (label the entry!). I will keep you informed about various possibilities as they arise throughout the semester.

Journal

Over the course of the semester, keep a journal in which you take note of the unfolding environmental changes that occur as we move from winter to spring and *record your responses to them*. You may want to document daily high and low temperatures, what the sky looks like, how the position of the sun and the length of daylight change as the season progresses, when you first notice certain birds or hear their songs, when leaves appear on the trees and flowers bloom. The purpose of this exercise is to heighten your awareness of the natural world that surrounds us—even on the Linfield College campus! Make two or three entries per week, and please type them before you turn each set in to me. I will collect them two or three times during the semester.

Group Projects

This assignment is intended to give you an opportunity to collaborate with several of your colleagues on a project that interests you and to share your findings with the rest of the class. I will provide you with some suggestions for projects and guidelines for carrying them out. You will be evaluated as a group. Therefore, it is important to agree, as a group, about what each person is responsible for and to work together to achieve a well-integrated presentation. I will make class time available for group work, and I will meet with each group separately during office hours. Group projects will not be tested on exams, but roll will be taken during student presentations.

Exams

There will be three exams. They will be largely short answer and objective in format and may include a take-home portion. The exams will cover lectures, videos and reading assignments, as well as comments made by me or other students during in-class discussions. Make-up exams will be given only for excused absences, such as illness. If you know you have a schedule conflict, make arrangements with me to take a make-up exam *prior to missing the exam.*

Field Trip

On Friday, April 25, we will go on a half-day field trip to the Trask Mountain Tree Farm, owned by Willamette Industries. This will be an opportunity to learn how private industries intensively manage their timberlands. The exact time of departure is not yet finalized, but plan on leaving at 8:00 am and returning at noon. I will notify the dean of students, who will notify your instructors, that this is an official class function and that you are required to attend. It is your responsibility to make arrangements with your instructors to make up assignments or exams. Do It Now! Write a one- to two-page journal entry summarizing what you learned on this trip.

Attendance and Participation

Clearly, the success of this course depends upon your willingness and eagerness to engage yourself with the material, to attend class regularly, and to participate in all activities. For example, occasionally you will be given in-class writing assignments which I will collect. Although they may not be graded, the effort and thought you put into completing the assignments will count towards "participation." We will also see several videos. For some of these, you will be given study questions or assignments relating to the topics. Although they will not be graded, you should be prepared to discuss them in class.

If you miss class for some reason, it is your responsibility to check with another student in the class to find out what we did in class that day and whether you missed an assignment or announcement. In short, I expect you to come to class regularly, be prepared to think about environmental issues and to write and speak about them.

Grading

Distribution of points:		*Letter grade:*	
Newspaper summary	25	A	90-100%
Community service	25	B	80–89
Journal	50	C	70–79
Group project	50	D	60–69
Exams	150	F	<60%
Attendance/participation	50		
	350		

Tentative Schedule

Feb. 11
Course overview
Read: Preface to the student

Feb. 13
Introduction to Environmental
  Science
Read: ch. 1; pp. 52-54

Feb. 18
Ecosystem structure
Read: pp. 54–57; 79–82

Feb. 20
Biomes
Read: pp. 114–130

Feb. 25
Biogeochemical cycles
Read: pp. 98–100

Feb. 27
Exam 1

Mar. 3
Energy Flow
Read: pp. 58–78; 82–98

Mar. 5
Video on greenhouse effect
Read: pp. 284–296; 305–307

Mar. 10
Ecosystem dynamics
Read: ch. 6

Mar. 12
Human population
Read: ch. 8

Mar. 17
Human population
Read: ch. 8

Mar. 19
Exam 2

Mar. 24–26
Spring Break

Mar. 31, Apr. 2, 7, 9, 14, 16, 21
Group projects
Readings to be assigned

Apr. 23
Evolution, biodiversity, and
    silviculture
Read: pp. 391–400

Apr. 25
Field trip: Trask Mountain Tree
    Farm

Apr. 28
No class

Apr. 30
Group project
Reading to be assigned

May 5
Economics and the environment
    (guest speaker)

Read: ch. 24

May 7
Politics and the environment
Read: pp. 38–49; ch. 25

May 12
Film on the Clean Air Act
Read: pp. 594–595

May 14
Ethics and the environment
Read: ch. 26

May 19
Video, "Earth First!"
Read: pp. 685–692

May 21
Course conclusion
Read: Epilogue

May 27
Final exam

NOTES

1. Ira Shor and Paulo Freire, A Pedagogy for Liberation (New York: Bergin and Garvey, 1987), p. 25.
2. Turnabout Map, Laguna Sales, 7040 Via Val Verde, San Jose, CA 95135.

SOURCES

M. F. Belenky, B. M. Clinchy, N. R. Goldberger, and J. M. Tarule, Women's Ways of Knowing: The Development of Self, Voice, and Mind (New York: Basic Books, 1986).

Paulo Freire, Pedagogy of the Oppressed (New York: Continuum, 1989).

Sandra Harding, The Science Question in Feminism (Ithaca: Cornell University Press, 1986), pp. 116–17.

Ira Shor and Paulo Freire, A Pedagogy for Liberation (New York: Bergin and Garvey, 1987).

B. J. Williams, "Timber, Part I: Trouble in the Colonies," Pacific Northwest 22, no. 12 (1988).

Economic Development

GABRIEL G. MANRIQUE

Learning Objectives

This course is designed to afford students an opportunity to acquire new knowledge, to analyze problems at increasing levels of sophistication, to utilize important communication and quantitative skills, and finally, to engage in reasoned discourse and conversation.

The discipline of economics is particularly suited to provide students with the opportunity to do all of the above tasks. This particular course on economic development incorporates these learning objectives as stated in the course objectives and expectations statement in the syllabus (see below). Students are expected to:

1. Acquire a significant amount of new knowledge. I have found the "value-added" of an economic development course to be substantial because the average college student has not had significant exposure to international studies, particularly dealing with the developing world.

2. Utilize the various theories, tools and concepts that economics provides to gain a better understanding of international issues and concerns. Since the course is offered to economics majors, there is the expectation that students will apply economic analysis to the study of the development process. This does not preclude the use of some interdisciplinary modes of learning. In fact, at certain points in the course I rely on material from other disciplines. However, it is made clear to students that while economic analysis does not exist in a vacuum, there is an "economic" way of thinking.

3. Engage in higher levels of analysis concerning development issues. While learning about developing countries is, by itself, an important learning goal, learning without the application of sophisticated analysis can degenerate into pedestrian or

common "wisdom" about the developing world. Such thinking almost always tends to be ethnocentric in nature, a tendency that we seek to avoid.

4. Engage in discourse through communication of his/her ideas as well as critique the work of others.

Target Audience

The course is offered as an elective for those majoring or minoring in economics. Students majoring in other disciplines may also take the course as an elective, provided that they have met the two prerequisite courses: principles of microeconomics and principles of macroeconomics. The prerequisites are important building blocks for the model building, data analysis and policy discussions that comprise the course.

The typical undergraduate who takes this course has had little or no exposure to, or knowledge of, developing countries. Occasionally, foreign students from lesser developing countries (LDCs) take the course, and, at least from an experiential standpoint, they have more awareness of the problems of development. However, I have noticed little difference in the level of sophistication of the economic analysis between the U.S. and LDC students.

In any case, economic development courses can contribute to efforts at campuses to internationalize the curriculum, enlarging the target audience.

Course Outline

The course outline reflects the attempt to reconcile, as realistically as possible, the characteristics of the target audience with the pedagogical objectives outlined above. I have found it best to offer the course in two-hour sessions because many of the class exercises and discussions require the continuity afforded by longer periods.

Segment 1: That Third World[1]

This segment of the course serves to acquaint the students with the various developing countries, their characteristics and their differences.

The first session begins with a map exercise where students are asked to locate countries on an unmarked map. While the class is not a geography class, studies of high school graduates have repeatedly shown an overall lack of knowledge about geography. Anecdotal evidence from my own classes supports these findings. The acquaintance with the names and locations of countries can increase student interest. As we begin to associate names with locations on the map, we also begin associating countries with different levels of development. I have found the map exercise a good way to start familiarizing students with the subject matter.

The second session of the course deals with numerous socioeconomic indicators that are common tools of the trade. This lays the foundation for further economic study and serves as a good review of economic terms and concepts. The session also introduces the different dimensions of development or underdevelopment and the various patterns of economic development. Thus, students learn at once that economic development is multidimensional. I have also used this session to introduce students to the idea that they must work with numerous data sets.

It is also important in this section to let the students know that the developing world is not composed only of poverty and destitution but that in almost all LDCs there are significant sectors that are highly modernized and wealthy. Students, particularly those at regional colleges and universities, are often surprised to learn that in some developing countries the way of life is more modern than what the average Midwestern student is accustomed to. This is important to note because it can counteract certain stereotypes; it can show that in many LDCs there exists a base for development; and it can also point out gross inequities that exist within LDCs.

Segment 2: Paradigms of Development, Growth and Change[2]

This segment of the course begins with about the third or fourth meeting. In it, students are encouraged to confront their own biases about the process of development, and to try to understand that the ways in which questions are framed, how data are analyzed, and the solutions we propose will largely be dependent on the paradigm we use.

Students in economics usually work with the neoclassical paradigm of markets. No attempt is made at first to use this paradigm or to critique it. I point out only that this is the dominant paradigm in economics and how it shapes some simple policy decisions, even in the U.S.

I also encourage students to discuss their own common perceptions of why the poor are poor, why certain peoples and countries act the way they do, and what specific solutions they see for the problems of underdevelopment. After we discuss the connections between perceptions and proposed solutions, we engage in an examination of our own eth-nocentrism. One encounters a natural resistance when ethnocentric views and solutions are challenged, but this is a crucial part of the learning process.

Segment 3: Domestic Issues and Sectors

In this segment of the course, we examine the specific parts of the economy and how they shape and are shaped by the process of economic development. This is also the segment where increasingly sophisticated economic models are introduced.

Economic applications readily surface in this section. For example, in the segment on population, once we have discussed the dimensions of population growth, students begin examining the relation to GDP growth and to per capita GDP growth. Then they can use economics to examine the debate about causality—does population growth retard GDP growth or does GDP growth lead to a reduction of population growth? Within this context, I have found it useful and appropriate to use economic concepts such as incentives and opportunity costs.

Policy discussions can also utilize economic theory extensively. For example, the students can discuss, assuming that countries want to limit population growth, various ways to achieve the goal. They can debate the relative effectiveness of family, market incentives, and changes in cultural attitudes towards women.

Income distribution is another segment that allows students to learn and to confront important questions regarding development. Measures of development such as the Lorenz curve and the Gini coefficient are useful tools, but the discussions extend beyond the statistics. I ask students to confront their own paradigm about the "correct" distribution of income. They examine how specific policies affect income distribution and whether or not specific development strategies are consistent with the desired distribution.

In this segment of the course, we also discuss sectoral issues and their role in economic development. The agricultural sector is always revealing for students because of the vast difference between agriculture in the U.S. and agriculture in the developing world. The ethnocentric views students have are partly shaped by their understanding of the structure of the agricultural sector in the U.S.; e.g., that bigger is more efficient. An understanding of agrarian societies in LDCs allows students to explore alternative solutions appropriate to Southern countries.

Segment 4: International Issues

While this segment is a continuation of the previous one, it also illustrates the interdependence among countries at various levels of development. Global interdependence is an important theme in the course.

Because the economic development of any nation, regardless of its level of development, cannot be viewed in isolation, we examine in this segment the various ties that bind countries—trade, investments, aid, debt. These ties bind developed countries to LDCs, and LDCs to each other. In the recent past, I have found the topic of third world debt to be most useful in demonstrating global interdependence, as well as to introduce the role of international multilateral organizations. Many students have only a vague knowledge of these important organizations but immediately become interested in the work of the International Monetary Fund and the World Bank.

In addition to examining global linkages, this segment explores the historical context and the political economy of development. We discuss such phenomena as colonialism, imperialism and multinational investments.

The use of economic models is continued in these classes, particularly those relevant to trade and investment. Since one cannot assume that the students have taken international trade and finance courses, it is necessary to use only the basic trade and investment models.

Simulations and role playing have increasingly become part of my teaching of this and other internationally oriented courses. Student evaluations of these simulations have been very positive. Some students have even begun to act as simulation facilitators at workshops and conferences. The most important lesson of such simulations is that linkages are pervasive in the world economy.

Course Requirements

The course requirements, particularly the three papers, reflect the course objectives as well as certain practical considerations for the students and the instructor. In particular, having students focus their research on one country for the entire term accomplishes several objectives.

First, it gives the student a sense of familiarity with a country—particularly important since the students have little or no background in international studies when they first come to the course. By focusing on one country, students learn to relate abstract discussion to a specific context.

Second, it conserves research time and material, which is sometimes necessary given library constraints. Students must be selective about which country they investigate, and they often have to rely on inter-library loans and new acquisitions, which must be ordered early in the term. This gives the instructor the additional benefit of being able to increase the library holdings for specific countries.

Third, it allows students to feel that they are making a significant contribution to the discussions. As the "resident expert" on a particular country, they can contribute the knowledge they have with less fear of duplicating what their classmates have said.

The first paper assignment is largely a familiarization exercise. However, in addition to researching the history and current situation of a country, students review relevant socioeconomic indicators for countries. These include the data from the World Bank's *World Development Report* and the United Nations' *Human Development Report*.

The second paper on specific issues is meant to accomplish three objectives: First, it should make the student think of countries as more than an amalgam of socioeconomic statistics. After the first paper, there is a danger that students will become fixated with the "number crunching" in development studies. This paper therefore focuses on pressing socioeconomic issues. Second, it should allow students to use whatever historical, social and cultural information they have learned in the first paper to analyze current problems in the country. Finally, it is an opportunity for students to share with the class their particular expertise.

For this paper, I suggest specific research topics, guiding students to those which most closely correlate with available materials. And close surveillance of student projects minimizes duplication of research in the class.

The third paper fosters the use of statistics and statistics software. Students analyze patterns of development using both cross-section and time-series data. Since students have had ample exposure to numerous socioeconomic indicators and development issues, the first step for this paper is to formulate hypotheses about patterns of development which can be tested using the available data. Next, students consult with me to identify the appropriate statistical tests and data; they then run statistical tests, analyze the results and conclude their paper with an explanation of their hypothesis, their results, and a discussion of the implications of their findings.

For students (and myself) the most time-consuming and frustrating part of this paper is the use of statistics software. At our university, we use SAS on our VAX system. Both the preparation of data and the running of statistical procedures require a significant investment of time for students. To ease students' work on SAS, I have converted much of the available socioeconomic indicators into SAS data sets, assigning each indicator an SAS-based variable name, label, and format.

I have also prepared step-by-step instructions (from logging on and running the most common statistical procedures to printing the statistical results) for the use of SAS on our VAX—using these economic development data sets as examples.

Has It Worked?

All courses that I teach, including this international economic development course, are evaluated by students at the end of the term. I use both a Likert-type questionnaire and a section that gives students the opportunity to comment.

Based on past student evaluations, it appears that this course has high value-added for student awareness and understanding. Among other things, this is most likely a function of the relatively low base of knowledge about the subject matter that students start out with.

Students have also commented on the usefulness of the course in learning the interrelatedness among various disciplines and issues. International economic development is a topic that lends itself to interdisciplinary learning.

Students have repeatedly commented on the amount of learning that they felt occurs during the class discussions. Of course, this presupposes that each student has the appropriate tools and framework for learning and that each student is able to contribute to the discussions. This has led me to believe that the series of three papers, in addition to the course readings, are effective ways to teach this course.

The most frustrating part for the students, and understandably so, has been the computer-related work. This results from a combination of the students' lack of experience in mainframe statistical software and of their weakness in statistics. This might be overcome by assigning smaller projects on the computer throughout the term.

Extensive readings are of course desirable in a course such as this. However, I have found that a heavy reading load results in confusion and lack of coherence in class discussions. I have therefore reduced the assignments to a few readings that highlight a different point of view from the material contained in the main textbook.

Every time I have taught the course, I have run out of time. Because I am unable to cover all the topics outlined in the syllabus, it has been necessary to cut some material from the section on domestic sectors (e.g., monetary policy). I have also found it saves time to steer clear of the more contentious ideological debates.

Possible Changes

The international economic development course is by nature very dynamic. We expect that its content will evolve, if only because its main subject matter—the developing countries—are evolving. We anticipate the following changes:

As noted above, we are considering offering versions of the course for noneconomics majors. This is in response to the increasing demand for global studies courses.

We must decide if Eastern Europe belongs in our teaching of international economic development. An alternative is to offer a separate course on Eastern European economic development.

With four decades of development experience to assess, we plan to devote more time in the course to studying the clear successes and failures of development experiments. We expect that with the decreasing level of ideological polarization, students and faculty will be better able to discuss and analyze what policies work for development and what approaches have not worked.

I do not intend to drop the third required paper on statistics; it may, however, be transformed into a series of group projects. This might reduce the level of student frustration and faculty consultation time.

The list of assigned readings will no doubt be revised as the tone of the debate about international economic development changes. Specifically, with the decline of the socialist/communist/Marxist paradigms, and with the increasing concern with U.S. domestic issues, we anticipate recasting the readings to highlight the mutual interdependence between rich and poor countries.

We anticipate the use of more simulations and role-playing sessions as a way of highlighting the interdependencies among nations. As mentioned, simulations and role playing have been very effective in fostering learning.

SYLLABUS

ECON 415—Economic Development
Spring, 1991
Instructor: Dr. Gabriel Manrique
Office: Somsen 310
Hours: 11–12 and 1–2 and any Pareto Optimal Time

Texts

Economic Development in the Third World, by Michael Todaro, Fourth Edition.
(Required)
Poverty Amidst Plenty: World Political Economy and Distributive Justice, by
Edward Weisband. (Required)

Objective

To provide the student with the opportunity to become familiar
with that group of countries that makes up the majority of this
planet—the third world—and to provide the student with the tools
and knowledge to analyze the process, costs and strategies of economic
development.

Expectations

It is assumed that the student is knowledgeable in the fundamentals
of economic analysis and is able to apply them to the subject matter. It
is also expected that the student remains up to date on events, issues
and decisions that pertain to the third world as well as its relationships
with the developed nations. A basic, working knowledge of algebra,
statistics and graphs for analysis is assumed by the instructor. Active
participation through questions, answers and pertinent comments is
strongly encouraged and suitably rewarded.

Grading

2 Periodic Tests	45%	A 90–100
Final Paper	25%	B 80–89
2 Reports	20%	C 70–79
Attendance and Participation	10%	D 60–69
		E 59 and under

Test Dates
April 17
May 20

Paper Due Dates
Country Report   April 8
Issues Report   May 6
Final Paper   May 23 (Final Exam Period)

Policy on Test Dates and Paper Due Dates

All of the test dates and paper due dates have been given to you ahead of time to give you ample time to prepare. Tests must be taken at the assigned time. *There will be no early or make-up tests.* Papers are due during the class period on the assigned dates. *Late papers will not be accepted regardless of the novelty of the excuse.*

Academic Honesty

Acts of academic dishonesty will not be tolerated. Anyone caught cheating will automatically receive a grade of zero for the test in question.

Anyone caught plagiarizing, that is, claiming what is essentially someone else's work as his or her own, will automatically receive a final grade of E for the course. The university may choose to impose additional penalties. Remember that submitting someone else's work as one's own after merely changing a few words or sentences still constitutes plagiarism. The proper citation must be given for any material taken from other sources.

Assigned Readings

The book by Todaro will be the main text. Readings from the book by Weisband will be assigned to supplement the material covered in the textbook as a way of adding to the ideological, historical and institutional dimensions of the subject matter. As such, you will be held responsible for all assigned readings even if they are not fully discussed in class. Other material such as films and data sets will also be introduced in class. You will also be responsible for those.

Course Outline

I.   That Third World (Todaro, ch. 1, 2)
II. Paradigms of Development, Growth and Change (Todaro, ch. 3, 4)
III. Domestic Issues

Poverty and Income Distribution (Todaro, ch. 5)
Population (Todaro, ch. 6, 7)
Unemployment (Todaro, ch. 8, 9)
Education (Todaro, ch. 11)
Agriculture (Todaro, ch. 10)
IV.   International Issues
Trade (Todaro, ch. 12, 14)
Finance (Todaro, ch. 13, 15)

Required Papers

A series of three papers is required for completion of the course. They are meant to provide you with a better focus as you study economic development in the third world.

All papers must be machine printed, double spaced. You will be graded on both substance and presentation. Any material taken from other sources should be given the proper citation in a separate "Footnotes" or "Endnotes" page. Consult a writing manual for the proper way to write footnotes.

1. Country Profile

For the first paper, you will write a country profile to familiarize you with at least one developing country. Select a third world country to write on, with the exception of the following: Brazil, Argentina, Singapore, Colombia, and the People's Republic of China. Each student must select a country other than their own.

For the country that you select, write a paper at least 5 pages long that describes:

A. The country's economic and social conditions as well as its economic performance. Use as much data as possible on social and economic indicators.

B. The recent history and political situation in the country. Include in this section as much information on current events as possible.

C. The economic structure of the country including its main industries, exports, imports, trading partners, etc. Include in this section information on the current economic climate and prospects of the country.

Due Date: April 8

2. Development Issues Paper

For the second paper, select at least two development issues or problems that are of major concern to the country that you selected in the first paper. (A partial list of issues is provided for you below.)

With that country as your focus, write a paper at least 5 pages long that describes:

A. The problem, its sources and its extent.
B. Its human, economic, and social ramifications.
C. The proposed solutions to the problems.
D. The probable impact on the U.S.A. and other developed countries.

Due Date: May 6
Suggested Issues:

1. The Year of the Child
2. Women and Development
3. Development and the Environment
4. Appropriate Technology/Products
5. Illiteracy
6. Hunger/Famine/Malnutrition
7. Debt
8. The Global Village
9. Income and Wealth Inequality
10. Unemployment/Underemployment/ Disguised Unemployment
11. Trade Protectionism
12. Overpopulation

3. Economic Data Analysis

The third paper will summarize the results of statistical analysis you will be performing during the quarter. You will be provided with computer access to a data set containing information on the nations of the world. You will also be taught the basics for using SAS, a statistics software.

Based on what will be covered in class, you will be able to compare countries as well as examine the relationships among economic and social variables. The contents of the third paper will describe what analysis you have done and your conclusions. The specifics of this paper will be made much clearer to you as we proceed with the course.

Due Date: May 23 (during the final exam period)

Additional Sources

Materials in addition to the readings to be assigned in the Weisband book.

"The Third World," by David Ziegler, *War, Peace and International Politics,* 4th edition, Harper Collins Publishers, 1987, pp. 391–402.

"Paradigms of Economic Development and Beyond," by Charles K. Wilber and Kenneth P. Jameson, *The Political Economy of Development and Underdevelopment,* 4th edition, Random House, 1988, pp. 3–27.

"The Development of Underdevelopment," by Andre Gunder Frank, *Monthly Review* (September, 1966), pp. 17–31.

"Can the East Asian Model of Development be Generalized?" by William Cline, *World Development* II, 10.

"Ethnocentrism and Third World Development," by Howard J. Wiarda, *Society* XXIV, 6, pp. 55–64.

"Easing the Debt Crisis," *Annual Editions, Third World, 91/92,* pp. 180–197.

"Inward- Versus Outward-Looking Policies," *Leading Issues in Economic Development,* by Gerald Meier, 5th edition, Oxford University Press, 1988, pp. 394–421.

"Human Resources," *Leading Issues in Economic Development,* by Gerald Meier, 5th edition, pp. 431–464.

One World, One Economy, documentary film produced by the International Monetary Fund.

World Development Report (various annual editions), The World Bank. (Pay particular attention to the indicators found in the statistical appendices.)

Human Development Report (various annual editions), United Nations Development Programme. (Pay particular attention to the indicators found in the statistical appendices.)

NOTES

1. The term is borrowed from Denis Goulet, "That Third World," *World Development: An Introductory Reader,* edited by Helene Castel, New York, 1971, pp. 1–24.

2. The term and some of the underlying ideas are taken from "Paradigms of Economic Development and Beyond," in Charles K. Wilber and Kenneth P. Jameson, *Directions in Economic Development,* University of Notre Dame Press, 1975, pp. 1–41.

Women in Development

CONNER BAILEY AND RUTH C. BUSCH

Overcoming Myopia

Since the early 1960s, Auburn University has played a prominent role in tropical fisheries development, both in training Third World scientists and through involvement in project activities in Asia, Africa and Latin America. Not until the mid-1980s, however, did the rest of this large land grant university begin to take part in international development activities. Despite token membership in the Southeast Consortium for International Development (SECID), faculty involvement in international development activities was actively discouraged; several faculty found it necessary to resign in order to work outside the United States. The official view was that the job of faculty at Auburn was to serve the needs of Alabama taxpayers. This position was reversed in the early 1980s when a new university president took office.

Given this history of parochialism, it took some time for the new policy to take hold and for a broad base of support for involvement in international activities to be built within the university as a whole. Several steps were taken to build such support. At the administrative level, an office of international programs was established to win contracts for implementation of development projects and to handle the increasing number of international students coming to Auburn as the university's graduate programs grew during the 1980s. Growth in graduate programs was tied to a new emphasis placed on Auburn as a research institution capable of attracting large contracts and grants. The same motivation lay behind the internationalization of Auburn University.

Faculty at Auburn responded to these new international opportunities in a variety of ways. In 1985, a loose group of faculty calling themselves the Third World Interest Group (TWIG) began to hold regular meetings and brown-bag seminars. Faculty at Auburn also began to become involved in the annual World Food Day activities which occur each October, presenting seminars on problems of hunger and development. At least two new courses on international development were established in 1986. During 1988, a group of faculty and students interested in women in development (WID) issues was formed, which also held working meetings and brown-bag seminars. Many women from campus were drawn to the WID meetings with a view towards identifying opportunities for involvement in international activities.

A parallel development to the globalization of Auburn University during the 1980s was the establishment of a women's caucus, a forum for women's issues in higher education. Additionally, a Women's Studies Program was established during the 1980s. This program coordinates courses that address women's issues. Undergraduate students at Auburn are able to earn a minor in Women's Studies if they take 30 quarter-hours of approved courses.

Conceiving a Course

The Women in Development course we developed at Auburn was established in response to a direct request from the director of the Women's Studies Program. The two of us have long years of international experience and a general interest in WID issues. One of us (Bailey) had worked in Southeast Asia while the other (Busch) had worked in the Middle East, Africa and Latin America. Busch also had served as the campus WID representative for the Southeastern Consortium for International Development (SECID).

There were some minor bureaucratic problems to be overcome before initiating this course. The two of us were from different disciplines and different colleges (rural sociology in the College of Agriculture, and anthropology in the College of Liberal Arts). Because most students involved in the Women's Studies Program were in the College of Liberal Arts, we decided it would be best to list the course in anthropology. Anthropology at Auburn is located in a joint department with sociology and social work and is linked to rural sociology through an interdepartmental masters degree program. Thus the structure for collaborative work existed.

The issue of disciplinary differences between us presented more opportunities than obstacles; each of us brought a perspective to the study of WID, but these perspectives tended to be complementary rather than contradictory in nature. For example, Busch's background in anthropology led her to draw attention to differences in gender roles at various stages of human evolution, while Bailey's focus on gender biases embedded in large bureaucratic structures like the World Bank drew attention to issues of political economy.

Course Preparation

Both of us had extensive field research experience relevant to the study of WID issues. However, neither of us had specialized in this area, so we both had to catch up on the explosion of literature in this field that occurred during the mid- to late 1980s. This was difficult because the course was being taught on an overload basis and without any release time for course preparation. The main incentives for us were the opportunity to expand our personal and professional relationship, and to get up-to-speed on an important topic.

The overall goal of the course was to familiarize students with the literature on women in development. Specific goals were to examine the variety of social and economic roles which women perform in tropical developing nations of the world, to assess the impact of development programs and projects on women, and to consider development alternatives that would improve the status and condition of women.

The course was made available to both advanced undergraduate and graduate students. Making the course available to undergraduates met the objective of contributing to the minor in Women's Studies. At the same time, we wanted to attract graduate students from fisheries and other programs around campus, particularly those with international experience. The course itself was run as a seminar where faculty and students alike were participants. We each took overall responsibility for directing class discussions on alternating weeks. We used two basic techniques in directing the seminar. One approach was for one of us to lead off with a 20–30 minute minilecture on the topic of the week, putting the readings into context and opening several lines of discussion for the next 2 hours. The second basic approach was to assign specific readings to particular students and have them be prepared to summarize the basic points and lead group discussions. This mix of instructors and approaches was well received.

Choice of Reading Materials

In planning this course, we decided to combine a mix of theoretical and descriptive readings. We wanted to place sufficient emphasis on theory so that students would understand the larger structural forces that create or increase gender inequalities in the development process. By the same token, we wanted to put some descriptive flesh on WID issues by examining particular case study materials. The case study approach, we felt, would help students understand the more theoretical materials and better appreciate the diversity of problems that fall under the rubric of WID.

As indicated in the accompanying course syllabus (see below), two texts and a diverse set of supplemental readings were selected. One text was a volume of 15 essays edited by Irene Tinker. As is frequently the case with such volumes, the quality was uneven. The introductory section and the sections on politics and challenging patriarchy were stronger than the section on intrahousehold distribution and control. Some chapters were based on particular cases, but most were of a broader, more theoretical nature. We decided to ground this theorizing, not only in our own experiences, shared in class discussions, but also in other readings, including the 1986 book by Margaret Leahy. Leahy examines the status of women in the United States, Mexico, the Soviet Union and Cuba. Her analysis focuses on social status, economic position and political rights, drawing attention to differences and similarities between capitalist and Marxist worlds. Leahy's book represents a good balance between theory and description, and remains relevant despite the recent collapse of the Soviet Union.

Having selected these two texts, we selected a number of supplementary readings to flesh out the course outline. We drew heavily from two edited volumes (Charlton, Everett and Staudt, *Women, the State, and Development*; and Parpart, *Women and Development in Africa*) for these additional readings, and brought in other readings as well.

Readings for the first week were intended to provide a broad overview of WID issues. Introductory readings from the two texts and the overview chapter from Parpart were used for this purpose. The readings and discussions gave students an understanding of the history behind WID and the forces promoting and delaying consideration of WID issues in the development arena.

The second and third weeks focused on case study materials. The first set of these readings focused on the United States, Latin America and the Carribean. What linked these readings was not so much a question of geography as the peripheral nature of women in capitalist economies of the Western Hemisphere. Two readings on the United States, for example, pointed out the reality of limits placed on the lives of many women in this country. The following week attention shifted to an examination of experience in socialist societies where political ideology would appear to have dictated more equitable treatment of women as a means of unleashing human potential in its fullness. The lesson here was that political ideology does not necessarily overcome ingrained cultural habits. Women in the Soviet Union, for example, have experienced over several generations many of the same problems faced by working women in the United States—the expectation that after a full day of work, it remains the woman's job to shop, clean, cook and raise the children. Leahy pointed out that only in Cuba was a systematic attempt made to alter this pattern through a conscious effort of addressing both male and female gender roles in a socialist economy.

Having explored the limits of political ideology in altering gender relations, during the fourth and fifth weeks we turned to WID issues in the Third World. The first set of readings focused attention on the role of the state and feminist perspective on the nature of societal development. The second set of readings continued this line of enquiry but shifted to examining the role of international development agencies in promoting or retarding consideration of WID issues.

At this point in the course we shifted direction back to concrete examples of the impact of developmental change on women. The argument was made that women bear major responsibilities that often go unrecognized and unrewarded. These responsibilities range from managing household economies to playing leading roles in agricultural production and marketing. Frequently, women's labor is undervalued by economists ("women have few alternative employment opportunities, so the value of their labor is near zero") and ignored by extension workers (who direct their efforts towards men, even in areas where women are the primary producers). In retrospect, this material should have been presented earlier in the course, in week four instead of week six—before consideration of the role of the state. This would have given us more empirical material to use in the more general theoretical discussions of weeks four and five, which focused on the political economy of development. This shift also would have allowed for a smoother transition to materials covered in week seven, which represent a feminist critique of development.

The last topic covered was women's roles in natural resource management. Two of the three readings assigned were focused on forestry issues. Among the common obligations of rural women in many developing nations is the provision of wood for cooking the family meals. Commercial logging and other human activities have dramatically reduced the local availability of firewood, making it necessary for women to spend enormous amounts of time to obtain fuel. For this reason, women have special interests in protecting forest resources. Addressing the positive contributions that women can play in natural resource management allowed us to end the course on a positive note.

Instructors' Assessment of the Course

Team teaching this course offered a number of advantages associated with crossing boundaries of gender and discipline, and expanding our base of geographical referents to use in seminar. As disciplines, anthropology and sociology share common concerns but also differ significantly in method and perspective. Working together in a classroom setting provided a valuable meeting point where commonalities and differences could be highlighted, both for students and for ourselves. For example, anthropologists frequently examine gender issues in comparative contexts which span time, culture and space. A sociologist may be less likely to consider gender relationships in early human societies, focusing instead on structural constraints impeding the advancement of women in society. Discussion of differing disciplinary perspectives was a positive feature of the seminar. Similarly, team teaching provided access to a wider range of field research experience, including the Middle East, Latin America and Southeast Asia. Finally, the fact that both male and female instructors were interested and involved in WID issues served to make the point that what we really were talking about was not only a matter of concern for women but also a matter of legitimate concern for anyone concerned with social justice and progressive change.

SYLLABUS

Anthropology 524
Women in Development
3–5 Credit Hours
(Fall 1990)

> Women constitute half the world's population, perform nearly two-thirds of its work hours, receive one-tenth of the world's income and own less than one-hundredth of the world's property. (United Nations, 1980.)

Women play central roles in agricultural production and marketing within most developing countries. In addition to these economic activities, women typically bear primary responsibility for food preparation, child rearing, collection of water and firewood, and other time-consuming domestic tasks. Frequently, women are responsible for managing the household economy, making key decisions affecting both family consumption and the adoption of new production technologies.

Until recently, these and other contributions by women to social and economic life were ignored or overlooked by development planners. The result was a series of unsuccessful development programs and projects. Even where development efforts were regarded as successful, ignorance of gender-based divisions of labor often have resulted in serious erosion of the status of women, either by eliminating their economic autonomy or by downgrading their economic and social roles.

The unique problems faced by women in development, as well as their unique potentials for contributing to the development process, have attracted increasingly active examination and debate. Most international development agencies now formally consider the issue of gender bias in their program reviews. Many of these agencies, as well as many universities, have professional and academic positions linked to the issue of women in development.

The objectives of this course are to familiarize students with the variety of roles played by women in the social and economic life of diverse tropical developing countries, to examine the impact of development programs and projects on women in developing countries, and to consider development alternatives that will improve the position of women.

Instructors

Dr. Ruth C. Busch, 6090 Haley Center, 844–2827
Dr. Conner Bailey, 313A Comer Hall, 844–5632

Texts

Irene Tinker. 1990. *Persistent Inequalities; Women and World Development.*
    New York: Oxford University Press. 302 p. HQ 1240 .P48 1990
Margaret E. Leahy. 1986. *Development Strategies and the Status of Women; A*
    Comparative Study of the United States, Mexico, the Soviet Union, and
    Cuba. Boulder: L. Rienner Publishers. 167 p. HQ 1240 .L43 1986

Supplemental Readings

Supplemental readings are on 2-hour reserve in the main library.
These can be requested either in the form of the original source (typically an edited volume) or a photocopy of the article or book chapter.

Prerequisites

Course available to Juniors, Seniors and Graduate students interested in issues of women and development.

This course counts towards fulfillment of the Minor in Women's
Studies at Auburn University.

Examinations

There will be one mid-term exam and one final exam. The exams
will combine multiple-choice/true-false questions with short-answer
and essay questions.

A list of essay questions will be distributed approximately one week
before the exam. The essay portion of the exam will be chosen from
this list. Students are encouraged to discuss these questions among
themselves before the exam. Each student will, of course, write their
own answers during the test.

All exams and research papers will be read and graded by both
instructors.

Variable Credit

Students taking the course for 3 hours credit are responsible for
readings and exams. Additional credit hours (up to 5 total credit
hours) can be earned through preparation of a research paper, subject
to approval of one of the course instructors.

Academic Honesty

The student academic honesty code of Auburn University will be enforced. This code is spelled out on pages 105–107 of the 1990–1991 Tiger Cub.

Evaluation

Students Signed up for 3 Credit Hours

220 course points

The mid-term and final examinations each are worth 100 points. An additional 20 points can be earned on the basis of class participation. The criteria used in determining points for class participation are as follows:

1. regular attendance;
2. active participation in discussions of assigned readings, showing evidence of having read and understood these materials;
3. creative contribution to class discussions evidenced by the ability to integrate assigned and outside readings, lecture and discussions, and personal experiences.

Students Signed up for 4 or 5 Credit Hours:

For those who write research papers, this total will be increased by an additional 50 points for each credit hour. Total course points for students signed up for 4 credit hours will be 270. Total course points for students signed up for 5 credit hours will be 320.

For All Students:

Course grades will be determined by points earned as a percentage of total course points, as follows:

A = 90% and above
B = 80–89%
C = 70–79%
D = 60–69%
F = 59% or less

Reading Assignments

NOTE: In order to participate effectively in class discussions, the material assigned should be read prior to class.

1 October

Introduction to Issues of Women in Development

1. Tinker. "A Context for the Field and for the Book." Ch. 1 of Tinker (ed.), pp. 3–13.
2. Boserup. "Economic Change and the Roles of Women." Ch. 2 of Tinker (ed.), pp. 14–26.
3. Leahy. "Women and Development: The Issues Defined." Ch. 1 of Leahy, pp. 1–13.
4. Eva M. Rathgeber. 1989. "Women and Development: An Overview." In: J. L. Parpart (ed.), *Women and Development in Africa; Comparative Perspectives*. New York: University Press of America. Pp. 19–32. HQ 1240.5 .A357 W66 1989

8 October
Case Studies from the Western Hemisphere
1. Leahy. "The Limits of Suffrage: Women in the United States." Ch. 2 of Leahy, pp. 14–46.
2. Monica H. Gordon. 1989. "Black Women in America: Coping with Paradoxes of Race, Sex and Class." In: J. L. Parpart (ed.), *Women and Development in Africa; Comparative Perspectives*. New York: University Press of America. Pp. 83–102. HQ 1240.5 .A357 W66 1989
3. Mary Turner. 1989. "Women and Development: The Caribbean and Latin America." In: J. L. Parpart (ed.), *Women and Development in Africa; Comparative Perspectives*. New York: University Press of America. Pp. 103–114. HQ 1240.5 .A357 W66 1989
4. Leahy. "The *Casa* Prevails: Women in Mexico." Ch. 3 of Leahy, pp. 46–64.
5. Joycelin Massiah. "Defining Women's Work in the Commonwealth Caribbean." Ch. 13 of Tinker, pp. 223–238.

15 October
Case Studies from Socialist Societies
1. Leahy. "Equality Creates a Double Burden: Women in the Soviet Union." Ch. 4 of Leahy, pp. 65–90.
2. Leahy. "The Revolution in the Revolution: Women in Cuba." Ch. 5 in Leahy, pp. 91–116.
3. S. Wolchik. 1989. "Women and the State in Eastern Europe and the Soviet Union." In: Charlton, Everett and Staudt (eds.), *Women, the State, and Development*. Albany: State University of New York. Pp. 44–65. HQ 1240 .W663 1989

22 October
The Political Economy of Women in Development
1. Tinker. "The Making of a Field: Advocates, Practitioners, and Scholars." Ch. 3 in Tinker, pp. 27–53.
2. Jaquette. "Gender and Justice in Economic Development." Ch. 4 in Tinker, pp 54–69.

3. S. E. M. Charlton, J. Everett and K. Staudt. 1989. "Women, the State and Development." In: Charlton, Everett and Staudt (eds.), *Women, the State, and Development*. Albany: State University of New York. Pp. 1–16. HQ 1240 .W663 1989
4. K. Staudt. 1990. "Gender Politics in Bureaucracy: Theoretical Issues in Comparative Perspective." In: K. Staudt (ed.), *Women, International Development, and Politics*. Philadelphia: Temple University Press. Pp. 3–24. HQ 1240 .W662 1990
5. Bunch and Carrillo. "Feminist Perspectives on Women in Development." Ch. 5 in Tinker, pp. 70–82.

Mid-Term Examination Week of 29 October

29 October

The Political Economy of Women in Development (continued)

1. Bourque and Warren. "Access Is Not Enough: Gender Perspectives on Technology and Education." Ch. 6 in Tinker, pp. 83–100.
2. Lim. "Women's Work in Export Factories: The Politics of a Cause." Ch. 7 in Tinker, pp. 101–122.
3. K. Himmelstrand. 1990. "Can an Aid Bureaucracy Empower Women?" In: K. Staudt (ed.), *Women, International Development, and Politics*. Philadelphia: Temple University Press. Pp. 101–113. HQ 1240 .W662 1990
4. N. Kardam. 1990. "The Adaptability of International Development Agencies: The Response of the World Bank to Women in Development." In: K. Staudt (ed.), *Women, International Development, and Politics*. Philadelphia: Temple University Press. Pp. 114–128. HQ 1240 .W662 1990
5. K. Jensen. 1990. "Getting to the Third World: Agencies as Gatekeepers." In: K. Staudt (ed.), *Women, International Development, and Politics*. Philadelphia: Temple University Press. Pp. 247–264. HQ 1240 .W662 1990

5 November

Women's Burdens

1. A. K. Sen. "Gender and Cooperative Conflicts." Ch. 8 in Tinker, pp. 123–149.
2. B. Senauer. "The Impact of the Value of Women's Time on Food and Nutrition." Ch. 9 in Tinker, pp. 150–161.
3. H. Papanek. "To Each Less Than She Needs, from Each More Than She Can Do: Allocations, Entitlements, and Value." Ch. 10 in Tinker, pp. 162–184.
4. M. McCall. 1987. "Carrying Heavier Burdens But Carrying Less Weight: Some Implications of Villagization for Women in Tanzania." In: J. M. Momsen and J. G. Townsend (eds.), *Geography and Gender in the Third World*. Albany: State University of New York. Pp. 192–214. HQ 1240 .G46 1987

12 November

Challenging Patriarchy

1. Mazumdar and Sharma. "Sexual Division of Labor and the Subordination of Women: A Reappraisal from India." Ch. 11 in Tinker, pp. 185–197.
2. Afonja. "Changing Patterns of Gender Stratification in West Africa." Ch. 12 in Tinker, pp. 198–209.
3. Obbo. "East African Women, Work, and the Articulation of Dominance." Ch. 13 in Tinker, pp. 199–222.
4. Kusterer. "The Imminent Demise of Patriarchy." Ch. 14 in Tinker, pp. 223–256.

19 November

Presentation of Research Reports
Thanksgiving break begins noon, Wednesday, 21 November

26 November

Women's Roles in Natural Resource Management

1. A. Molnar. 1989. "Forest Conservation in Nepal: Encouraging Women's Participation." In: A. Leonard (ed.), *Seeds: Supporting Women's Work in the Third World*. New York: The Feminist Press at The City University of New York. Pp. 98–119. HQ 1240.5 D44 S43 1989
2. M. Schmink. 1989. "Community Management of Waste Recycling in Mexico." In: A. Leonard (ed.), *Seeds: Supporting Women's Work in the Third World*. New York: The Feminist Press at The City University of New York. Pp. 123–138. HQ 1240.5 D44 S43 1989
3. I. Dankelman and J. Davidson. 1988. "Women and Forests: Fuel, Food and Fodder." Ch. 4 of Dankelman and Davidson, *Women and Environment in the Third World*. London: Earthscan Publications Ltd. Pp. 42–65. HQ 1240.5 .D44 D36 1988

30 November

Research Papers Due

3 December

Final week assignments to be determined. Students are encouraged to make suggestions regarding topics and material to be covered. Thursday, Dec. 6th is the last day of class.

7 December

Dead Day. Time and date of final exam will be determined.

World Politics and Economy: The Political Economy of Development

EDWARD WEISBAND

The course outlined below is designed to enable introductory students to work toward an understanding of certain major concepts relevant to world poverty, including: political economy, international division of labor, social and political development, global politics and distributive justice. The syllabus itself, after all one of the initial engagements the teacher has with the students, plays an integral role in establishing and maintaining the learning objectives facing the students. And it does so not merely by identifying *what* the goals are but by suggesting *how* they are to be achieved.

The mission of this course, as conveyed through the syllabus, is ultimately to engage student imagination in ways that reveal the inextricable linkage between moral discourse, theoretical insight and analytical precision. Students must function effectively within these three modes of discourse, learning to aspire to theoretical rigor, analytical clarity, and, above all, moral or philosophical centeredness. But they do so within the context of a plea for humility. For as the syllabus suggests, the quality of theoretical discourse is not to be measured by the answers any theory provides but, rather, is measured by the richness of the questions theories provoke.

The syllabus outlines a sequence of topics and learning strategies. Lectures begin by describing the plight of small-scale farmers in developing countries. At first the pace of the course is deliberate. Students must grapple with their image of the world as a place of prosperity and well-being for most people, and, in particular, with the moral as well as intellectual issues that arise as a consequence of the basic fact that misery pervades human existence in the modern world.

The Theoretical and the Concrete

The pedagogical and learning missions of this course include comprehension of both texts and subtexts. Both must be made explicit in class and by means of the syllabus. One major component of the course is therefore exploration of certain central propositions which comprise the analytical frameworks of competing developmental theories.

Development, like all great concepts in social science and theory, does not exist apart from one's intellectual orientation to it. For example, liberal conceptions of markets, dependency approaches to underdevelopment, Marxist theories of imperialism, basic needs strategies, sustainable forms of agricultural development—these and many other similar and familiar notions—all represent subtextual theoretical orientations in that they frame the very perspectives which students must establish in their own minds simply in order to comprehend the concrete character of development. Students must be able to look through many lenses if they are truly to see.

As the course proceeds, the skein of problems relevant to development unravels. For example, the impacts of industrialization policies, of trade policies, of import substitution policies, of monetary policies that overvalue or undervalue domestic currency, the various effects of capitalism, of cash cropping, of urban push and rural pull, are represented to students as parts of a larger composite, a mosaic, as it were, that must be grasped in its entirety to be understood at all.

In addition to shifting between the theoretical and the concrete, students are asked to shift from micro to macro perspectives, perspectives that might be envisioned in terms of bottom-up or top-down. They are introduced to the plight of poor rural or of peasant families, of the urban slum-dweller, or of the marginalized, or of the migrant, or of the entrepreneur within the informal sector, etc. Such individuals become prototypical of entire developmental processes such as industrialization or uneven growth, as well as of development policy.

Further, students learn how to assume more world or internationalist and less parochial perspectives by confronting the fundamental proposition that poverty in any one country reflects, in many instances, the poverty that exists in many countries, and that poverty anywhere feeds off of poverty everywhere.

The Syllabus and the Course

A syllabus should be more than a list of assignments. It must do more than merely outline requirements. A syllabus calls students into imaginative and moral presence by attracting them to the great challenges that lie before them. It represents an invitation for dialogue and mutuality. It must reveal systematic and deliberate concern on the part of the teacher for the subject at hand and for the student. Only then may a teacher expect the reciprocal from any student.

The syllabus below is thus an open letter to students. It reveals the internal dialogical process which I, the teacher, use in making pedagogical choices such as assigning texts and organizing sequence. But more importantly, it indicates why I believe in the importance of this topic. It suggests why one should care about it. It declares over and over that intellectual life is part of one's moral and ethical existence. And it shows that care for others in development is a moral obligation, one that must be tempered by intellectual and analytical integrity.

This coexistence in the classroom between intellectual rigor and moral reflection is illustrated by two evaluation exercises, designed to introduce activist forms of connected learning into the instructional framework of the course.

First, students are required to submit a policy position paper at the end of the semester. This is an especially important learning exercise given the structure of the course and the pedagogical format which informs it. The actual syllabus includes a model outline of how such a position paper might be organized. This model is presented in order to induce students to think and to analyze concrete policy issues systematically and, most important, with a clear view to the theoretical implications of their analysis.

Thus the pedagogical aim of this assignment is to encourage students to integrate theoretical analysis with an attempt to advocate a specific policy solution to a problem. It is this combination of theoretical analysis and policy advocacy that is crucial to student learning and to intellectual development as defined in this course.

Too often undergraduate students shy away from abstraction and theoretical analysis. On the other hand, relativism, in which all opinions are deemed to operate at equivalent levels of validity, often dominates student's ways of knowing. This assignment thus provides, though not in so many words, a lesson in epistemology, a lesson in which theoretical methods and procedures must be combined with debate over policy choices, values, and meanings.

Another exercise introduced by the course revolves around a final debate. One of the most exciting ventures in teaching occurs through peer learning. In this case, a number of students are asked to respond to a series of questions before the entire lecture class. Those students who are deemed to have best answered the question are granted extra credit toward their final grade. But the real point of the exercise is to create a learning environment in which students actually conduct a final review of the entire course. What is essential here is that the set of questions raised by the instructor and graduate teaching assistants in the debate are formulated with a view to the final examination. The questions raised in the debate, students are informed, will reappear in some reconstituted manner in the final essay exam question, and so it is useful for students to attend the final debate, and they often do so enthusiastically.

The syllabus shows how each segment of the course attempts to draw the linkages between grand policy and its impacts upon the lives of real people. Meanwhile, each segment of the course explores how people in developing countries can and often do shape their own lives and the worlds in which they live.[1]

Structural Constraint and Human Agency

Students' senses of right and wrong and of good and bad become important instructional allies to the teacher able to muster them in the service of intellectual growth and progress. This is certainly true in many topical areas, but no more so than in teaching poverty and development within a context framed by the tensions between structural constraint and human agency and values.

No teacher should fail to provide students with some basis for interpreting the various impacts of structural determinants on processes of development. The term, "structure," conjures up the full array of positional relationships in development. Terms such as "underdevelopment," "immiseration," "class," "marginalization," indeed, the entire lexicon of development, are virtually grounded in notions of structure.

How does one explain the structural element of social order and of social systems? In the context of development theory, the intricacies of international division of labor, of comparative and competitive advantage, the relationship of capital to labor, the mobilities of factors of production, the efficiencies of economies of scale, the transfer of technology and the migration of jobs all provide rich examples of the systemic structural location of human activity, ultimately permitting teachers to enable students to distinguish the movable from the intractable. It encourages students to think about the nature of human agency, of the role of human values, of the impact of human vision and struggle in development. Structures of all kinds, including class structure, help "position" both the privileged and the disadvantaged. Thus structures create distributional outcomes through which the fate of millions are filtered. But despite the structural constraints that restrain or, at least, limit the possibilities of distributive justice, it is human agency, purpose, goals, and vision which still play the major roles in any process correctly labeled "development."

A syllabus retains its role as the primary teaching aid precisely because it conveys the character of a teacher's vision of the impact of human will and intentions upon society. It allows a teacher to express hope for the future despite all the immovable structural forces that hinder developmental efforts. And it demonstrates over and beyond any other lesson that what each of us does for others in development truly matters. For knowledge based upon vision breeds the kind of hope that tempers idle dreams with true understanding, the kind of understanding which development as a subject for teaching requires and surely deserves.

SYLLABUS

World Politics and Economy II

Department of Political Science   Prof. Edward Weisband
IS 2056   Spring, 1992

The Basic Proposition: Poverty amidst Plenty

This course is dedicated to an understanding of a single basic proposition: Wealth generates poverty. We ask the question: How can this be? How is it that the very source or solution to the problem of poverty is itself the very vector that promotes and expands it?

Posing the problem in this manner requires us to do more than merely describe. The problem we have posed engages us in a quest for theoretical explanation. Now we must seek to explain why poverty and destitution is the plight of more than two-fifths of the human family. Description, even dramatic depiction, although they represent initial conceptual steps along the way, are insufficient grounds for understanding. If we wish to struggle for social change, for human betterment, for amelioration of human misery and squalor, we must learn to distinguish between human agency, on the one hand, and the social, economic, and political frameworks or constraints in which human values and policy choices operate, on the other. And to be able to do this requires us to confront the study of political economy and the nature of theoretical analysis.

The Theoretical Task of Students in Political Economy

Poverty is nothing if not a problem in political economy and thus in theoretical discourse. What does this mean? What are theories and why do we need them? One way to respond is as follows:

First, theories seek to explain complex reality or phenomena that defy common sense or intuitive understanding.

Second, theories never prove, in that the measure of a successful theory is gauged by the richness of the questions it allows us to raise rather than by the answers it provides. The task of theoretical discourse is to get the question right. Why wealth promotes poverty is such a question, and the mere act of posing it represents a new level of theoretical understanding and insight. Once a theory is said to have proved something it no longer remains a theory as such, but moves on to a new status such as a law or principle.

Third, theories operate intellectually in ways that require alternate explanations or contrasting ways of thinking and reasoning. Too often we think either in terms of facts or in terms of opinions. In such an analytical scheme, facts are "hard" and opinions are "soft." The consequence is a misguided notion that all opinions are always equally correct or useful. But social understanding is not a taste. Examining poverty is not like a preference for chocolate rather than strawberry ice cream. We have to earn our intellectual spurs before we have the right to exert our opinions. Thus opinions or value-judgments must be informed by a theoretical quest in which alternate ways of interpreting reality, contrasting visions of the social truth, conflicting languages and concepts are all introduced in pursuit of systematic investigation and analysis.

Fourth, the primary theoretical task in studying political economy focused on poverty and development is to establish a multidisciplinary perspective on alternate forms of explanation of why and how development and poverty expand or operate in a world economy of contrast and uneven growth.

A World of Contrast

The world economy provides a lesson in contrast: uneven growth represents the salient feature of the world economy. The very conceptual terms that characterize or explain why and how the world economy emerged in the way it has imply disparity between rich and the poor, haves and have nots, North and South, First and Third Worlds, core and periphery, Advanced Developed Countries (ADCs) and Lesser Developing Countries (LDCs).

Not that such terms are unchanging. The concepts of First and Third Worlds imply the existence of the Second World of Communist states or command economies relevant to the Cold War; recent maturation of the Newly Industrialized Countries (NICs), moreover, reveals the extent to which the world economy has witnessed social and economic transformation in such countries as South Korea and Mexico. National as well as regional economic conditions change and thus so must our concepts that describe and explain such conditions.

Nonetheless the assumption on which this course is predicated suggests that despite whatever change or progress in the world economy we have witnessed in the last forty years of modern developmental experience, economic growth will continue to accentuate the contrast between intensive wealth and extensive poverty. The human condition is a study of poverty amidst plenty and it behooves us to understand why as well as to explore what policies might be pursued to relieve and to remedy this.

This course is thus dedicated to the examination of poverty and development. Poverty assails the human family as no other scourge in the modern world. One-fifth of the world's population faces absolute violation of the basic capacity for people to sustain themselves physically. Vast populations, numbering billions of people, face various forms of chronic deprivation. Such destitution exists in a world economy that produces wealth on an unprecedented scale. We ask why, and, in asking why, we raise three connected questions:

1. What is poverty?
2. What is a poor economy?
3. What is development?

Such questions present us with the overriding intellectual mission of this course.

International Development Policy: The Realm of Choice

Just as theoretical explanation involves a quest for understanding, based on an ability to explain causes as well as on a capacity to describe effects, our stress upon the importance of policy engages us in a dialogue over choices. It is here, in the realm of policy, that the relevance of human decisions, values, meanings, intentions, interests, objectives, goals, aims, and purposes all become central to our study.

The examination of alternate theoretical perspectives on poverty and development, although crucial, may sometimes lead to a kind of paralysis. The problems presented by poverty seem so overwhelming: the political and economic forces that generate and sustain poverty often appear more, rather than less, intractable, the more we understand how they function.

Yet such a sense of futility is inappropriate given the magnitude of the misery we must survey. Struggle is a necessary component of all developmental strategies and approaches. Hope for a better world must continue to encourage us all to participate in discussions and debates over the most effective means and methods of pursuing development. And this involves us in an exercise devoted to development policy and decision. For policy is the arena in which choices have to be made and the choices involving developmental policy are fraught with significance for the many whose future survival depends upon the decisions that are made.

Policy choices are double-edged swords. LDCs, by definition, confront complex problems that tend to be closely intertwined both in their origin and in their solution. In studying the political economy of development, from the perspectives of policy choice and decisions, we shall learn that one of the fundamental difficulties facing poor countries is that so often the policy solutions for development which they pursue in turn become the very sources of the policy problems they must resolve.

Throughout the forthcoming semester, we shall examine the wide institutional nexus which exists within the world economy relevant to development:

We shall examine the practices of institutional actors such as international financial institutions and multilateral development assistance banks such as the World Bank.

We shall take a careful look at the policies of conditionality associated with the International Monetary Fund (IMF) and the process of international monetary management relevant to what we shall call "structural adjustment."

We shall examine international markets, division of labor, and the principles of free trade liberalism based upon notions of comparative advantage relevant to international trade policies. We will examine various preferential schemes such as that established by the Lome Convention to see if they assist LDCs. We shall contrast import substitution schemes with policies organized by the precepts of "export promotion."

We shall review the operations and policies of the General Agreement on Tariff and Trade (GATT), an intergovernmental organization established in 1947 to promote free and open trade practices. We shall pay particular attention to the multilateral trade negotiations (MTN) promoted by the GATT to advance the principles of free trade throughout the world.

We shall review past and present MTN rounds such as the Kennedy, Tokyo, and especially the Uruguay Trade Rounds, which involve LDCs and their interests in new and unprecedented ways.

We shall discuss a major new actor in the private sector relevant to development policy and strategy, namely, the Transnational Business Enterprise, and the advantages and disadvantages it brings to LDCs through its package of capital investment, technology transfer and managerial know-how. The world economy is witnessing a major restructuring based on a new world structure of production. Terms such as "economies of scale," "flexible specialization," "strategic competition," "sectoral protectionism," "neomercantilism," all reflect these changes, as does the overarching concept of transnational division of labor. We shall examine these concepts in order to concentrate on their relevance to an understanding of how the new dynamics of world production intrude on LDCs and shape the policy decisions LDCs must take.

We shall survey the regional attempts at integration designed to promote economic development. Do free trade zones and integrated markets work to promote or impede national development?

We shall begin this series of policy perspectives by analyzing the plight of small-scale agricultural producers. This returns us to our central theme: wealth creates poverty. If we need one explanation as to why the poor become poorer everywhere in developing countries, that explanation resides in policies that favor urban areas over agrarian or rural regions, that promote industrialization rather than agricultural development, that advance the interests of large-scale enterprises over the interests of small-scale entrepreneurs and farmers. Small-scale farmers, the very key to development, are thus forced into misery, malnutrition, migration. They leave their villages and homelands to form slums around cities. And as they do so, they expand the poverty line that renders development policies less capable of reducing poverty than ever before.

Finally, we shall examine the consequences of poverty for women. Poverty is the ultimate women's issue. Poverty hurts women in excruciating ways. It is often the women who tote jugs of clean water for miles and miles each day to sustain their families. It is women who directly bear the pain and the anguish of high levels of infant mortality. It is women who work the hardest and the longest hours but consume the least food in many poor countries. And it is the relationship of women to development that is key to future advance of LDCs and to the enhancement of justice.

Course Examinations, Exercises and Evaluation

Requirements for Evaluation

Evaluation in the course involves three exercises:

1. Two essay examinations based on lectures as well as reading assignments (40%);
2. A final examination based on lectures and reading assignments conducted during final examination week (25%);
3. The Policy Position Paper due the final week of classes (25%);

4. Class participation in discussion sections as assessed by Graduate Teaching Assistants and based upon regularity of attendance and engagement in discussion (10%).

Books for Purchase

Students are required to purchase the following books. Each is designed to contribute to a student's learning experience.

World Bank, *World Development Report 1991: The Challenge of Development*, New York, NY: Oxford University Press, 1991.

Michael P. Todaro, *Economic Development in the Third World*, 4th ed., White Plains, NY: Longman, 1990.

Robert S. Walters and David H. Blake, *The Politics of Global Economic Relations*, 4th ed., Englewood Cliffs, NJ: Prentice-Hall, 1991.

Edward Weisband, ed., *Poverty amidst Plenty: World Political Economy and Distributive Justice*, Boulder, CO: 1989.

Charles K. Wilber and Kenneth P. Jameson, *The Political Economy of Development and Underdevelopment*, 5th ed, New York: McGraw-Hill, Inc., 1992.

Reading Assignments and Topics

PART I. THE POLITICAL ECONOMY OF DEVELOPMENT

First week: Poverty and Development
World Development Report, v–xii, Chap. 1.
Todaro, Introduction, Chap. 1.
Weisband, Statement of Purpose, Introduction.
Wilber and Jameson, Part One.
   Second week: What Is a Poor or Developing Nation?
World Development Report, Chap. 2.
Todaro, Chap. 2; Chap. 3, pp. 86–99; Appendix 3.2, pp. 108–113.
Weisband, Chap. 1, Readings #1–6.

PART II. DOMESTIC DEVELOPMENTAL PROBLEMS AND POLICIES—INCOME DISTRIBUTION

Third week: Measuring Income Distribution
World Development Report, Chap. 3.
Todaro, Introduction to Parts II and III, pp. 139–141; Chap. 5, pp. 143–170, 175–186.
Weisband, Chap. 2, Readings #7–10.
   Fourth week: Population and Development
World Development Report, Chap. 4.
Todaro, Chaps. 6, 7, pp. 214–221, 224–236.

Fifth week: Domestic Strategies for Development
Weisband, Reading #11 and Reading #16.

Sixth week: Employment and the Problem of Rural-Urban Migration
Todaro, Chap. 8, pp. 237–249, 251–253, 254–255, Chap. 9.

Seventh week: Rural Development, Agricultural Transformation, and Educational Policies
Todaro, Chaps. 10 and 11.
Wilber and Jameson, Part Four.

PART III. INTERNATIONAL DEVELOPMENTAL PROBLEMS AND POLICIES—TRADE THEORY AND PRACTICE

Eighth week: Trade Theory, Development, and the Liberal International Economic Order
Blake and Walters Chaps. 1 and 2.
Todaro, Chap. 12.
Weisband, Part Three, Chap. 7, Readings # 28, 29, 30, 31.

Ninth week: Trade Policy Debates—Export Promotion versus Import Substitution
World Development Report, Chap. 5.
Todaro, Chap. 14, pp. 427–435, 438–440, 443–445, 447–465.

Tenth week: The International Monetary and Financial System and Development
World Development Report, Chap. 6.
Blake and Walters, Chaps. 3 and 5.
Todaro, Chaps. 13 and 17.
Weisband, Part Three, Chap. 7, Reading # 31.
Wilber and Jameson, Part Three.

Eleventh week: The Transnational Organization of Production and Development
Blake and Walters, Chap. 4.
Todaro, Chap. 15.
Weisband, Part Two, Chap. 5, Readings #21, 22, 23, 24.
Wilber and Jameson, Part Five.

Twelfth week: Policy Debates in Development
World Development Report, Chap. 7.
Blake and Walters, Chaps. 5, 6, and 7.
Wilber and Jameson, Part Six.

PART IV. DEVELOPMENT THEORY AND DEBATE—CAPITALISM AND UNEVEN GROWTH

Thirteenth week: Critical and Neoimperialist Theories of Domestic and International Development

Todaro, Chap. 3, pp. 63–64, 68–69, 72–99; Appendix 3.1, Chap. 4.
Weisband, Part One, Chap. 3, Readings #12, 13, 14, 15; Part Two, Chap. 4,
   Introduction and Readings #17, 18, 19, 20.
Wilber and Jameson, Part Two.
   Fourteenth week: Development and Social Justice
World Development Report, Chap. 8.
Todaro, Chap. 18.
Weisband, Chap. Six, Readings #25, 26, 27; Conclusion, Readings #28, 29,
   30, 31, 32.
Blake and Walters, Chaps. 8 and 9.
Wilber and Jameson, Part Seven.

The Policy Position Paper: The Summation

All students are required to submit by the last of day of classes a policy position paper. A policy position paper analyzes a concrete policy
issue in a systematic way, that is, in a way designed to integrate theoretical analysis with policy choice and advocacy. A policy position
paper may assume the format outlined below:

1. Statement of the problem or policy issue within the context of the economy or society of any specific country or
   subset of countries;
2. An examination of the historical origins of the problem;
3. An assessment of the significance of the problem for the
   development of the particular society;
4. An analysis of the domestic political, economic and social
   constraints upon policymaking;
5. An analysis of the international political, economic and
   social constraints upon policymaking;
6. An exploration of the relevant theoretical explanations
   pertaining to the nature of the problem;
7. A survey of the relevant intergovernmental organizations
   relating to the problem and a review of their role in this
   regard;
8. A delineation of policy choices and their consequences;
9. Policy recommendations and their justification;
10. Conclusions.

The last portion of this syllabus (see below, Policy Issues in Development) lists possible topics relevant to your policy position paper. This
list is based on topics mentioned in a variety of sources including the
books required in this course, especially the Todaro text. But no such
list, however lengthy, is exhaustive, and students should feel free to

select their own policy issue or problem according to their intellectual or ethical interests and professional aims.

The Final Debate

Students are provided an opportunity to review all materials presented in the course prior to the final examination by means of the final debate and review.

Two students from each discussion section are selected, one by the students in the section, one by the Graduate Teaching Assistant presiding over the section, to participate in the final review and debate. The debate and review is conducted the week before finals. During the course of the debate, the instructional staff will pose a set of no less than seven questions to the teams selected. Each set of questions will focus on one of the concrete clusters of policy problems or issues listed below. At least one of these questions, concentrating upon policy analysis, will appear on the final examination.

The team which, in the judgment of the staff, responds most effectively to these questions during the debate and review, will receive a half letter grade elevation in their final grade.

The educational objectives of the debate encourage students to examine policy-related problems and issues, especially those confronting poor and lesser developing countries. Therefore, questions posed on the final examination as well as during the final debate and review, revolve around policy related matters. Students are requested to think, not only in general theoretical terms about world economy and development, but also in concrete policy-oriented ways.

Policy Issues in Development

I. DOMESTIC POLICY ISSUES IN DEVELOPMENT

1. Population in Development

    a. Population Growth, Social Welfare, Rural and Urban Poverty;
    b. Population Growth, Education, and Literacy;
    c. Population Growth and Food Supply;
    d. Population Growth and Health Delivery;
    e. Population Growth, Income Distribution, and Gross National Production: Hypothesized Linkages;
    f. Population Growth and World Resources Depletion;
    g. Population "Hawks" versus Family Planning;
    h. Family Planning and Human Rights;
    i. Development With Population Programs.

2. Rural Development and Agricultural Transformation in Development

    a. From Peasant Subsistence to Specialized Commercial Farming;
    b. Technological Change and Innovation;
    c. Land Reform and Other Policies in Rural Development;
    d. Modernizing Farm Structures to Meet Rising Food Demands;
    e. Changing Rural Environments to Improve Living Standards.

3. Water and Food Policies in Development

    a. Water and Irrigation Programs in Development;
    b. Water Policy Issues and Conflicts;
    c. Water and Women;
    d. Water and Children;
    e. Water and Work;
    f. Famine, Hunger, and Malnutrition;
    g. Policy Debates Regarding Availability of Food;
    h. Food Production and the Role of Agribusiness;
    i. Consumption and Distribution of Food.

4. Public Health and Health Care Delivery in Development

    a. Economic Development and Health;
    b. Curative Health Programs in Development: Financially Viable or Not;
    c. Curative Care Delivery in Rural and Urban Development: Women and Children;
    d. Disease Vectors: Smallpox, Malaria, Diarrhea;
    e. Infant Mortality and Mortality Rates in LDC's;
    f. Health Organizations and Networks: WHO, Doctors Without Borders, Save the Children Fund.

5. Education and Human Resources in Development

    a. Public Educational Expenditure and Enrollments;
    b. Educational Opportunities and Educational Demands;
    c. Education and Economic Growth;
    d. Education and Social Equality;
    e. Education, Internal Migration, and Population Growth;
    f. Education and International Migration;
    g. Education and Rural Growth;
    h. Educational Policies: Internal and External.

6. Environmental Problems in Development

    a. Resources and Development; The Experiences of LDCs;
    b. World Supply and Demand for Material Resources;
    c. Energy and Development;
    d. Environmental Considerations and Industrial Pollution;
    e. Extensive Agriculture and Decertification;
    f. Environmental Degradation and the Food Supply;
    g. Development and Natural Ecosystems;
    h. Environmental Degradation of Marginal Lands: The Sahel and the Demise of Nomadism.

7. Development and Military Expenditures

    a. The Impacts of Military Expenditure upon Income Distribution, National Economic Growth, and Standards of Living;
    b. Arms Production, Sales, and Trade in Third World Countries.

8. Strategies for Development

    a. The Nature of Development Planning;
    b. National Development Planning: Pro and Con;
    c. Crisis in Planning;
    d. Developmental Strategies and Planning:
        i. Neoclassical Growth Models;
        ii. Revolutionary;
        iii. Redistribution with Growth;
        iv. Basic Needs;
        v. Self-Reliance and Popular Participation;
        vi. Integrated Rural Development in a Social Market Economy.

II. TRADE ISSUES IN DEVELOPMENT

1. Trade Theory and Policy in Development

    a. Trade and Development: The Example of NICs;
    b. Trade and Income Distribution;
    c. Trade and National Economic Growth;
    d. Terms of Trade in North-South Exchange;
    e. Fixed Resources, Employment, and the International Immobility of Capital and Skilled Labor;

f. Factor Endowments and Comparative Advantage: The Problem of Specialization;
g. Trade, Underemployment, and Resource Underutilization: Vent-for-Surplus;
h. International Factor Mobility and Transnational Business Enterprises;
i. Internal Factor Mobility and Leveraged Markets.

2. The Trade Policy Debate: Export Promotion versus Import Substitution
   a. Agricultural and Manufactured Exports and Imports;
   b. Tariffs, Infant Industries, and the Theory of Protection;
   c. Foreign Exchange Rates, Exchange Controls, and Devaluation of Currency;
   d. Terms of Trade, South-South Exchange, and Regional Development;
   e. Trade Policies: Tariff and Nontariff Barriers;
   f. Trade and Economic Nationalism: Neomercantilism and the Intervention of the State;
   g. Strategic Competition and the Impact on Development.

3. The Trade Regime of the Liberal International Economic Order and Development

   a. The GATT, Multilateral Trade Negotiations, and Lesser Developing Countries;
   b. The Principles of Most Favored Nation, Non-Discrimination and Reciprocity in Trade Relations;
   c. The Kennedy, Tokyo, Uruguay Rounds: Success and Failure;
   d. Special Schemes of Preference and Development: The Lome Convention, STABEX, Others;
   e. The Group of 77, UNCTAD, and the NIEO.

III. CAPITALISM, PRODUCTION, AND THE TRANS-
NATIONAL BUSINESS ENTERPRISE IN DEVELOPMENT

1. Industrial and Postindustrial Capitalism and the Problems of Uneven Growth

   a. Modes of Production Analysis;
   b. Research and Development and Production in Modern Technology;

    c. Technology Transfer and the Knowledge Structure of the World Economy;

    d. The Organization of Global Production under Conditions of Advanced Capitalism;

    e. Product Cycle Theory and High Tech;

    f. Technological Imperatives and Global Restructuring;

    g. Postindustrial Capitalism, Outsourcing, and Models of Development.

2. Transnational Business Enterprise and Development

    a. Transnational Business Enterprise and Direct Foreign Investment in Development;

    b. Transnational Business Enterprise in Host Developing Countries: Policy Issues and Debates;

    c. Private Foreign Investment: Debates on Developmental Policy for and against Private Foreign Investment;

    d. Key Policy Issues:

        i. International Capital Movements;

        ii. Displacement of Indigenous Production;

        iii. Extent of Technology Transfer;

        iv. Appropriateness of Technology Transfer;

        v. Patterns of Consumption;

        vi. Social Structure and Stratification;

        vii. Income Distribution and Dualistic Development.

3. Work, Labor, and Unemployment: The Emergent Crisis

    a. Labor Underutilization;

    b. Growth and Employment Levels;

    c. Appropriate Technology and Employment;

    d. Industrialization, Labor Policies, and Development;

    e. Labor Policies in Dependent Development.

IV. THE MOVEMENT OF PEOPLES IN DEVELOPMENT: INTERNAL AND EXTERNAL DYNAMICS OF MIGRATION

1. Urbanization and Rural-Urban Migration

    a. Migration and Development;

    b. The Todaro Model and the Meier Model: Urban Pull and Rural Push;

    c. Migration Policies and Linkages to Other Policy Areas;

d. The Need to Reduce Imbalances in Urban-Rural Employment Opportunities;

e. Urban Job Creation and the Problem of Urban Unemployment;

f. Education and Urban Unemployment;

g. Wage Subsidies and Artificially Induced Unemployment;

h. Employment and Rural Development;

i. The International Labor Organization, the International Labor Convention, and International Standards Applicable to Transient Labor.

2. International Migration and Development

a. The International Mobility of Labor;

b. The Unwanted Concept of "Economic Refugee";

c. The Underclass of Migrant Workers and Global Cities;

d. The Domestic Social Consequences of Migration;

e. International Labor Policy Development and International Migration.

V. INCOME DISTRIBUTION, FISCAL, AND MONETARY POLICY ISSUES IN DEVELOPMENT

1. Income Distribution and the International Poverty Line

a. Income Distribution and Relative Poverty;

b. Measuring Income Distribution, Lorenz Curves, Gini Coefficients, and the Kuznets Hypothesis;

c. Variations in Equality of Income Distribution and Patterns of National Economic Growth;

d. Policy Perspectives on Income Distribution and Development.

2. Income Distribution and Domestic Fiscal Policies

a. Altering the Functional Distribution of Income through Policies Designed to Change Relative Price Factors;

b. Modifying the Size Distribution through Progressive Redistribution of Asset Ownership;

c. Reducing the Size Distribution at the Upper Levels through Progressive Income and Wealth Taxes;

d. Increasing the Size Distribution at the Lower Levels through Direct Transfer Payments and the Public Provision of Goods and Services;

   e. Redistribution of Per Capita Income versus Growth in Gross
      National Income and Product;
   f. The Killick-Todaro List of Fiscal Policies and the Savings
      Gap.

3. Monetary and Fiscal Policy, International Finance, and the Debt
   Crisis

   a. The International Financial System and International
      Reserves;
   b. Structural Problems and Balance of Payments Adjustments;
   c. International Indebtedness and Problems of Development;
   d. IMF Stabilization Policies or Conditionality: Pro and Con;
   e. Regional Developmental Banking Institutions and their
      Policies.

4. Foreign Economic Assistance and Development

   a. A Profile of Bilateral Foreign Economic Assistance:
      i.   American Style;
      ii. Japanese Style;
      iii. Dutch Style.
   b. Multilateral Aid Programs: The Role and Policies of the
      World Bank and Related Institutions;
   c. The Role and Policies of the United Nations Developmental
      Program (UNDP);
   d. The Domestic Impacts of Foreign Economic Assistance in
      LDCs;
   e. Policy Arguments for and against Foreign Economic Assis-
      tance.

VI. THE POLITICS OF ECONOMIC DEVELOPMENT: HUMAN RIGHTS, SOCIAL JUSTICE, AND CRITICAL PERSPECTIVES

1. Political Development and Economic Development

   a. Authoritarian versus Democratic Regimes and Development;
   b. Human Rights, Political Regimes, and Development.

2. Social Justice and Development

   a. Equality and the Quest for Standards of Distributive Justice;
   b. Inequality and the Quest for Standards of Distributive Justice.

3. Critical Theories of Development and the Dual Economy

   a. The Colonial Dual Economy;

   b. The Creation and Entrenchment of Political and Economic Elites;

   c. External Economic Dependence;

   d. The Modern Export Enclave Economy;

   e. International Equality and Dependence;

   f. From Dependence to Dependency;

   g. The Latin-American Dependency School;

   h. Dependent Development and Underdevelopment;

   i. Marxist and Neo-Marxist Theories of Imperialism and Neoimperialism: Prebisch, Lewis, Frank, Sunkel, Amin;

   j. Critical Views of Capitalist Development in Asia and Africa.

NOTES

1. Recently, I developed the notion of "constructivism" as a pedagogical approach in teaching issues in development. This emphasizes how individuals, in particular how women and peasant farmers, "construct" the social circumstances of their lives when caught in the dynamics of social change and development; see "Justice and the Challenges of Constructivist Pedagogy: Normative Perspectives in Teaching Political Economy," in Lev Gonick and Edward Weisband, eds., *Teaching World Politics: Contending Pedagogies for a New World Order*, Boulder: Westview Press, 1992.

PART 3

Annotated Bibliography

INTRODUCTION

Welcome to the Annotated Bibliography.

We invite you to think of this section as a large and friendly book-store, a teachers' bookstore, packed with books selected for classroom use and syllabus design. What follows is a brief floor plan to make your shopping more productive and more enjoyable.

What's Here and What's Not

Confronted with the vast and varied literature of development, and the format of *Teaching Global Development*, we realized that this bibliography must be select rather than comprehensive. And like all selections, ours has its idiosyncrasies.

First, in recognition that development is a rapidly growing, rapidly changing field, the bibliography emphasizes recent scholarship. Titles published before 1983 have been systematically excluded, and books from the past five years—since 1988—were strongly preferred. Our presumption is that works of enduring value published more than ten years ago are well enough known that they need no rehearsing here, while most of the monographic literature of that age is no longer appropriate for classroom use. Recognize, however, that a number of pedagogically effective classics will not figure in these pages.

Second, we preferred classroom veterans over untried texts. In com-piling the annotated syllabus section and working with faculty in a variety of contexts, we have gathered hundreds of syllabi, and it is from them that we drew most of the titles reviewed below. It is true that a substantial number of books, especially those appearing very recently, are recommended without classroom experience. But in the main, this is a collection of taught texts.

Third, we confess that this is an opinionated bibliography: we tended to include books we liked. Negative reviews do appear, largely to warn faculty from texts with inviting titles or misleading pitch. Most of the volumes, however, are recommended for use in one or another classroom context. Laboring under tight limitations of space, we have opted for what is helpful rather than for what is not.

Fourth, the bibliography is restricted to *books*: you will not find journals, films, videos, on-line educational products or other nonprint resources reviewed here. These important lacunae are similarly due to limitations of space, and, as a corrective, we direct you to the following alternative bibliographies for nontraditional sources:

Bob Keesey's contribution to the present volume, "Why the Humanities Should Be Incorporated in Development Education," is a treasure trove of music, film, and nonfiction useful in undergraduate teaching. Keesey provides annotations and teaching pointers in his discussion.

Patricia Kutzner's *World Hunger*[1] contains an up-to-date, annotated listing of periodicals, audiovisual resources and computerized references which should prove a useful adjunct to the present bibliography. Kutzner also includes a section on "landmark monographs" which surveys many pre-1983 classic texts omitted here.

And be sure to consult the institutional periodical literature of the field, where you will find much of the most recent research on development. While scholarly journals are sometimes too advanced, too narrow, or too technical for undergraduate use, annual reports and occasional papers issued by organizations such as the United Nations Development Program, the World Bank, Bread for the World and Worldwatch Institute are frequently outstanding and merit the attention of undergraduate educators.

"The Instructor's Electronic Tool Kit: Personal Computers and Audio Visual Aids for Development Education" was prepared for this book by Rich Ryan, director of the Center for Food and Hunger Education at the Imperial Valley Campus of San Diego State University. Ryan's brisk survey of nontraditional teaching resources was not included, again due to constraints of space, but will appear in the journal, *Development TeachNet*, in late 1993. Readers are invited to contact the IHA Office on Education for ordering information.[2]

How The Bibliography Works

This bibliography is organized into eight "window themes" or conceptual rubrics: Development and Theory; Economics; Environment; Food and Hunger; Gender; Democracy and Grassroots Power; Interdependence; and Refugeeism. Dividing the literature of development studies, with its disciplinary sweep and thematic breadth, is a tortuous endeavor: many alternative formulations are of course possible.

Selected on the basis of timeliness, relevance and classroom utility, the themes all represent windows into broader issues in development.

Conceptually, the categories are self-explanatory, with the possible exception of "Development and Theory." Here we have collected titles about ethics and development, development theory, the problem of development per se, as opposed to its constituent parts, and many books focused on politics in the Third World or the political dimension of development. Classifying the books proved a vexing and imprecise science: the problematics of development cut across disciplines and are often multifocused. We have assigned each title by its central theme, but many listed in one area could as easily have been placed in another. Remember to consider all rubrics relevant to your classroom topic.

The reviews themselves follow a two-paragraph formula: in the first paragraph, we sketch the structure, main themes and interpretive core of the book under review; in the second, we evaluate classroom utility, level of difficulty and likely student response. The annotations are thus designed to save the instructor time and expand her perspective of the literature by identifying texts appropriate for a variety of pedagogical purposes.

We hope you find the development educators' bookstore helpful. Come often, and browse as long as you like.

NOTES

1. Patricia Kutzner, *World Hunger: A Reference Handbook*, Santa Barbara and Oxford: ABC-Clio, 1991. The book also contains a useful section on "Facts and Data" about hunger and development.

2. Contact *Development TeachNet*, Interfaith Hunger Appeal Office on Education, 475 Riverside Drive, Suite 1630, New York, NY 10115; telephone (212) 870–2035.

Development and Theory

Andrain, Charles F. *Political Change in the Third World* (Boston: Unwin Hyman, 1988). 296 pp.

In this work of comparative political science, Andrain creates theoretical models to illustrate how "sociopolitical structures, beliefs, and public policies cause Third World political change." The flow of political decision making, he argues, is defined by fixed systems, or what Weberian social scientists call "ideal types." Andrain, however, proceeds to add empirical flesh with discussions of Vietnam, Cuba, Chile, Nigeria and Iran. These nations, in Andrain's analysis, represent sharply contrasting paradigms. Their governments are differentiated by political beliefs, the power of social groups, the power of political organizations, and ways of processing basic policy issues. Andrain demonstrates that excessive bureaucracy threatens the vitality of these Third World nations. A centralized and hierarchical system undermines a community's capacity to tolerate pluralism and to mobilize citizens at crucial junctures. Andrain thus reminds us that economic development requires a firm groundwork of equality and decentralization. To flourish, he concludes, a nation must be able to win over the hearts and minds of its citizens to development projects.

Highly conceptualized, and weighted down with occasionally obfuscating jargon, Andrain's book will frustrate professors seeking a pragmatic approach to Third World social and economic issues. Andrain focuses on issues raised by comparative political science, and this work will best serve senior-level seminars on the nations and regions he covers. Development issues are only implicitly discussed and are subordinate to politics and government. Despite its attractive title, therefore, this volume seems destined exclusively for advanced courses in political science.

Apter, David. *Rethinking Development: Modernization, Dependency and Postmodern Politics* (Newbury Park, CA: Sage Publications, 1987). 236 pp.

"[T]he underlying theme of this book is that 'systematically' development will generate democracy, but it will not do it easily, and there are snares along the way...." Such is the author's assessment of the changing shape of the political world, and with it the development process. Part 1 describes the relationship between development and the state. Part 2 asserts the inherent conflict between development and statist politics. Apter's concern is to avoid violence and foster development, both in the less-developed nations and in the industrialized economies of the world. In critiquing current political development, he constructs new theories which place needs before ideology.

This is a tough-minded and provocative political science text, and students will benefit most if they also bring some political science expertise to their reading. And as *Rethinking Development* has such a broad perspective, instructors will want to supplement this text with monographic material on particular regions or nations.

Attwood, Donald, Thomas Bruneau, John Galaty, eds. *Power and Poverty: Development and Development Projects in the Third World* (Boulder: Westview Press, 1988). 186 pp.

This collection of eight diverse case studies examines the evolving relationship between state and society as forged by development projects. The book's organizing principle is concerned with the question of "whether efforts to achieve economic growth can be made compatible with social justice." The authors contend that development in and of itself does not improve the lives of people. While focusing on different regions, the author are linked by a commitment to comprehend the development process as inherently political; they seek to establish that the struggle against poverty entails empowerment before technological advancement. Their approach calls attention to the interests of players who compete over projects. In the context of irrigation projects, seed programs and credit policies is revealed a similar pattern of movement from victimization to politicization by peoples as diverse as forest dwellers in the Amazon and nomads in Eastern Africa. Bureaucratic controversies, cultural disruptions, ethnic rivalries and other obstacles are exposed as essentially political conflicts involving the advancement of some at the cost of others. The interdisciplinary dedication of the editors assures the inclusion of the voices of anthropologists, sociologists, as well as economists and political scientists.

The critical focus of these essays should be welcome in all courses on development. Its coherent argument spans a variety of programs and regions; the uncluttered and substantive writing renders each essay a perfect two-day assignment for juniors and seniors to complement more narrative studies. These essays can contribute as well to courses focused on regional development: The Indian subcontinent and Africa are particularly well represented here. In such courses, the student will be well prepared to understand the broader significance of each case study.

Ayres, Robert L. *Banking on the Poor: The World Bank and World Poverty* (Cambridge: MIT Press, 1983). 282 pp.

The theme of this book, according to the author, is "Robert S. McNamara's efforts to reorient the World Bank toward a more explicit concern with poverty alleviation in the world's poorest countries." It briefly outlines the historical evolution of the Bank, and then focuses on the transformations effected under McNamara's presidency. Ayres discusses the Bank's institutional structure and activities and the external constraints placed upon its operations before turning to a close examination of the Bank's poverty-oriented approach to rural as well as urban development. The book also addresses the many criticisms leveled against the Bank from both the right and the left, adopting instead a centrist view, from which the Bank is seen as "an agent of reform."

In addition to published sources, this book is based on confidential documents made available to the author, as well as on approximately 300 interviews conducted with staff and officials of the World Bank. It may be the most comprehensive examination of the operations of the World Bank in recent years and is essential reading for students of international development, whether they agree or not with the author's conclusions as to the ultimately positive role of the Bank.

Ball, Nicole. *Security and Economy in the Third World* (Princeton, NJ: Princeton University Press, 1988). 432 pp.

"Does expenditure in the security sector of Third World countries hinder their development, or does it, as some analysts have suggested, promote the development process?" While Ball appears to believe the former is true, her thorough study of the theoretical and practical evidence seriously entertains the latter possibility as well. The first part of the book describes the most recent theoretical, empirical and methodological frameworks into which the evidence can be cast. Part 2 relates a number of facets of the debate in terms of specific cases in various developing countries. Questions of resource diversion, debt, human capital and the development role of security spending are all dealt with in exhaustive detail.

The sheer heft of Ball's impressive study will be daunting to most beginning students, as will the author's recourse to the jargon of political economy. (Ruth Leger Sivard's partisan, but fascinating and concise, *World Military and Social Expenditures* annual will better serve first- and second-year students.) Advanced curricula can easily include the second, empirical section of the book, however, and those seniors planning on careers or graduate work in the development field are urged to peruse part 1 as well. The subject matter may initially appear somewhat narrow in scope, but in today's multilateral world, its importance must not be underestimated.

Black, Jan Knippers. *Development in Theory and Practice: Bridging the Gap* (Boulder: Westview Press, 1991). 224 pp.

In this highly critical account of the theories and practices that fall under the rubric "development," Black evaluates both abstract explanatory models and various practical strategies. She discusses the foreign assistance policy of the United States and other donor countries and institutions, paying particularly close attention to whose interests were best served by the programs. She considers as well the development strategies of Third World nations and organizations themselves, including import-substitution, export-led growth, commodity cartels, and revolutionary strategies. The book also explores various issues of acute, contemporary urgency: the gender bias in development, prospects for the ecology, refugees, and the debt situation of developing countries. The text concludes with descriptions— from the perspective of an agent in the field—of what goes wrong in the implementation of assistance programs and why they often fail the people they are intended to benefit.

This book will prove an informative and thought-provoking resource in introductory courses on development issues. Black makes her own views clear, yet her analysis remains sharp and her treatment of the subject rigorous.

Cernea, Michael, ed. *Putting People First: Sociological Variables in Rural Development*, 2nd ed. (New York: Oxford University Press, 1991). 575 pp.

This lucid volume has been broadly adopted as a central text in courses of the sociology of development and other upper-division courses concerned with the *practice* of development. First published in 1985 by the World Bank, then revised and expanded in 1991, *Putting People First* articulates a burgeoning, if perhaps still minority view within the Bank: that "people are—and should be—the starting point, the center, and the end goal of each development intervention." As such, the book represents a perspective somewhat at variance with the conventional image of the Bank.

The contributors draw on World Bank cases to inform their discussion; therefore, the book is of real value in courses examining the details of development. The chapters ("Technical and Social Change in Currently Irrigated Regions"; "Social Analysis in Rural Roads Projects") are occasionally technical and are not for beginners. But this is no mere collection of case studies. The explicit argument that social organization is at the heart of the development enterprise makes *Putting People First* an effective, experientially-grounded reader for teachers who wish to focus on a participatory or grassroots vision of development.

Clapham, Christoper. *Third World Politics: An Introduction* (Madison: University of Wisconsin Press, 1985). 197 pp.

Clapham's book is a clear, succinct introduction to the nature of politics in the Third World and the basic analytical paradigms employed by scholars to assess them. He discusses the position of Southern countries in the international arena, the demise of the colonial state and the birth of independent nations, the management of the state and the economy, the role of the military, and the nature of revolutionary regimes.

This book is ideal for students with no prior knowledge of the subject. The annotated bibliography, divided by topic, offers suggestions for further reading, making it a useful source for first-year students preparing research papers.

Commins, Stephen K., ed. *Africa's Development Challenges and the World Bank* (Boulder and London: Lynne Rienner Publishers, 1988). 243 pp.

The contributions to this volume are divided into three parts. The first addresses the operations of the World Bank as they relate to sub-Saharan Africa. A presentation of the World Bank's perspective on development in the region is followed by assessments of the Bank's approach from the viewpoint of two African nations, Tanzania and Zambia. The second part of the book is devoted to analyses of the difficulties faced by donor nations in general as they seek ways to support policy reforms, and examines the politics of decision making within the African states themselves. Part 3 addresses broader issues of the political economy, from the relationship between bureaucratic growth and economic stagnation to the long-term impact of the structural adjustment strategy advocated by the World Bank and the IMF.

The essays in this book not only provide a critique of World Bank policy but also discuss the difficulties of other development approaches, considering the political and economic conditions within the African nations themselves. Students in their second or third year of study who wish to begin focusing on the relationship between African states and international donor institutions will find the essays in this volume, along with the bibliographies, a helpful resource.

Coombs, H. C. *The Return of Scarcity: Strategies for an Economic Future* (Cambridge: Cambridge University Press, 1990). 171 pp.

An eclectic gathering of essays and addresses by the former governor of the Australian Reserve Bank, *The Return of Scarcity* offers practical advice from an insider. According to the author, the two great opposing forces in the current development debate are quality of life and production growth. Quality of life, to Coombs, is the most important issue. The selections cover science and technology, population growth, resource management and the world economic order.

Informed by classical economics and development theory, Coombs's work presents a picture of the development debate in terms easily understandable to the American undergraduate. Readers can benefit from both his hindsight as a former bureaucrat and his insight as a devotee of development studies. The issues presented are salient and easy to understand, limited only by space and the author's particular point of view. Instructors should focus on those selections directly pertinent to their particular course, as there is some repetition of ideas and information among articles.

Ensign, Margee M. *Doing Good or Doing Well? Japan's Foreign Aid Program* (New York: Columbia University Press, 1992). 198 pp.

Basing her work on column upon column of statistics, Ensign's controversial book tackles four main questions: "What drives Japanese foreign assistance? Is this an example of mercantilist strategy to develop and control markets and/or a reflection of Japan's desire for international acceptance and prestige, through 'burden-sharing'? What is the impact of Japanese ODA on the less-developed countries that are the recipients of Japanese economic assistance? What does Japan's new status as a leader in foreign aid mean for the United States and for the world economy?" Her conclusions refute Japan's claims that its foreign aid program is no longer merely a tool of its commercial interests.

Although this book may be too dry for introductory students, instructors should familiarize themselves with its conclusions, which counter the popular conception that Japan's foreign aid loans are in the process of being untied from their exports. Solidly argued, the book has caused a stir in Washington as well as Tokyo.

Estes, Richard J., ed. *Internationalizing Social Work Education: A Guide to Resources for a New Century* (Philadelphia: University of Pennsylvania Press, 1992). 286 pp.

"The publication of this volume reflects a fundamental change that is occurring in American social work education, i.e., the shift toward a more international view of the profession and its potential leadership role in promoting international social development." Essentially a guide to the resources in the field of international social work education, this book includes brief essays concerning a wide array of subjects, from human rights to AIDS to working with selected population groups. Each essay is followed by a basic bibliography for the subject.

Students and instructors involved in international development at the grassroots level will find this book indispensible. For those students who are thinking of pursuing a career in internationally focused social work, this book includes a chapter on planning a career in that field.

Faaland, J., and J. R. Parkinson. *The Political Economy of Development* (London: Francis Printer, 1986). 265 pp.

This scholarly work approaches development economics as history, theory and empirical application. It focuses on the process of development, using Bangladesh and Mozambique as case studies of two distinct paths to economic growth. The authors' principal contribution is their rigorous analysis of the nuts and bolts of policy formulation: Projects to increase agricultural and industrial output, for example, are examined through appropriate statistical evidence, economic models, political objectives and longterm goals. The case studies conclude with an evaluation of current innovative practices. The complex of issues that economic reformers face in Bangladesh and Mozambique is treated in its full particularity—here, development economics is assigned its rightful place among social and political concerns. The authors challenge the traditional bipolar socialist vs. market-driven solutions to development. In sum, this study covers the full range of issues implied by its broad title.

The authors themselves recommend this book for the British equivalent of juniors and seniors. Its statistical underpinning and complex arguments might be forbidding for younger students. But professors of development economics and the recent history of the Indian subcontinent and Africa will find this a helpful text for upper-level courses. It is a model study in the development field for its interdisciplinary focus; its nonideological and substantive core make it most worthwhile for undergraduates to study in great depth. It would thus be best utilized in seminars for intensive readings.

Fry, Gerald W., and Galen R. Martin. *The International Development Dictionary* (Santa Barbara, CA: ABC-Clio, 1991). 445 pp.

Designed as "a basic reference work," the *Dictionary* draws on economics, political science, sociology, demography, history, geography, psychology and anthropology, reflecting not only a wide disciplinary scope but also "a wide range of ideological perspectives." The authors divide their book into four parts: development thinkers, leaders and practitioners; basic concepts; analytical concepts; and movements, projects and organizations. Each entry consists of a descriptive paragraph and a brief assessment of the entry's "significance." All of the entries are cross-referenced.

With only 457 entries, the dictionary is far from comprehensive but will more than suffice in an undergraduate environment. It will be a book that students can and will refer to for their entire course of development studies from undergraduate work up to the graduate level. The writing is concise and evenhanded, and all the material is presented to the reader as if he or she has no prior knowledge of any aspect of development.

Hancock, Graham. *The Lords of Poverty: The Freewheeling Lifestyles, Power, Prestige and Corruption of the Multi-Billion Dollar Aid Business* (London: Macmillan, 1989). 234 pp.

In the words of the author, "This book is an attack on a group of rich and powerful bureaucracies that have hijacked our kindness ... those that administer the West's aid and then deliver it to the poor of the Third World in a process that Bob Geldof described as 'a perversion of the act of human generosity.'" This indictment of bureaucracies limits itself to official agencies, for the most part, although it also takes passing shots at a few NGOs that, in general, "rarely do significant harm; sometimes they do great good." The targets hit head-on are USAID, the World Bank and Britain's Overseas Development Administration. In addition to picking apart the bureaucrats, Hancock also sets out to "question aid as such."

This ambitious and iconoclastic book deserves space on undergraduate syllabi. It best serves those courses devoted to the ethics and practice of development. Writing for a wide audience, Hancock is quite passionate and often witty in his indictment, but he never forgets to marshal salient, occasionally surprising, facts to support his arguments. Provocative and important, *Lords of Poverty* will work well in seminars where students can respond to Hancock's charged argument.

Harrison, Paul. *Inside the Third World: The Anatomy of Poverty* (New York: Penguin, 1981; reprinted 1987, with a revised overview). 514 pp.

Harrison sets out to write "a non-academic general survey of the entire field of development problems," and, despite the potential pitfalls of such an approach, he succeeds admirably. After identifying the roots of underdevelopment in climate, colonialism and "the fascination of Third World leaders . . . with western models of development," Harrison examines the situation today as well as the future prospects for the poor in Africa, Asia and Latin America. Major issues addressed include the problem of agriculture and land distribution, urbanization and industry, hunger, overpopulation, undereducation, the global economic system and the domestic politics of Third World nations.

Harrison's book is ideal for first-year students struggling to build a framework on which to hang future studies in development. Instructors may choose to use *Inside the Third World* as a basic introductory text, using other sources to deepen students' understanding of the complexity of the many subjects treated by Harrison.

Hettne, Bjorn. *Development Theory and the Three Worlds* (New York: Longman, 1990). 296 pp.

"There can be no fixed and final definition of development, only suggestions of what development should imply in different contexts." That said, Hettne embarks on an "intellectual history" of development thinking, tracing it from postwar attitudes in the industrial West through dependency theory to changes in formulation based on Third World scholarship and globalization.

Hettne tries to be both factually exhaustive and reflective, all within the limited space of 300 pages. This leads him to gloss over certain aspects of development theory that he assumes his readers already know. So, while his conciseness may appeal to first-year students of development, Hettne's work ought to find its place only on those introductory syllabi containing other, more issue-specific texts. More advanced students will find *Development Theory and the Three Worlds* a useful distillation of history and theory and an excellent springboard for further theory building.

Isbister, John. *Promises Not Kept: The Betrayal of Social Change in the Third World* (West Hartford, CT: Kumarian Press, 1991). 240 pp.

John Isbister's *Promises Not Kept* is an ambitious attempt to fill a significant lacuna in the literature available to teachers of undergraduate courses on Third World development. It is intended as a basic text on development for undergraduate general education courses, interdisciplinary team-taught courses and also for supplementary use in disciplinary courses in political science, economics or sociology. The first chapter includes an effective and balanced appraisal of the varieties of poverty and the ways it is measured, mixing vignettes and primary readings with drier statistical material. Another chapter, "Explanations of Underdevelopment" introduces the major interpretive schools of Third World studies: modernization, dependency and Marxist. This summary requires some reduction, and Isbister handles it with commendable subtlety.

On political questions, such as Isbister's chapter on the United States' proximate responsibility for much of the world's poverty, a necessary frankness often sinks into polemic, and some of the solutions he suggests—such as worldwide debt amnesty—fail to take into account the complexity of the problem at hand. Nevertheless, Isbister's accessible account delivers the basic blocks for building undergraduate understanding of Third World development. *Promises Not Kept* should make a meaningful addition to many lower-division development syllabi; with such an introductory text in hand, faculty can more confidently assign impressionistic readings and explore selected topics more deeply in lectures and discussions.

Jaffee, David. *Levels of Socio-Economic Development Theory* (New York: Praeger, 1990). 218 pp.

A rather advanced textbook on development theories, *Levels* addresses various schools of thought, not one by one, but rather on the basis of the levels of society they address, from individual to organizational, societal to global. Each level is scrutinized and critiqued as to its strengths and weaknesses by a social scientist who seeks to penetrate the trappings of sociological and scientific jargon in order to assess the actual utility of each level of discourse. Individualism receives the most intense criticism, while organizational theories are, to Jaffee, of the most utility. Global theories, new as they are, offer the most room for improvement and modification.

Jaffee's philosophical rigor and reflective approach to his subjects balances nicely with a careful, interdisciplinary study of theory, leaving few stones unturned. The sheer variety of ideas and evidence compensate for a painstaking and somewhat dry writing style. Advanced students of development theory will benefit from Jaffee's thoughtfulness and discipline while beginners are recommended to look elsewhere (e.g., Alvin Y. So, 1990: reviewed below).

Klare, Michael T., and Daniel C. Thomas, eds. *World Security: Trends and Challenges at Century's End* (New York: St. Martin's Press, 1991). 427 pp.

Though not concerned per se with the Third World, this collection contains several contributions directly bearing on development. Relevant essays include Joseph Collins's "World Hunger: A Scarcity of Food or a Scarcity of Democracy," Vincent Ferraro's "Global Debt and Third World Development," and Nicole Ball's "Militarized States in the Third World." Moreover, the balance of the volume, including chapters on environmental security, human rights and ethnic conflict, treats the Third World in the broader context of contemporary globalism.

Klare and Thomas have gathered a repository of brief, sophisticated and readable essays by leading scholars on the full range of "global" issues. Faculty looking to highlight interdependence or teach development education as part of a global curriculum would do well to consult *World Security*. And those teaching courses more strictly focused on development and the Third World might find a valuable reading or two here as well.

Klitgaard, Robert. *Tropical Gangsters* (New York: Basic Books, 1990). 281 pp.

Tropical Gangsters sets out to paint a picture rather than to analyze a theory; it "tries to tell a story and capture a mood" of a country in the process of economic reform. Klitgaard spent two-and-a-half years in Equatorial Guinea, where he was an administrator for a World Bank–sponsored economic reform project. In very personal and human terms, he addresses the important issues facing students of development. Important questions are raised—and lived out, such as the role of international aid; how to promote change while respecting what already exists; and who are the "tropical gangsters"? (are they corrupt government officials, or are they foreign capitalists and aid workers?). The controversial aspects of structural adjustment policies are witnessed, as are the institutional hurdles of economic reform policies.

Klitgaard can be criticized for the somewhat paternalistic attitude evidenced in his writing; he suggests that his role, and that of the World Bank, is that of a doctor administering healing medicine to the sick patient. He is also guilty of making sweeping generalizations about the entire continent based on his experiences in one country.

Education must involve critical thinking, and it is for this reason that this book, despite its undeniable flaws, merits consideration for elementary-level syllabi. It provides a refreshing break from dry, theoretical analysis, and the assumptions and attitudes inherent in the writing should stimulate lively classroom discussion.

Kusterer, Kenneth, Mike Rock and James Weaver. *Capitalism with a Human Face: Achieving Broad-Based Sustainable Development* (forthcoming, 1994).

This volume, prepared by the experienced and excellent teaching team based at American University and the Development Studies Program, could well become the standard textbook for undergraduate development education in the 1990s. Though only several of the chapters were available for review before our own book went to press, this book will span the field with sophisticated but terrifically teachable chapters on subjects such as "Freedom to Develop: Democracy, Freedom and Human Rights"; "Sustainable Development: What It Is and How to Achieve It"; and an updated treatment of paradigms of development. While the book recognizes and exposes the unfortunate results of 1980s development policy, the interpretive slant is somewhat optimistic, yielding the notion that progress along the road to sustainable development is possible, if difficult and uneven.

Perhaps most remarkable is the book's overall exposition of development economics: while it presupposes no prior knowledge of economics, the authors convey a nuanced and complex perspective in accessible prose. Designed for undergraduates by teachers of undergraduates, *Capitalism with a Human Face* will deserve consideration for your syllabus. Watch for it.

Kutzner, Patricia. *World Hunger: A Reference Handbook* (Santa Barbara, CA: ABC-Clio, 1991). 359 pp.

World Hunger provides a one-stop information source and guide to exploring the causes and consequences of global hunger and the policies intended to reduce its incidence.

Kutzner has produced a long-needed handbook which provides a useful foundation for policy choices and research. Accurate and useful bibliographies and profiles of key organizations and individuals in the fight on hunger are included. This resource deserves space in the working libraries of academics, development specialists, students, advocates and concerned members of the general public.

McCleary, Rachel M., ed. *Seeking Justice: Ethics and International Affairs* (Boulder: Westview Press, 1992). 165 pp.

In her introductory essay to this volume Rachel McCleary provides the philosophical framework within which discussions of ethics in international affairs can take place, introducing the concepts of the morality of means and ends, and of distributive justice. The essays themselves, which are followed by discussion questions designed to spur classroom debate, apply this conceptual framework to specific cases: the U.S. invasion of Panama; the 1972 Vietnamese peace negotiations; the Third United Nations Conference on the Law of the Sea; the IMF's relationship with Nigeria; GATT; and the preservation of the Amazonian rain forest.

Written specifically for undergraduate students, this book will surely be of great use in the classroom, in that it will stimulate readers and challenge them to form their own opinions concerning questions that they may not have yet thought through.

Manor, James, ed. *Rethinking Third World Politics* (London and New York: Longman, 1991). 283 pp.

Attempting to promote a new approach to the study of Third World politics, the editor and contributors to this volume stress the limitations of the two paradigms that dominate the field. The first of these, the political development paradigm, views the course of Third World politics as an evolution toward liberal Western political systems, while the second, the dependency paradigm, predicts that Third World nations are consigned to the globe's political and economic periphery. In the editor's words, both schools of thought "approached political systems in search of structural determinants which in our view were seldom present." The essays in this volume stress the need for "thick description" of the realities of politics in specific nations, and of the long-term historical background, in place of the development of parsimonious models. The essays are divided into three parts: "Conceptualizing Third World Politics," "The Theatrical and Imaginary Dimensions of Politics," and "Political Institutions and State-Society Relations."

Students well advanced in the study of political systems will find this book thought provoking. The papers concerned with the creation

and institutionalization of political symbolism and discourse are particularly interesting. Because the issues and the regions treated in this
volume are diverse, instructors will likely wish to focus on those essays
most relevant to their syllabus when making assignments to students.

Martin, Mitchell T., and Terry R. Kandall, eds. *Studies of Development and
Change in the Modern World* (New York: Oxford University Press, 1989).
458 pp.

The editors assert that "not all social change can be characterized as
development." In pursuit of what can be termed true developmental
change, they have collected a series of studies of development as a
product of history, molded by modern capitalism and structured around
cores and peripheries. These Marxist approaches to development are
especially concerned with the world system of politics and markets,
rather than regional or national questions. At the same time, the contributors take a critical look at both classical Marxism and neo-Marxism. Case studies of Latin America and the Caribbean are included to
substantiate the editors' theories.

A product of careful research with a dedication to radical, new perspectives on development, *Studies* fails only in its geographic limita-
tion. The highly theoretical nature of this collection will pose difficulty
for beginners, but second- or third-year students of political economy
ought to relish the well-reasoned arguments and heavily researched
case studies presented here.

Midgley, James, and Anthony Hall, eds. *Development Policies: Sociological Perspectives* (Manchester and New York: Manchester University Press,
1988). 154 pp.

All of the articles in this volume address the issue of sociological
involvment in development policy. Each essay discusses a specific
issue, such as the planning and implementation of foreign-aid funded
development programs, social research and development policy, women
and development, community participation, and agrarian development and state intervention, all from a sociological perspective.

This book will certainly prove useful for sociology courses focusing
on development but may also have something to offer students of
development administration as they become familiar with the methods
and possible contributions of a variety of disciplines.

Nafziger, Wayne E. *Inequality in Africa: Political Elites, Proletariat, Peasants and
the Poor* (Cambridge: Cambridge University Press, 1988). 204 pp.

Rejecting the World Bank/IMF strategy for economic growth in Africa, Nafziger employs a political economy analysis to demonstrate that only through increased democratization and distribution of resources can equality in Africa be achieved. He examines the history and causes of inequality, from the colonial legacy to the contemporary global economic system, and shows how the ruling elites have managed to co-opt labor, how they favor urban areas to the detriment of rural areas, and how they use education as a tool to insure the perpetuation of their class's control. In addition to class discrepencies, he examines regional and gender inequalities in the African economy as well.

As an introduction to the economic and political disparities within Africa this is an exemplary volume. With a minimum of jargon, it manages to convey the essential elements of the contemporary African development dilemma. Students of development and contemporary Africa will find this a very useful book.

Nash, Manning. *Unfinished Agenda: The Dynamics of Modernization in Developing Nations* (Boulder and London: Westview Press, 1984). 148 pp.

"Modernization is the growth in capacity to apply tested knowledge to all branches of production; modernity is the social, cultural, and psychological framework that facilitates the application of science to the process of production." Nash explores the historical background and the sociological implications of these two concepts from an anthropological perspective, moving from the impact of colonialism to the political decision making which determines who profits from the application of economic and social modernization policies. He addresses such central themes as the convergence and divergence of the forms that modernization takes, the function of religion and education and their effect on the move towards modernity, and the effects of modernization on the traditional social order.

This concise, highly readable book offers students a real taste of what modernization has meant for different people in different places at different times, while at the same time depicting the system of global interdependence as a whole. It is a fine book for first-semester students, as it addresses political, social and economic forces simultaneously, showing the relationships among them.

Nichols, Bruce, and Gil Loescher, eds. *The Moral Nation: Humanitarianism and U.S. Foreign Policy Today* (Notre Dame, IN: University of Notre Dame Press, 1989). 321 pp.

This book focuses on two central conflicts that define the discourse of humanitarianism and public policy: the problematic disjuncture of moral principle and political expedience; a disturbing lack of synergy between PVO relief efforts and official foreign policy objectives. The first section of the book explores the different philosophies of humanitarianism and their significance in relation to U.S. foreign policy. This is followed by a more specific historical review of the political and legal determinants of American foreign assistance and international humanitarian efforts. The second half is devoted to the examination of particular regional issues: human rights in Central America and famine relief in the Horn of Africa.

Represented in this volume are the diverse perspectives of journalism, academia, government and the NGO community. Students will find *The Moral Nation* an accessible text that clearly and compellingly presents a critical examination of the ethical, political and material dimensions of contemporary humanitarian relief.

Packenham, Robert A. *The Dependency Movement: Scholarship and Politics in Development Studies* (Cambridge, MA: Harvard University Press, 1992). 362 pp.

Born in Latin America in the late 1960s, the "dependency school" explicitly challenged the prevailing assumptions and approaches of development economics, with a profound effect on academic theory and political policy which continues to the present. Packenham studies the history of the dependency movement and the context of dependency ideas, focusing on the criticisms leveled against the system of dependent capitalism and proposed alternatives to it. He traces the influence of these ideas in both Latin America and the North, and explores the ways in which they have transformed the debate in the field of development economics. In addition, he examines the politicization of scholarship to which many of the dependency writers contributed.

As the author himself points out, this is "the first comprehensive assessment" of the dependency movement by a non-Marxist scholar. For students interested in a critical analysis of the substance of the dependency paradigm it will therefore prove very useful. It is, however, a highly specialized work, relevant only to advanced studies in the field of development theory.

Ramirez-Faria, Carlos. *The Origins of Economic Inequality between Nations* (London: Unwin Hyman, 1991). 318 pp.

This book provides a survey and taxonomy of theories which have sought to explain the phenomenon of international economic inequality. Ramirez-Faria identifies these theories as "the postwar orthodoxy of developmentalism and its denial in the contemporary laissez-faire, neo-liberal reaction; and the two main branches of marxist analysis: the dependency branch . . . and. . . [the] class struggle branch." The book traces the historical development of these models and demonstrates the interactions between them.

Excellent for providing students with a framework for approaching theories of the inequality among nations, the present volume is well suited for inclusion in first-year development courses.

Randall, Vicky, and Robin Theobold. *Political Change and Underdevelopment: A Critical Introduction to Third World Politics* (Durham, NC: Duke University Press, 1985). 219 pp.

Written for use in undergraduate courses on the politics of development, this text seeks to canvas the major theories employed to evaluate political and economic development in the Third World, and to demonstrate their transformation over time. Randall and Theobold explore the concepts of modernization, dependency theory, the politics of class within Third World nations, and the political role of the military. The book endeavors not merely to present but also to critique the various frameworks for analysis and to provide the student with some idea of how political institutions in the Third World actually operate.

Political Change and Underdevelopment offers a solid introduction to the major themes and issues involved in the politics of development, and will provide undergraduates with a sturdy framework for more advanced study.

Seitz, John. *The Politics of Development: An Introduction to Global Issues* (New York and Oxford: Basil Blackwell, 1988). 194 pp.

Seitz studies the Third World and the wider world for political causes of widespread wealth and poverty. He is especially concerned with the persistence of poverty in even the most industrialized and affluent nations. A political-scientific approach is taken to population, food, energy, the environment and technology in turn. Each section briefly summarizes the current status of its topic and explores the various political factors—regime type, international relations—that may have led to it. Nuclear power, the most highly politicized and potentially globally hazardous technology, forms the basis of two case studies.

This book "focuses on the role politics plays in solving certain key problems which have accompanied economic development in both the developed and less developed nations of the world." Because its focus is global and because it seeks positive political solutions to what some may consider apolitical problems, this volume can appeal to a broad curricular and disciplinary audience. The writing is simple and fairly jargon-free. Instructors ought to bear in mind, however, that a political approach to development has its limits. Look elsewhere for complementary texts on cultural, environmental and other approaches to the same issues.

So, Alvin Y. *Social Change and Development: Modernization, Dependency and World-System Theories* (Newbury Park, CA: Sage Publications, 1990). 282 pp.

Written specifically for undergraduates, *Social Change and Development* sets out to show that the modernization, dependency and world-systems schools "are very much alive." This is, for all intents and purposes, a primer in development theory. For each of the three "schools," So addresses five issues: how each emerged; how they differ; their "classical" roots; the criticisms they draw; and their proponents' response to this criticism. Taking each theory in turn, So describes their history and context, their strengths and weaknesses, and the newest literature in the field (specifically those writings which best answer the critics).

So is admirably objective. With each theory, he plays advocate and devil's advocate, not only clarifying specific features of each construct, but also apprising students of the most useful critical approaches to such matters. He writes well and he writes for nonspecialists. These studies keep each theory alive and relevant to any ensuing undergraduate study of development. Introductory classes on development in general or on theoretical approaches to development will be greatly enriched by this book.

Somjee, A. H. *Development Theory: Critiques and Explorations* (London: Macmillan, 1991). 185 pp.

Too often the social sciences, developed in Europe and the United States, "miss out on some of the peculiar, often crucial, problems of non-Western societies." Somjee addresses such oversight with a review of development theories articulated in Latin America and Asia as well as in the industrialized West, "taking into account the actualities of grassroots development experiences." The book includes a case study of rural India, illustrating how "enmeshed forces" increase poverty despite economic reform.

Somjee's work is well researched and carefully argued. The need to involve the poor in their own development—and the dangers that arise when the poor are excluded—informs the argument to great effect. While *Development Theory* may be too complex for beginners, more seasoned students will find many difficult questions raised here, especially after studying more orthodox theories of development without the aid of Somjee's critical eye.

Staudt, Kathleen. *Managing Development: State, Society, and International Contexts* (Newbury Park, CA: Sage Publications, 1991). 283 pp.

This book begins with an examination of the language and concepts used in the field of development, and considers the factors of culture and politics as they affect the development process. It then surveys the structure and composition of national development institutions, international development agencies, and nongovernmental organizations. The final chapters focus on two specific areas of development: agriculture and health. Cases, both hypothetical and real, are included at the end of each section, which are meant to engage the student in exercises in problem solving in the context of conditions that might be faced by a development manager in the field.

Staudt outlines the institutional environment in which attempts at transforming the social and economic conditions of individuals must be carried out. As a book more concerned with praxis than discourse, *Managing Development* is best suited to courses concerned with the implementation, rather than the formulation, of development policy.

Steidelmeier, Paul. *The Paradox of Poverty: A Reappraisal of Economic Development Policy* (Cambridge, MA: Ballinger Publishing Co., 1987). 318 pp.

Steidelmeier bases his analysis of hunger and poverty on four variables: (1) population, resources and scarcity; (2) technology; (3) power and social organization; and (4) culture. It is his contention that the latter two variables deserve much more attention in the current development debate. To this end, he sets forth "the outlines of a sound and effective development policy . . . [that] is value critical." Each of the four variables is explored in depth, culture to an extraordinary extent.

The emphasis on ethics and culture is what sets this book apart. By carefully defining his terms, the author can both summarize and address many of the most pressing questions of the development debate. The global scope of the work offers the reader perspective but occasionally leads to overgeneralization. Lively writing and the paucity of jargon make this volume suitable for an introductory course on issues of poverty or political economy in general.

Weisband, Edward, ed. *Poverty amidst Plenty: World Political Economy and Distributive Justice* (Boulder: Westview Press, 1989). 270 pp.

Recognizing the lack of adequate pedagogical materials for the student seeking an introductory survey of the concepts and issues involved in the study of the world political economy, the editor of this volume has set out to provide a book that "combines the advantages of a systematic text with those of a broad anthology." The chapters are divided into three parts: "The Political Economy of Development," "The Political Economy of Uneven Development," and "The Political Economy of States in the Liberal International Order." Each chapter contains readings representative of various, often conflicting, perspectives:

> Original materials by the editor introduce each part and each reading. By emphasizing fundamental concepts, units of analysis, analytical assumptions, theoretical frameworks and normative approaches, these introductions assist the reader in locating each reading within the broad spectrum created by contending analytical and normative perspectives in world political economy.

Although the numbers of issues and viewpoints introduced may at first seem overwhelming, this book is ideal for use in the classroom because it forces students to compare many different ideas and thus to develop the foundations for their own personal approach to the issues. *Poverty amidst Plenty* has quickly and understandably emerged as a classroom standard: it provides the stimulus for provocative classroom discussion while introducing students to the conceptual vocabulary necessary for further, more specialized research.

Whitaker, Jennifer Seymour, ed. *How Can Africa Survive?* (New York: Harper and Row, 1988). 264 pp.

This is a collection of essays on general topics of the current crises in Africa. Most of the essays concentrate on understanding Africa as a postcolonial political entity. A number of them study the synthesis of African culture with Western political and economic models imposed on various nations before independence. Others describe the relationship between the problems faced by various African nations and the industrialized societies of Europe and the United States.

How Can Africa Survive? would best serve students in an introductory seminar: the book is admirably broad but not analytically deep. Nevertheless, Whitaker's straightforward writing style ought to appeal to first- and second-year students of African society, while her careful evaluation of sources for further reading provides a stepping stone for those who wish to study the subject in greater depth.

Wilber, Charles K., ed. *The Political Economy of Development and Underdevelopment*, 5th ed. (New York: McGraw-Hill, 1992). 611 pp.

This book is "designed to be used as a standard textbook in advanced undergraduate and beginning graduate courses. The readings emphasize the political economy rather than the narrowly economic approach and issues." The contributors factor in questions of social structure, political systems and cultural values with the raw data of technology, income and growth. The readings, often radical in tone, but fairly balanced nonetheless, cover theory, history, agriculture, industry and human rights—as well as more general readings on possible solutions to the development crisis.

Instructors need not pay the "advanced undergraduate" design of the book much heed. The sheer variety of viewpoints and levels of discourse will enrich any student's understanding of political economy. Professors can easily find material here suitable for beginners or experts. Contributors include Deepak Lal, Amartya Sen, Paulo Freire and Frances Stewart, all controversial, original and opinionated thinkers. With good reason, the volume is among the most frequently assigned by undergraduate educators, and its popularity has allowed regular updating to insure continuing high quality and relevance.

Williamson, Jeffrey G. *Inequality, Poverty and History* (Cambridge, MA, and Oxford, UK: Basil Blackwell, 1991). 151 pp.

Does industrialization breed inequality? Does it increase poverty? In four transcribed and edited lectures, Williamson answers these questions by bringing the debate about development economics into the realm of economic history. Using the first Industrial Revolution as his starting point, he arrives at four conclusions: (1) the initial rise in inequality at the start of the revolution gave way to an aggregate rise in equality by the twentieth century; (2) while poverty did not rise, the rate of escape from poverty was slowed where inequality was greatest;

(3) inequality did not inhibit nonhuman capital accumulation; and (4) rising inequality did inhibit human capital accumulation. The lectures are concerned with inequality and the Industrial Revolution; migration to cities; accumulation and inequality; and poverty policy and industrialization.

Williamson is a somewhat conservative scholar, and although he recounts his economic history with an eye to today's Third World, he never takes into account the simple differences between the contemporary South and yesterday's North. Nevertheless, advanced students of political economy may want to read these lectures for their wealth of historical information and considerable scholarship in the area of industrialization. Much of this could provoke fiery discussion in senior seminars.

Economics

Blake, David H., and Robert S. Walters. *The Politics of Global Economic Relations*, 3rd ed. (Englewood Cliffs, NJ: Prentice-Hall, 1987). 248 pp.

A comprehensive primer in the politics of the global economy, this book addresses such issues as the world monetary order; the role of the multinationals; foreign aid to poor states; and technology transfer.

The authors' aim is to expand the conceptual framework for the study of the global political economy rather than to reach final solutions. Therefore, they take the time to investigate the claims of all sides of the debate while providing good references for further reading. This makes their book extremely useful for beginning students.

Cook, Paul, and Colin Kirkpatrick. *Macroeconomics for Developing Countries* (London: Harvester Wheatsheaf, 1990). 200 pp.

In their presentation of the basic principles of macroeconomic theory, the authors assume a model representative of the "typical" economic structure and institutional framework of developing countries, seeking to avoid "the uncritical application of advanced economy models to the very different conditions found in developing countries." They begin with an introduction to the concepts of aggregate demand and supply, assuming a closed economy with no government sector. They then discuss money supply and the financial sector, factoring in the role of government. This is followed by an examination of demand and supply factors in the open economy. Thus the presentation of the theoretical framework moves from the simple to the more complex. The remainder of the book is devoted to the consideration of policy issues: fiscal and monetary policy, balance of payments policy, and inflation policy. A discussion of stabilization policy includes an examination of the impact on developing countries of both the demand side and the supply side approach.

This book is intended as an introductory text. However, students lacking general familiarity with the economic conditions prevailing in the developing world may have difficulty relating the theoretical framework presented here with the reality it is meant to explain. Therefore, it may prove most beneficial to students in the second year of development study, or when the book is used in conjunction with case study material in the first year.

Gemmell, Norman, ed. *Surveys in Development Economics* (London: Basil Blackwell, 1987). 390 pp.

This collection of essays deserves brief mention as an effective response to a real gap in the teaching literature. Each of the ten contributions surveys a broad theme in development economics, such as trade policy and industrialization, agriculture and economic development, or poverty inequality and development.

The sophisticated essays include fine overviews of the relevant literature, and the book is thus a bonanza for students preparing research projects. These *Surveys*, which presume familiarity of intermediate economics, can play an important supporting role in upper-division courses.

George, Susan. *A Fate Worse Than Debt* (New York: Grove Weidenfeld Press, 1990). 300 pp.

Susan George asks three primary questions: How did the world debt crisis come about? Who was profiting by the system that brought it about? And how have the policies that have been enacted in order to allow debtor governments to avoid moratoria or default affected the lives of the poor within the debtor nations? While condemning the IMF's austerity programs, George sees the Fund as merely a tool that serves the interests of private banks, the U.S. government and, by extension, the elite classes within the debtor nations, consigning the majority to poverty. She presents case studies of African and Latin American countries that have been subject to IMF adjustment programs, thus providing examples for her contention that such programs have exacted a high price in human misery.

George writes in clear, jargon-free prose and assumes no prior knowledge of the issues involved. First-year students will find this book a lucid, very readable introduction to the subject. To others with more advanced knowledge it might serve as a reminder that the machinations of governments and other institutions have a direct effect on the lives and livelihoods of many millions of people.

Ghatak, Subrata. *An Introduction to Development Economics* (London: Allen and Unwin Ltd., 1986). 397 pp.

The open-ended and inviting title of this tome is somewhat misleading, for this is a densely quantified textbook in the theory of development economics. Ghatak's primary interest is to abstract the arguments of Keynesian, neoclassical, Marxist, and other models, and to illustrate the dynamic laws of each paradigm. The application of growth theory to less developed countries is studied through formulas whereby production, capital, labor and investment are reduced to logical symbols, and their interrelationships to mathematical equations. Ghatak proceeds to apply this analysis to resources for development. The resulting input-output ratios are examined for their calculable effect on population, poverty and income distribution. Here, too, the terrain remains solidly quantified. The author's positivist assumptions extend even to the statistical probability of human suffering. Finally, the study turns to newer concepts of development. Economic takeoffs are broken down by Ghatak into models incorporating the variables of savings, investment, capital stock and income. In a cursory conclusion, Ghatak argues that only a major emphasis on agricultural, rather than industrial, production will advance less developed countries.

A professor of development economics will find only the most advanced undergraduates prepared to penetrate this forbidding book. The author assumes readers' rigorous training in economics and statistics. The volume favors no regions and makes no compromises with readers seeking narrative coherence. Perhaps a few seniors with an intensive background in development economics will be methodologically equipped to use this book; however, it cannot be recommended as a true introduction to the topic.

Gillis, Malcolm, Dwight H. Perkins, Michael Roemer and Donald F. Snodgrass. *Economics of Development* (New York and London: W. W. Norton, 1983). 599 pp.

The authors, all at one time or another instructors of Harvard University's introductory undergraduate course on the economics of development, have attempted to devise a textbook that might serve as the foundation of a development syllabus. The book is organized into five parts. Part 1 explores what prevents development from taking place and what kinds of structural change occur once growth is under way. Part 2 "deals with how human resources are transformed in the process of economic development, and how that transformation contributes to the development process itself. Part 3 is concerned with how capital is mobilized and allocated for development purposes." Part 4 focuses on international trade and interdependence. Part 5 examines institutional reform from the perspective of the varying sectors of the economy.

The authors believe that "economic theory tends to take the *institutional context* (the existence of markets, of a banking system, of international trade, etc.) as given. But development is concerned with how one creates institutions that facilitate development in the first place." This issue provides the focus of the book. The authors have definite opinions of their own, stemming from their basic neoclassical economic orientation, yet where controversy exists they point it out. This rigorous text covers a large area without passing into oversimplification and will provide first-semester students with a good framework for future study.

Griffin, Keith. *World Hunger and the World Economy and Other Essays in Development Economics* (London: Macmillan, 1987). 274 pp.

The ten essays in this volume are concerned with a number of different issues in a number of different countries. The title essay argues that "the fundamental cause of hunger . . . is the poverty of specific groups of people, not a general shortage of food." In "Rural Poverty in Asia," Griffin tries "to understand how poverty can increase despite growth of production and on elucidating the policies necessary to combat poverty." A review of communal land tenure systems defies the negative attitude of Western policy-making circles, suggesting that communalism can in fact "make a positive contribution to rural development." Three essays in the volume concern the economic reforms introduced in China in 1978, and two deal with the Ethiopian economic crisis and agricultural development. The last two articles examine economic aid to the developing nations and the effects of the debt crisis on poor nations.

All of the essays in this volume are thought provoking, but they span a wide range of specificity. The title essay, for instance, is a good introduction to the subject, whereas "Problems of Agricultural Development in Socialist Ethiopia" will be more useful to students seeking more specialized knowledge.

Hill, Polly. *Development Economics on Trial: The Anthropological Case for a Prosecution* (Cambridge: Cambridge University Press, 1986). 198 pp.

What a nifty little book. Hill is up to two things here: first, she launches a polemic against the orthodox practice of development economics, arguing that it suffers from clumsy ethnocentrism and a near-complete failure to understand the importance of cultural context. Then, she presses the case for the relevance of economic anthropology to development economics, a perspective which, she laments, has been "habitually ignored."

Short, smart and fun to read, this book will work with undergraduates. It contains direct attacks on the pillars of development economics—including many reviewed elsewhere in this section—and, as such, it creates intellectual dialogue with most standard approaches, forcing students to revisit the assumptions of development strategies. This book deserves real consideration.

Lal, Deepak. *The Poverty of "Development Economics"* (Cambridge, MA: Harvard University Press, 1985). 153 pp.

Deepak Lal's critique of development economics takes a hard look at what the author calls the *"dirigiste* dogma" current in the field. It is his belief that such economics amount to little more than an excuse for widespread government interventionism in affairs better left to the vicissitudes of the marketplace. "Imperfect markets are superior to imperfect planning." He arrives at his conclusions by means of a concise but compelling deconstruction of development economics as both an academic discipline and a social science, concluding that it is little more than a digression from "legitimate" economics based on a few anomalous paradigms.

This controversial work defending traditional economics will ruffle more than a few feathers. But Lal's is a compelling argument well presented. Claiming little interest in politics left or right, the author concentrates on economic issues. Indeed, this apolitical approach may be the book's great weakness, as it is difficult to study any aspect of development in such a vacuum. Lal's work is best suited for more advanced students wishing to explore theoretical issues.

Lombardi, Richard W. *Debt Trap: Rethinking the Logic of Development* (New York: Praeger, 1985). 217 pp.

More than simply "a description of the impact of multinational banking in the Third World" this book is a critical history of development attitudes in the West and an appraisal of the economic and political "disorder" that operates between Northern and Southern nations. The author strays far from his original purpose—describing the current morass of moral and fiscal indebtedness into which First and Third World nations have brought themselves—but it is worth the trip.

Debt Trap is one of the few books available that attacks ethical questions of lending and borrowing in language that undergraduates can easily understand. Lombardi expresses his opinions within a carefully presented historical and theoretical framework from which students in discussion groups can draw their own conclusions. What is important is that Lombardi has written a book about the dilemma of debt that is not all numbers but is, rather, a portrait of the ethical debits and credits exchanged between two very different communities.

Meier, Gerald M. *Emerging from Poverty: The Economics That Really Matters* (New York: Oxford University Press, 1984). 258 pp.

This extremely effective volume is a survey of the theory and practice of development economics in the postwar period. Meier covers the range of issues faced by economists who search scholarly, technical, and activist means of securing subsistance for all. He breaks down the history of development economics into its conceptual and institutional components, and compares strategies applied to the underdeveloped world. A straightforward chronology guides the reader from the birth of the World Bank and International Monetary Fund at the Bretton Woods Conference and through the career of many U.N. and international development agencies. Meier is particularly adept as an authority on economic models, and he skillfully conveys the thorny controversies between the neoclassical system, the Keynesian system, and more recent paradigms, such as the school of dependency. In a final section, "The Underdevelopment of Economics," Meier concludes his overview with an imaginative assessment of the successes and failures of various developmental efforts. He makes the case ultimately for the convening of Bretton Woods 2 to rethink and recast the international public sector.

A measure of this book's achievement is its usefulness to all levels of undergraduate curricula, although its level of analysis would best suit sophomore- or junior-level courses. It is ideal as the textbook for a survey course in development economics. It also will take pride of place in classes on famine, underdevelopment and international agencies, where it would serve as a background reading of postwar economic policies. Only its emphasis on centralized organizations and economic models would render it less than serviceable to courses with a regional specialization.

Meier, Gerald. *Leading Issues in Economic Development*, 5th ed. (New York: Oxford University Press, 1989). 566 pp.

Revised five times since its first appearance in 1964, the 1989 edition of *Leading Issues* remains among the most useful texts in development economics. This dense volume tackles definitions and dimensions of development problems, competing paradigms, development strategies for Southern countries, urban-rural exchange (here teachers might want to offer comparative readings with the Todaro text, reviewed below; see also Edward Weisband's syllabus in part 2), project appraisal and much else. The text offers both sweep and depth: at once micro- and macroeconomic analysis, it provides a window on both the discourse and praxis of development economics.

Admirably thorough, nicely adapted to the complexity of the subject and effectively revised to remain current, this is, simply, a textbook, with all the good and some of the bad that attends such volumes. There is not a whole lot more to say: if you teach development to undergraduates, you're probably already familiar with this book. If not, it's time to get acquainted.

Nafziger, E. Wayne. *The Economics of Developing Countries* (Englewood Cliffs, NJ: Prentice-Hall, 1990).

This is an introductory textbook designed for undergraduate courses in development economics. It introduces the basic principles and concepts of the field, as well as specific theories of economic development, before focusing in more detail on the factors of economic growth: natural resources, population, demographics, human resource development, technical progress, capital formation, investment, and the like. It examines various domestic resource policies, as well as the role of external finance and international trade in the development of Southern economies. The final chapter is devoted to priorities for international development in the late twentieth century.

Each chapter concludes with a summary, along with a list of terms to review and questions to discuss. For students with no prior knowledge of development issues, this is a clearly written, well-structured presentation which offers a fine foundation for future study.

Nelson, Joan M., ed. *Economic Crisis and Policy Choice: The Politics of Adjustment in the Third World* (Princeton: Princeton University Press, 1990). 378 pp.

Why do some governments respond immediately to signs of economic difficulty, while others waver indecisively for years? How is the decision reached whether to use short-term remedies or to adopt a longer-term strategy of adjustment? Why have structural reforms forged ahead in some countries and failed to get off the ground in others? The contributors to *Economic Crisis and Policy Choice* aim to

answer these questions by looking at the politics of economic adjustment in thirteen different countries and nineteen governments. Before
examining how adjustment policies have fared in various countries,
the authors provide the reader with a clear understanding of the components of adjustment, as well as an examination of orthodox and
alternative thinking on stabilization and adjustment. This helpful
overview is followed by a comparative study of the political dimensions
of adjustment in Latin America, in small democracies (Costa Rica,
Jamaica and the Dominican Republic) and the debt crisis in the
Philippines.

This is an excellent resource for courses focusing on the political
aspects of the economic crisis of the developing world thoughout the
1980s. When taken as a whole it provides an across-the-board survey
of the political economy of adjustment. Piecemeal, the essays are lucid
case studies that students can refer to as the basis for research papers.

Onimode, Bade, ed. *The IMF, the World Bank and the African Debt*, vol. 1 and
   2 (London and New Jersey: Zed Books, 1989). Vol. 1, 244 pp; vol. 2,
   208 pp.

In this two-volume collection, African scholars and public officials
challenge the IMF and World Bank policies for structural readjustment
and economic development, addressing economic impact in volume 1
and social and political impact in volume 2. The essays include theoretical perspectives on the current African debt situation, as well as
case and sectoral studies.

The Latin American debt crisis, which has involved enormous sums
of money borrowed from commercial banks and thus has threatened
the stability of the international monetary system, has received the
bulk of media and diplomatic attention. But the African debt problem,
involving more governmental or multilateral money, has often inflicted greater pain on a more impoverished population. These volumes
go a long way toward illuminating the dimensions and context of the
debt crisis in Africa. The essays, which might easily be assigned piecemeal, are suitable for both beginning and advanced students of Africa
and/or the global debt problem.

Pool, John Charles, and Steve Stamos. *The ABCs of International Finance:
   Understanding the Trade and Debt Crises* (Lexington, MA: Lexington
   Books, 1987). 138 pp.

This book is an extremely useful introduction to the mechanics of
international trade and finance, and to the historical evolution of the

international monetary system and the accumulation of debt by the U.S. and various Third World countries. Chapters treat the role of international trade in the world economy; the world of international finance; the international monetary system; and the U.S. and Third World debt crises. Because the authors consider the Mexican debt situation particularly troubling, they devote an entire chapter to it. The book concludes with a rather gloomy forecast for the future.

These ABCs are superb for first-year students who have no previous knowledge in the area of international trade and finance. A simple framework for future studies, the book provides an interesting and challenging read.

Ranis, Gustav, and T. Paul Schultz, eds. *The State of Development Economics: Progress and Perspectives* (London: Basil Blackwell, 1988). 653 pp.

Nearly all of the papers in this collection were presented at a 1986 symposium organized in celebration of the twenty-fifth anniversary of the founding of the Economic Growth Center at Yale University. Their objective is to present the lessons learned in the field of development economics over the past quarter-century, as well as to assess the direction that the field will take in the future. The first part of the book presents the changes in development economics in historical perspective and provides an overview of macroeconomic theory. Part 2 addresses the development experience in Latin America, Africa and Asia, and examines the theoretical constructs, along with policies which stem from them, in socialist developing countries. Part 3 examines specific microeconomic issues as they relate to particular economic sectors and markets. Such issues include the investment in human capital through specialized training, interest rate policies in LDCs, the impact of technology on productivity and economic growth, and external borrowing by LDCs.

Although the editors do not claim to have canvased all the issues, *The State of Development Economics* provides a fairly comprehensive look at the field. Second- and third-year students of development who are not focusing their studies on economics per se will likely profit much from this book, as it provides an overview of the discipline with a minimum of "econobabble."

Reynolds, Lloyd G. *Economic Growth in the Third World: An Introduction* (New Haven and London: Yale University Press, 1986). 149 pp.

Taking as a representative sample thirty-four countries on three continents, Reynolds examines the trends in long-term growth in the

Third World from the mid-nineteenth century to the present, identifying for each nation the turning point when the economy began to grow at an accelerated pace and per capita income began to rise. In contrast to the common view that economic growth in the Third World did not begin until the post–World War II era, Reynolds holds that countries throughout Africa, Asia and Latin America, many still colonies at the time, experienced rapid economic growth beginning as early as 1840, with two-thirds of his sample having reached the turning point before the outbreak of the First World War. Reynolds examines the pattern of intensive growth in various countries at different times, and compares the growth performance in the years between 1950 and 1980, focusing on the factors which may have contributed to, or frustrated, economic growth in those years. The final chapter considers the function of government as it relates to economic growth.

Derived from Reynolds's more detailed *Economic Growth in the Third World, 1850–1980*, this book is geared to students and is thus composed primarily of the more general material included in the first book. Students will benefit from this bird's-eye view of the economies of the Third World over the period of more than a century, especially if it is used in conjunction with texts focusing on the political and social changes that were taking place coterminously.

Sachs, Jeffrey D., ed. *Developing Country Debt and the World Economy* (Chicago: University of Chicago Press, 1989). 335 pp.

Comprehensive as it is, this volume is actually a precis of a multivolume compendium of reports on debt in the developing world commissioned by the Project on Developing Country Debt. The present volume includes studies of "debt crises that occurred before World War II, political factors that contribute to poor economic policies in many debtor countries, the role of commercial banks and the IMF during the current crisis, the effect of developed countries' economies on the debtors, as well as possible solutions to the debt crisis." The rest of the book is devoted to summaries of case studies of Argentina, Brazil, Indonesia, Mexico, the Philippines, South Korea and Turkey. All of this is ably introduced by Sachs in a concise review of all aspects of the crisis.

This book is suited to an undergraduate's reading level, if students bring to it some prior understanding of the debt crisis and the world monetary system. Any student of macroeconomics will profit from this collection of some of the best current scholarship on debt. *Developing Country Debt*'s only drawbacks are its insistently top-down perspective and the editor's choice of mid-level Third World economies as subjects of study.

Sheahan, John. *Patterns of Development in Latin America* (Princeton: Princeton University Press, 1987). 399 pp.

This study focuses on three sets of issues: the persistence of poverty in Latin American countries; the nature of economic relationships between these countries and the outside world; and the association between the changes toward market-oriented economic systems and the increase in political repression. Part 1 is directed to the economic problems common to the countries discussed—poverty, unemployment, external trade and ownership of land—while part 2 looks at how the patterns of response by the individual countries contrast with each other. The early industrialization and violent reactions which marked Argentina and Brazil are compared to Chile's reformism and militant monetarism. Revolutionary alternatives are also explored in looking at Cuba and Peru (under Velasco). And the "middle-road market economies" are illustrated by the examples of Mexico, Costa Rica and Colombia. The issues are then pulled back together in part 3 to analyze how the political and economic relationships interact. Sheahan discusses a "more modern kind of repression" which has the special characteristic of combining free-market economies with destruction of democratic institutions. This leads into a discussion of the role, and the interests of, the United States in relation to poverty, repression and dependence in Latin America.

Sheahan's concentration on the three central themes of poverty, external relationships and the association between political repression and market forces omits a broad historical picture which is necessary for the beginner student. The intermediate student will, however, find his analysis, especially that of the connection beween repression and market trends, interesting and useful.

Todaro, Michael. *Economic Development in the Third World*, 4th ed. (New York and London: Longman, 1989). 698 pp.

With an emphasis on "the analysis of critical development problems from a combined theoretical, empirical and policy-oriented perspective," Todaro's book is probably the most comprehensive college text available on development. It covers both macro- and microeconomic themes, bringing a number of disciplines to bear on its analysis. The focus here is not on models or theories (although it is certainly informed by them) but on actual cases of poverty, inequality, unemployment, debt and rural stagnation. State structures and local and international institutions come under study along with the economic dynamics of the Third World in Todaro's "problem- and policy-oriented" instruction.

This important, thorough work is, along with Meier's *Leading Issues*, the standard textbook for development economics. It is structured in such a way that students with little or no background in economics may gain as much from it as more advanced students. The fourth edition contains new chapters on the debt crisis, and other chapters have been updated to reflect the changing terms of the development debate. Todaro's text remains among the best and most widely assigned for the economic dimensions of development studies.

Environment

Adams, W. M. *Green Development: Environment and Sustainability in the Third World* (Routledge: London, 1990). 225 pp.

In recent years, developers and industrialists have been paying more attention to the environmental impact of their projects both at home and abroad. Adams chronicles the "greening" of development and seeks to evaluate its effects on the political economy of the developing world. In brief case studies, the author examines green development's effects on the welfare of various communities and nations and describes the extent of change in their environmental landscapes. The essential question is whether developers really are more conscientious now than before or are merely paying lip service to popular notions of environmental responsibility.

Beginning students may have some trouble with Adams's book, as the case studies are brief and few, the bulk of the text consisting of evaluations of green development programs and the evaluation of various theories, both the author's and others'. Advanced students can glean much valuable information from *Green Development*, thanks to the author's thorough examination of the current literature on the topic.

Anderson, Anthony, ed. *Alternatives to Deforestation: Steps toward Sustainable Use of the Amazon Rain Forest* (New York: Columbia University Press, 1990). 281 pp.

After defining the current crisis and offering various hypotheses as to its origin, Anderson's collection proceeds to offer several remedies for deforestation in the Amazon basin. Aware of the need for interdisciplinary approaches, the editor convenes experts from various fields. Botanists and biologists offer essays on preserving the vast Amazonian genetic resources. Anthropologists and economists offer constructive alternatives to current methods of resource management in the region.

Each author provides his or her own footnotes, allowing students at all levels to pursue a particular literature in greater depth. And, given the carefully segmented construction of the book, teachers can assign only those portions immediately relevant to a particular course. Some chapters may be slightly difficult for beginners, but the volume will prove versatile for courses or modules focusing on the intersection of environment and development.

Bartelmus, Peter. *Environment and Development* (Boston: Allen and Unwin, 1986). 96 pp.

This introductory text explores the problematic relationship between environmental imperatives and economic growth. The author addresses the problem at a national and subnational level, identifying various environmental problems and offering grassroots approaches to solving them. The book consists of four parts: definitions of environmental and economic concerns; an assessment of current environmental crises; a guide to planning solutions to these crises; and strategies for implementing such plans. The latter guidelines arise from Bartelmus's considerable experience at the United Nations. The centerpiece of the book is the author's theory of "ecodevelopment": a basic approach to the integration of environment with development planning. He describes various models and potential models of ecodevelopment and weighs their relative merits.

Environment and Development is a simple book, very useful for beginning students. Many of the definitions and descriptions of environmental issues are simply thumbnail sketches. Little attention is given to the various and complicated debates raging between and among economists and environmentalists. Nevertheless, this concision makes for compelling reading and will apprise students of the basic issues of the debate.

Bhagavan, M. R. *Technological Advance in the Third World* (London: Zed Books Ltd., 1990). 156 pp.

The inroads of technology and the concomitant reorganization of people and resources in the developing world are the subjects of Bhagavan's history of the rise of industrial capitalism in poor nations. The author isolates four states of technological sophistication, from the high-tech industries of Korea and Mexico, to the low- or no-tech economies of Bangladesh and the Dominican Republic. There is also a summary of the technological situation in the Third World as of 1990, broken down by industry (manufacturing, mining, service, etc.). The third, and most provocative, section of the book is concerned with the technological empowerment of Third World peoples and the environmental disasters brought on by burgeoning and shrinking capitalist industries.

As it is a rather earnest bit of advocacy literature, the tone of *Technological Advance* may distract some students from the substance of the book. Nevertheless, Bhagavan has successfully combined issues of polity, economy and science—natural and industrial—into a cohesive picture of the dangerous interdependence between rampant "growth" in business (often represented by distant Western European and American bosses) and the land and people of the planet's threatened majority.

Broad, Robin, with John Cavanagh. *Plundering Paradise: The Struggle for the Environment in the Philippines* (Berkeley and Oxford: University of California Press, 1993). 185 pp.

A book of stories about people fighting to change their future, *Plundering Paradise* seeks to show what Third World environmentalism is and to shatter the myth that only rich people in richer countries care about the environment. Instead, it argues, poor people in a country like the Philippines are most dependent on natural resources for survival and have become the core of a vibrant movement for sustainable, equitable and participatory development. The authors also examine how Southern activists can and are linking up with social movements in the United States.

This very engaging book should not be limited to courses on environmental issues. It provides a clear picture of the position of labor in the Philippines, as well as that of the grassroots political organizations and their struggles against both the government and big corporations.

De Onis, Juan. *The Green Cathedral: Sustainable Development of Amazonia* (New York: Oxford University Press, 1992). 280 pp.

De Onis, a journalist and naturalist, describes humanity's strange relationship with the often mystifying Amazon basin. At times a highly personal account, *The Green Cathedral* covers the history of Amazonian exploration, exploitation and deterioration, all the while admitting that, while certain concessions to the survival of the forest may be made, humans will be exploiting the forests of Brazil forever. Part 1 researches the biological diversity and planetary necessity of Amazonia, while part 2 is a history of the region's development. Part 3 offers various strategies for reforming the use of the forest without giving it back up to nature.

While some may argue with the author's premise that sustainable development can be achieved in Amazonia, there is no doubt that this is a valuable contribution to the debate. Of greatest value is the author's historical account of explorers' and exploiters' utter mystification at the sight of the vast tropical wilderness. Of good use to instructors of development is the final chapter, which explores the possible role of NGOs in regulating development. De Onis's prose is brisk and detailed, more journalistic than scholarly, and therefore accessible to beginners, while he offers more advanced students of development ample food for thought and dispute.

Diamond, Irene, and Gloria Feman Orenstein, eds. *Reweaving the World: The Emergence of Ecofeminism* (San Francisco: Sierra Club Books, 1990). 320 pp.

The overall voice of *Reweaving the World* is probably a far cry from most anything the typical undergraduate has ever heard. Indeed, the editors have gathered essays that contribute to a fundamental shift in ecological perspective. Divided into three sections, the book first takes an historical approach, recounting the origins of ecofeminism in prepatriarchal societies and in our own, and includes such subjects as Demeter and the Eleusinian mysteries. Part 2 draws political connections to ecofeminism, and part 3 offers various feminist solutions, tried and untried, to current ecological problems.

For sheer variety of topics, this collection is hard to beat. While it is not directly related to development per se (with the exception of Vandana Shiva's "Development as a New Project of Western Patriarchy") the questions it raises can all be applied in a development curriculum. None of the material is highly technical, and the tone varies from the historical to the poetic to the political scientific. Instructors with limited space in their syllabi will be best served by selecting readings from parts 2 and 3. And, even where feminism is not a central concern, the text will work well in courses designed to promote brisk and provocative dialogue on environmental issues.

Engel, J. Ronald, and Joan Gibb Engel, eds. *Ethics of Environment and Development* (London: Bellhaven Press, 1990). 264 pp.

The editors of this volume have sought to "begin to clarify, from a multi-cultural perspective, the ethical principles at stake at the centre of the World Conservation Strategy—'sustainable development.'" To this end, they have gathered the writings of environmentalists from religious, philosopical and ethical groups around the world.

Instructors who find it difficult to integrate longer philosophical essays on nature into development curricula will have no trouble selecting concise articles on ethics, environment and development. Such texts will be welcomed by philosophically minded students of any level, provided they are familiar with the concept of sustainable development.

Gradwohl, Judith, and Russel Greenberg. Illustrated by Lois Sloan. *Saving the Tropical Forests* (Washington, DC: Island Press, 1988). 207 pp.

After an introductory essay on the gravity and causes of deforestation, the authors proceed to show the importance and variety of conservation projects in lowland tropical rainforests. Four sections of case studies describe particularly successful projects, many of which go against the grain of conventional wisdom. The authors isolate four types of projects: (1) forest reserves; (2) sustainable agriculture; (3) natural forest management; and (4) tropical forest restoration. They draw material from Africa, Asia and Latin America.

The scientific realities behind politics and economics in environmentally threatened areas are carefully clarified, offering students a view of ecology beyond rhetoric. The naturalist's perspective on social scientific issues, often lacking in other such books, is here clearly presented for the lay reader. In addition, *Saving the Tropical Forests* acts as a primer on grassroots environmental action. Its exhaustive explorations of political, economic and ecological perspectives, coupled with the nuts-and-bolts realities of the case studies, make this book a useful introduction to issues of sustainable development in the dwindling rainforests.

Harrison, Paul. *The Third Revolution: Environment, Population and a Sustainable World* (London and New York: I. B. Tauris and Co. Ltd.,1992). 356 pp.

This is essential reading for anyone seeking to understand the issues involved in the debate about the relationship between the environment and the economy. Harrison begins by framing the debate, and then looks back at the history of human dominion over the earth, pointing up the environmental factors which contributed to the agricultural and the industrial revolutions. His "third revolution" is a hypothesis as well as a challenge: Will humankind successfully adapt to the pressures of environmental degradation that humankind itself has engendered?

Harrison considers a plethora of major issues, from biological diversity to deforestation, the environmental impact of cities, population, pollution, and climate change. And, in the process, he evaluates numerous ideological perspectives, from the free-market conservative to the socialist. His personal position: "No one is free of some ideological baggage, and I don't claim to be. But the largest suitcase in my luggage is marked Empiricism." Students of all levels will benefit from Harrison's clearly written and very engaging book.

Hecht, Susanna, and Alexander Cockburn. *The Fate of the Forest: Developers, Destroyers and Defenders of the Amazon* (New York: Verso, 1989). 226 pp. Index, bibliography, and notes. Illustrated.

In the classroom, this book would function at best as an introduction to the history and problems of the Amazon rainforest. In a series of brief chapters, the authors describe each stage in the history of the use of the Amazon's resources from the colonial era to the present. The narrative presents a picture of continual decline in the diversity and availability of those resources and the consequent effects on indigenous populations, colonists and the forest itself.

Hecht and Cockburn have collected data from a broad array of sources—historical, literary and scientific—yet they fail to delve deeply into any single aspect of Amazon history. The book, therefore, tends to preach to the already converted, asking few difficult questions of itself or the reader. The appendixes, containing glossaries of Portuguese and botanical terms as well as interviews with various advocates of Amazon preservation, are perhaps more useful to the student than the rest of the work. The bibliography is long but needs thorough annotation to be at all helpful; the notes tend to be more explanatory than bibliographic.

Hurst, Philip. *Rainforest Politics: Ecological Destruction in South-East Asia* (London: Zed Books Ltd., 1990). 303 pp.

Rainforest Politics describes the historical, cultural and political forces behind forest destruction in Indonesia, Malaysia, Papua New Guinea, the Philippines and Thailand, taking each country in turn. Each report lists the effects of forest loss; the development of current policy; the causes of deforestation; and prospects for new policy. As the title indicates, Hurst views much of the destruction of the forests as politically motivated. The final chapter outlines the political factors common to all of the countries under review.

Hurst emphasizes the need for indigenous land use alternatives to replace short-sighted logging drives, and he touches on issues of international relations and law, successfully assembling data and argumentation into a readable and compelling introduction to one aspect of environmental politics. If nothing else, students will learn from this book how the complexities of a common problem can differ from country to country.

Ives, Jack D., and Bruno Messerli. *The Himalaya Dilemma: Reconciling Development and Conservation* (London and New York: Routledge, 1989). 295 pp.

"This book seeks to examine the basis of the widely supported prediction that the Himalayan region is inevitably drifting into a situation of environmental supercrisis and collapse . . . ." Concluding that the situation is even worse than generally thought, the authors propose their own theoretical interpretation and policy suggestions.

The book offers upper-level students a chance to take a single region and look at it from a number of conflicting perspectives, hopefully honing their own critical skills along the way.

Leonard, H. Jeffrey, et al. *Environment and the Poor: Development Strategies for a Common Agenda* (New Brunswick, NJ: Transaction Books, 1989). A volume from the Overseas Development Council "Policy Perspectives" series. 222 pp.

Concerned with the relationship between poverty and the environment and the need for long-term infrastructural change, these essays discuss irrigation, desertification, rainforest depletion, hillside agriculture, urbanization and ecosystem preservation. Instead of focusing on the contention between economic growth and environmental destruction, Leonard and his colleagues concentrate on the unmistakable correlation between environmental degradation and poverty. The goal is to design a single set of policy instruments to address all of these problems while never losing sight of the human cost of environmental decline.

Although Leonard raises questions of sociology and ecology, his focus is on policy issues. The complex questions of policy analysis and the detailed scrutiny of environmentalism might be too much for a general course on development, but *Environment and the Poor* will contribute greatly to ecological development studies.

MacNeill, Jim, Pieter Winsemuis and Taizo Yakushiji. *Beyond Interdependence: The Meshing of the World's Economy and the Earth's Ecology* (New York and Oxford: Oxford University Press, 1991). A Trilateral Commission book. 159 pp.

The 1992 Rio de Janiero Earth Summit presented many scholars with an opportunity to grapple with the dilemma of promoting economic growth without placing the planet at risk of environmental collapse. The Trilateral Commission provides a laundry list of environmental issues placed in world economic perspective, offering industrialized nations possible solutions to such problems as ozone depletion and carbon dioxide buildup.

The authors focus on industrial Asia, America and Europe, paying scant attention to possible grassroots action in the developing world. However, despite its problematic Northern focus, *Beyond Interdependence* offers a concise summary of current environmental issues suitable for an introductory course.

Mathews, Jessica Tuchman, ed. *Preserving the Global Environment: The Challenge of Shared Leadership* (New York and London: W. W. Norton and Company, 1991). 362 pp.

The preparation of this book was initiated by the American Assembly in collaboration with the World Resources Institute with the aim of providing a framework for the development of policy concerning the role the United States should play in confronting global environmental issues. Each paper included in this volume deals with a specific factor influencing the environment, from population growth and deforestation to diplomatic initiatives aimed at protecting the ozone layer and the environmental implications of economic policies. Using this collection of essays as background reading, the participants of the American Assembly met in 1990 to discuss the issues raised therein, and to issue a report.

This book is meant to spur scholarly research in environmental issues in addition to making concrete suggestions for policy development. It concentrates within one volume examinations of topics that range through the fields of foreign policy, environmental science, international law and economics, and thus serves as a good starting point for the study of environmental policy. One drawback for students: the book contains no bibliography.

Meadows, Donella H., Dennis L. Meadows and Jorgen Randers. *Beyond the Limits: Confronting Global Collapse, Envisioning a Sustainable Future* (Post Mills, VT: Chelsea Green Publishing Co., 1992). 300 pp.

Beyond the Limits is the sequel to the same authors' *The Limits to Growth* (New York, 1972), a study of the potential unsustainability of production and growth in a world of finite resources. While that volume predicted catastrophe in a century, this entirely rewritten assessment considers the dangers more imminent.

The book is simply and carefully written, going as far as to explain the mathematics behind exponents and providing teachers with instructions on how to use this and other models. *Beyond the Limits* is a useful tool in first- and second-year classes on sustainable development and macroeconomics, although all students would profit greatly from it.

Milbrath, Lester W. *Envisioning a Sustainable Society: Learning Our Way Out* (Albany, NY: SUNY Press, 1989). 403 pp.

In this thoughtful, wide ranging and often personal essay, Milbrath advocates changes in human behavior from the level of government policy down to individual activity. Along the way, he discusses the current state of development, characterizing it as wantonly destructive and in need of reform. Similarly, he builds cases against traditional left-right politics, belief paradigms, work ethics, education and technology.

This is a provocative book, carefully paced, with each argument leading to a conclusion that bolsters the author's theme. Instructors will probably have difficulty excerpting particular sections and may therefore be compelled to omit the book altogether from already crowded syllabi. Students of development and environmental ethics, however, will profit greatly from Milbrath's reflective approach to the social and environmental sciences, especially as his concern is with sustaining a human ecology.

Porter, Gareth, and Janet Welsh Brown. *Global Environmental Politics* (Boulder, CO: Westview Press, 1991). 208 pp.

While ecological concerns may appear self-evident to many students, the political underpinnings of environmental degradation and improvement may not be so obvious. *Global Environmental Politics* is not an inappropriate place to begin learning about the transnational political dynamics of development and industrial growth. The book offers a brief history of environmental politics and politicians, followed by brief outlines of the issues: air pollution, ozone depletion, whaling, ivory poaching, waste disposal, mining, global warming and forest clearing. Much of the text is concerned with the interaction of North and South. The authors conclude by offering three possible approaches to reconciling political differences with ecological necessities.

Porter and Brown bring a wealth of statistical information and often very technical observation to this book. Nevertheless, the most dense material is relegated to charts and diagrams, and the more technical aspects of political science, as well as the historical minutiae, can be figured out with the aid of the glossary and chronology. The text itself consists of thoughtful, self-contained essays that would fit well on any political science or environmental syllabus.

Redclift, Michael. *Sustainable Development: Exploring the Contradictions* (New York: Routledge, 1987). 221 pp.

Eager to break disciplinary boundaries, Redclift has written a critique of the social sciences' effectiveness in the realm of ecology. By contrasting economic theories (Marxism, capitalism, etc.) with environmental realities, the author seeks to rectify academic misunderstandings of the world around us. But above all, the book describes "the destruction of life support systems and their creation," showing along the way how the environment, like politics and economics, fits into a long process of change and is not merely a static form.

Despite its apparently concrete approach, many readers will find this to be a highly theoretical text. A great deal of political science and economics go into Redclift's arguments. Although he is careful to make this information as readable as possible, Redclift relies quite heavily on the jargon of political economy and, at times, the hard sciences. Beginning students may have trouble keeping up with *Sustainable Development*, but those with background in either the social sciences or ecology will find Redclift's rigorous critique a welcome challenge.

Repetto, Robert. *World Enough and Time: Successful Strategies for Resource Management* (New Haven, CT: Yale University Press, 1986). A World Resources Institute book. 147 pp.

The 1984 Global Possible Project assembled scientists and resource managers to discuss effective, feasible means of protecting the world's resource base while fostering growth in the developing world. While the papers presented there (and available through WRI) were highly technical, Repetto's synthesis of the debates and conclusions is not. The author believes that actual growth is lagging behind potential growth, and that progress can be made without endangering precious resources. Indeed, the right kind of progress can better sustain these resources. The book offers policies for fostering growth; suggests useful policy instruments in the private and public sectors; summarizes actual and possible development policies in nine resource sectors—"feasible initiatives in each . . . sector that, if widely adopted, would have the greatest beneficial effect on human welfare."

The reading level is not particularly difficult, and, as was the author's intent, technical terms and concepts are kept to a minimum or carefully explained for the nonspecialist. Repetto does not address the legitimacy of the growth model itself, which instructors may want to take up as a topic of class discussion. What he does offer is a grand tour of politically centrist technocratic responses to the dual problems of underdevelopment and environmental decline.

Schmink, Marianne, and Charles Wood. *Contested Frontiers in Amazonia* (New York: Columbia University Press, 1992). 387 pp.

This anthropological and demographic study follows the activities of various people representing various interests—political, economic and social—in the Amazon frontier in the decade following the building of roads through the heart of the rainforest. Essentially, the exploitation of the frontier was the result of a contest for resources among peasants, miners, Indians, politicians and others. Further affecting this frontier struggle were remote national and international influences. A brief introductory chapter outlines the historical background from European incursion to the twentieth-century militarization and deep exploration of the forest.

Contested Frontiers is an historical and historiographical account of the exploitation of the Brazilian forest. Not only does it provide a factual record, but it also draws a more nuanced picture of the human interactions occurring in the tropics. Conflicts do not always cast huge developers against landless peasants, and, when they do, the peasants do not always lose. A brisk narrative style and a wealth of anecdotal information make this a gripping read, while the sheer weight of the scholarship involved will provide students with a great resource for their own studies of the region. The book is thus as useful in a senior class as in a first- or second-year survey course.

Seager, Joni, ed. *The State of the Earth Atlas* (New York: Touchstone Books, Simon and Schuster, 1990). 127 pps.

This book consists of thirty-seven maps of the world and its parts, which describe, through color coding and other keys, the nature, scale and distribution of the most important global environmental and ecological problems—problems which effect every aspect of development work and development studies. Each map, covering two facing pages, serves as a compact almanac of a particular issue, providing a wealth of information, and serving as an excellent stepping stone to further inquiry and discussion. "Habitat" maps show population density and growth, and species extinction; "Food and Water" maps depict resource distribution, subsistence patterns, chemical fertilizer use, desertification and the fate of fisheries; "Shelter" maps describe urban sprawl, coastal crisis, waste, sewage and air quality. There are also maps concerned with energy, industry, defense, consumerism and global warming. In addition, there is an international table of environmental indicators plus detailed narrative commentaries on each map.

The State of the Earth Atlas is a concise, comprehensive portrait of global interconnectedness. It is profoundly instructive, and the maps are beautiful. Of great importance is the editor's view (a view that guides the entire volume) that "most of the deterioration in our environment is the direct or indirect consequence of particular human arrangements of economic and political power superimposed on vulnerable ecological systems." The atlas, which clearly shows linkages between all fields of study that feed into the interdisciplinary approach of development studies, is an indispensable resource for educators and students alike.

Southgate, Douglas D., and John F. Disinger. *Sustainable Resource Development in the Third World* (Boulder and London: Westview Press, 1987). 177 pp.

This book presents the papers that came out of an international symposium staged in 1985 to address the technological and institutional challenges of sustainable development of natural resources in the Third World. The opening arguments present the difficulties facing individuals and agencies attempting to mount resource conservation projects, and stress the importance of evaluating the impact of these projects. Subsequent papers offer suggestions as to how to evaluate the impact of the projects, taking in such considerations as the affected population's willingness to change, the nature and degree of institutional change, and the distribution of the costs and the benefits. The closing chapters are case studies of various projects in the Dominican Republic, Barbados, Kenya, Colombia and India. Each case study illustrates the importance of "sustainable development of natural resources as a necessary approach to the confrontation of world problems." The vital importance of taking into account the local and human realities when designing environmental policy and resource development projects is stressed throughout each of the essays.

All of the essays are easy to read and can provide the beginner with a complete picture of resource development, the problems it faces, its technical aspects, and the evaluations necessary to increase its sustainability.

Stern, Paul C., Oran R. Young and Daniel Druckman, eds. *Global Environmental Change: Understanding the Human Dimensions* (Washington, DC: National Academy Press, 1992). 308 pp.

This published report of the Committee on the Human Dimensions of Global Change offers a "five-point plan for a national research program on the human dimensions of global environmental change." The committee consists of twelve social scientists and two natural scientists. The report's stress on social science derives from the committee's belief that, as current environmental damage is anthropogenic, so, too, should people take responsibility for repairing that damage, and environmentalists should confront human behavior in their efforts to preserve nature.

While the report does offer a thumbnail history of environmental change, its greater concern, and greatest asset, is setting parameters of study, suggesting new methods of data gathering, and generating an interdisciplinary dialogue among sciences. Past anthropogenic changes in the environment are compared to potential uses of human organization to correct such changes. Because much of this material is concerned with promoting new ideas and courses of action as yet undefined, the text reads at times like a work in progress. Nevertheless, it is a simple, clearly written source of new ideas that can possibly lead students to developing environmental perspectives of their own.

World Commission on Environment and Development. *Our Common Future* (Oxford and New York: Oxford University Press, 1987). 400 pp.

The WCED is an international group of scholars and politicians organized by the UN to study issues of environmental sustainability. *Our Common Future* is the commission's "global agenda for change," a high-level study of the world's economic and environmental degradation which labels and assesses those challenges that are common to humanity as a whole. Along with the assessments come possible solutions, arrived at by the consensus of the commissioners.

Amidst the usual calls for institutional reform and multilateral action, the editors have included exerpts from speeches made by the various delegates, showing readers the wide range of strongly held opinions that the world's most influential scholars and politicians actually hold about pressing environmental issues. For this, if not for its geographical ecumenism, *Our Common Future* should be included in all levels of development teaching.

Food and Hunger

Alamoir, Mohiuddin, and Poonam Aroral. *Providing Food Security for All* (New York: NYU Press, 1991). 269 pp.

The political economy of food production and distribution is the focus of this demanding study. Contending that food security is an "economic proposition not just a welfare responsibility," Alamoir and Aroral align themselves with advocates of empowerment as an alternative to excessive dependency on relief. This is no idle slogan: The premise of their book is that universal access to land—matched by employment opportunities—must replace food aid as a solution to world hunger. Brandishing an exhaustive array of macroeconomic data, they argue that access to an adequate food supply can eventually be guaranteed for all on household, national, and global levels. To achieve this, they advocate no less than the overhaul of domestic policies within all Third World nations. This entails the transformation of economic structures, in particular, credit networks, transportation facilities, environmental policies and access to markets.

In this contentious and erudite work, Alamoir and Aroral have achieved a true global synthesis on food security. At first glance, the eighty-six tables and ten appendices, most of extreme complexity, lend this study the oppressive feel of an academic tome. But the persevering advanced student with a macroeconomic background in development studies will find the authors' conclusions original and persuasive. This book is critical to advanced courses in development economics as a comprehensive treatment of the hard but vital path to economic autonomy.

Commins, Stephen K., Michael F. Lofchie, and Rhys Payne, eds. *Africa's Agrarian Crisis: The Roots of Famine* (Boulder: Lynne Rienner Publishers, 1986). 236 pp.

The essays in the first section of this book provide an overview of the agricultural crisis in Africa, as well as a survey of food policies in sub-Saharan Africa and an examination of government regulation of rural markets. The second section is devoted to analyses of the relationship between public policy and agricultural productivity in specific contexts, such as the impact of international and domestic development programs on the peasants of Liberia. Other essays in this section focus on policy issues in Ghana, Tanzania, Morocco and Kenya. The third section presents two case studies which analyze the impact of the external factor of donor policy on African agriculture.

Students focusing on the intersection between policy and production will find this book very useful. The case studies are a valuable resource for those focusing research on individual countries. Professors wishing to provide their students with concrete examples of more general questions might select one reading from each of the three sections.

Currey, Bruce, and Graham Hugo, eds. *Famine as a Geographical Phenomenon* (Dordrecht, Boston, and Lancaster: D. Reidel, 1984). 202 pp.

This collection of articles by scholars in a number of disciplines addresses such issues as the effect of famines on demographics, the relationship between war and famine in Cambodia, the circumstance of famine amidst plenty in the Caribbean, the compilation by the British of the Indian Famine Codes, and the impact of famine on women in Bengal. Also considered are methods for planning emergency food relief in times of famine, as well as food crisis management and relief in general.

The book is intended for use with undergraduate students of geography.

Dreze, Jean, and Amartya Sen, eds. *The Political Economy of Hunger*, vol. 1: *Entitlement and Well Being* (Oxford: Clarendon Press, 1990). 492 pp.

This is the first volume of revised versions of papers given at a 1986 meeting of the World Institute for Development Economics Research (WIDER); two more are to follow. The editors and contributors, "concerned with diagnosis and causal analysis as well as policy research," focus on African and Asian plus a smattering of Latin American topics, ranging from "An Independent Press and Anti-Hunger Struggles" to "Rural Women and Food Production in Sub-Saharan Africa." The result is not merely an academic picture of the quality of life in developing regions, but a portrait drawn by the self-perceptions of the inhabitants of such regions.

Students in their third or fourth year of college, comfortable with interdisciplinary research, ought to enjoy the eclectic arrangement of topics in Sen and Dreze's collection. This very eclecticism, however, reduces the volume's usefulness as a whole. Instructors will be best served by directing interested students to particular essays, although some are general enough to include on any syllabus.

Erb, Gene. *A Plague of Hunger* (Ames, IA: Iowa State University Press, 1990). 127 pp.

For students unfamiliar with issues of world poverty, hunger and development, this book will serve as a good point of departure. Originally appearing in the *Des Moines Register*, the material is divided into two sections. The first introduces the problem of world hunger, which it explores in the varied contexts of particular countries, including Honduras, Ethiopia, Egypt, Zimbabwe and South Korea. It also addresses briefly the issue of world debt and provides a cursory look at the various quests for solutions to the problem of world poverty and hunger. Part 2 focuses more specifically on foreign-owned plants in Mexico and their effect on the lives of the poor.

In addition to journalist Erb's simple, concise text, the book is replete with photographs, candid portraits of people in the countries under consideration. This emphasizes the human factor, which is Erb's primary intention. Because the book is such an easy read, instructors of first-year students may wish to assign it in the first week in order to level the playing field between those students who follow developments in the Third World through the news media and those who do not.

Fletcher, Lehman B. *World Food in the 1990's: Production, Trade and Aid* (Boulder, CO: Westview Press, 1992). 368 pp.

The papers and edited discussion transcripts that appear in this volume were first presented in a four-session workshop held in September, 1989. Anticipating international economic and policy trends in the 1990s, they focus on such issues as the relationship between the operation of world food markets and the food security concerns of developing nations, the implications of a possible liberalization of global agricultural trade for world food production and distribution, and the role U.S. foreign economic assistance should play vis-à-vis the world food system. Also discussed is how agricultural trade and policy reforms in both industrialized and developing countries might contribute to a more secure food supply as well as global economic growth.

Each essay is followed by a response paper, which makes this volume quite useful for spurring classroom debate, and the selected statistical tables contained in the appendix will prove helpful to students preparing research papers. An advanced knowledge of macroeconomic theory and some familiarity with the major issues involved in world trade and economic development are necessary to profit fully from this work.

Foster, Phillips. *The World Food Problem: Tackling the Causes of Undernutrition in the Third World* (Boulder, CO: Lynne Rienner, 1992). 367 pp.

Like the other important book about the world food problem published in 1992 (Nan Unklesbay's *World Food and You*, discussed below), *The World Food Problem* is a highly detailed, often technical overview. Foster first documents the staggering proportions and deadly toll of malnutrition, then identifies the failure of food security—the nexus of economic, demographic and health variables—as the cause, and finally evaluates competing public policy choices.

This is a careful and impressive work of scholarship. Foster moves deliberately from evidence to conclusion, from one definition to the next. The writing is methodical, clear and not ungraceful. Frankly data driven, the volume is loaded with graphs, tables and equations. For sophisticated students concerned with the global food problem, this is the state of the art. Others, less advanced or less focused, it may well intimidate.

Goodman, David, and Michael Redclift. *Refashioning Nature: Food, Ecology and Culture* (London and New York: Routledge, 1991). 279 pp.

This book is an attempt "to formulate an integrated framework of how the modern food system developed, and how this system works." Issues such as the effects on women's role in the labor market on the increasing commoditization of food, changes that have taken place in the social organization of farming in Europe, and the emergence of the modern agrifood system are taken up, as well as such subjects as biotechnology and the food system, and the relationship between the modern food system and the environment.

The essays in this book deal with both developed and underdeveloped regions. They make important reading for those third- and fourth-year students interested in the technologies, infrastructures, and consequences of modern food production and distribution.

The Hunger Project. *Ending Hunger: An Idea Whose Time Has Come* (New York: Praeger, 1985). 430 pp.

Included here are such topics as population, food, foreign aid, national security and the New International Economic Order. Students and instructors alike will find the appendices invaluable, as they provide information on terminology, suggested reading, and how to contact hunger relief organizations. Full-page photographs accompany the text.

This is an ideal introductory-level text. It will provide first-year students not only with the basic facts about world hunger but also with an overview of the approaches and perspectives concerning the major issues around which the international debate about ending hunger revolves.

Lappe, Frances Moore, and Joseph Collins. *World Hunger: Twelve Myths* (New York: Grove Weidenfeld, 1986). A Food First book. 208 pp.

World Hunger: Twelve Myths is an introductory text designed to present the basic issues of food security while at the same time correcting popular misconceptions about hunger and development. The authors introduce the book with a chapter called "What is Hunger?" The myths themselves are presented one at a time in a simple fashion and followed by brief rebuttals. The rebuttals lead into more detailed discussions of particular cases in point. Some examples of myth: "The Green Revolution Is the Answer" and "The Free Market Can End Hunger."

More than any other book of its kind, *World Hunger* will inform and entertain students beginning a course of study in Third World development. The environment, gender, money and population all have a place in this mythology. Lappe's and Collins's desire to inform and mobilize Americans in the face of widespread ignorance is equaled only by the clarity of their logic and the relevance of the data they marshal against each myth. The book is also easy to teach from. Instructors may wish to assign a myth each week and have their students research the evidence in greater depth and report their findings to the class. More advanced students, already familiar with hunger issues, may wish to refer to the reading lists and resource guides at the back of the book. Activists as well as scholars, the authors have also provided a guide to U.S. and international hunger organizations.

Minear, Larry. *Humanitarianism under Siege: A Critical Review of Operation Lifeline Sudan* (Trenton, NJ: The Red Sea Press, 1991). 215 pp.

This book reviews the massive relief effort launched in 1989 by the international community with the objective of providing assistance to the many civilians starving as a result of the Sudanese civil war. After providing the historical context and assessing Lifeline's work on a month-by-month basis, Minear considers issues of politics, sovereignty, and conflict resolution as they related to the relief effort. The final chapter explores the ways in which Operation Lifeline Sudan might serve as a model for future humanitarian relief efforts.

Subsequent crises in Somalia and Bosnia underscore Minear's assertion that "Lifeline's significance extends well beyond the Sudan." This is a clearly written, informative book for students at all levels.

Newman, Lucille, ed. *Hunger in History: Food Shortage, Poverty and Deprivation*
(Cambridge, MA: Basil Blackwell, 1990). 429 pp.

The results of the interdisciplinary work of Brown University's
World Hunger Program, Newman's collection offers a broad array of
essays dedicated to the better understanding of hunger. Specialists in
their respective fields, the authors of these essays grapple with population models and archaeological theories in order to explain how and
when societies grow short of food. The book is divided into three rough
periods: the prehistoric era, early civilization, and industrial and postindustrial society.

Although convenient, the periodization of this collection may be its
major flaw. A chapter that conflates Mesopotamia and medieval European society is bound to confuse students who lack background in one
or both of these eras. On the other hand, such a synthesis could broaden
the horizons of students as yet unfamiliar with the global nature of
human development. Teachers may find it best to use different sections
of the text with different classes, as the range of technical language and
subject matter is somewhat broad.

O'Neill, Onora. *Faces of Hunger: An Essay on Poverty, Justice and Development*
(London and Boston: Allen and Unwin, 1986). 178 pp.

"This book asks *whether* and *why* development should be pursued,
not only by the poor and vulnerable, but by the rich and powerful." At
a time when popular interest in development is peaking while the
interest of the rich and powerful in development is waning, O'Neill's
philosophical inquiry into assisting the poor is quite welcome. In addition to offering reasons why the rich should continue (or begin) to help
the poor, O'Neill generates rubrics of ethical deliberation, assessing
motives of assistance—from the most idealistic to the coldly utilitarian.

Applying Kantian philosophy to the "finite and vulnerable rational
beings" who seek to help others or themselves may seem at first irrelevant to undergraduate development studies. Nevertheless, O'Neill
demonstrates convincingly that it is just as often the motives behind
development initiatives as it is the initiatives themselves that determine the success or failure of the initiative. This is a thoughtful essay
that does not dictate any particular attitude other than the author's
own belief that assistance must continue. It leaves the way open for
more thoughtful students to generate their own ethics of development
using the author's ideas as guideposts. *Faces of Hunger* will be accessible
to beginners in development studies, while its compelling subject and

unblinking ethical examinations will provoke quite a response from those well along in their studies.

Raikes, Philip. *Modernising Hunger: Famine, Food Surplus and Farm Policy in the EEC and Africa* (Portsmouth, NH: Heinemann Publishing, in Collaboration with the Catholic Institute for International Relations, 1988). 280 pp.

Commissioned to study the African food supply without reference to trade proved an impossible and fruitless task for Philip Raikes, so he broadened the scope of his research to study how Africans benefit and suffer from trade in food with their neighbors to the North. The book is in two parts. An introductory section gives historical, political and economic background to the "food gap" and discusses its implications. The following section outlines the international implications of the food shortage, especially in relation to the European Community, which, being Africa's biggest trading partner, has much to do with the reliability of the food supply.

Raikes is a specialist in economics who has put together a study of a difficult topic for other specialists to use as a policy-making tool. Less experienced students can find much simpler texts on the African food problem. Part 1 and the first two chapters of part 2 can serve as a comprehensive introduction for students already well versed in political economy and economics but with little knowledge of African topics. The text itself is dense and the number of variables guiding any one of the author's arguments will confuse many readers. Nevertheless, Raikes takes pains to construct a coherent picture of a complicated situation.

Seavoy, Ronald. *Famine in Peasant Societies* (Westport, CT: Greenwood Press, 1986). 479 pp.

Seeking to demonstrate historical parallels between subsistence crises in the East and West, Seavoy draws together four peasant societies in a sweeping indictment of the politics of hunger. Famines in England, Indonesia, India and Ireland are described and analyzed with an eye to their avoidable causes. European references include the killing crises induced by the bubonic plague in the fourteenth century and the potato famines of the nineteenth century, which are deftly juxtaposed to starvation among the Bengali in the 1870s and among the Javanese in the 1960s. It is Seavoy's contention that none of these famines was inevitable; each was provoked or aggravated by outside intrusion upon the traditional practices of subsistence food production. Seavoy thus affirms the essential rationale of peasant societies and seeks to inspire political protection for the customs of peasants, whose collectivist wisdom, he argues, is superior to encroaching market forces—the bête noir of this book. Seavoy concludes that only action in the political sphere will assure a food surplus, for "the assumptions and terminology of economics do not apply to subsistence cultures."

Readable and provocative, Seavoy's book speaks to college students of all levels. Ideal particularly for comparative history courses, his arguments will intrigue students in any of the social sciences. Seavoy is attentive to the particular contributions and methodology of each discipline, giving this book the broadest possible audience. It is also free of jargon or of shorthand references to obscure scholarly debates. In sum, this is a definitive book for a college course on the causes of famine and on the structure of traditional peasant societies.

Tullis, F. Lamond, and W. Ladd Hollist, eds. *Food, the State, and International Political Economy: Dilemmas of Developing Countries* (Lincoln: University of Nebraska Press, 1986). 351 pp.

Agriculture is the core issue of these ten essays. These authors situate food firmly within the global web of market forces, international policies, the environment and production technologies. Their interdisciplinary treatment of agricultural issues seeks to encourage government policies that will equitably control production, pricing, and distribution on the international market. Demonstrating the inadequacy of laissez-faire market forces and of pure technological responses such as the Green Revolution to feed the world, these authors are also unified in their commitment to depoliticize food. Many of these studies expose the manipulation of technologies or contributions by donor nations to enhance diplomatic relations with select client states. In a context where food is allowed to become a political weapon, they argue, aid will never follow true need. But to depoliticize, they remind us, is not to diminish the role of the state. The book's lesson, in conclusion, is that principled state intervention in distributing relief, stabilizing markets, and minimizing risks to individual producers is critical to food security on a global scale.

These essays by agricultural economists, political scientists, nutritionists, and sociologists will engage upper-level students of all these disciplines. The coherence and lucidity of these authors, unified by their Keynesian approach, will spur real discussion. Their commitment to an interdisciplinary approach to development education renders this a model study of this growing field.

Unklesbay, Nan. *World Food and You* (Binghamton: Food Products Press, 1992). 444 pp.

World Food and You is described as "a complete guide to nutrition and world food issues." "Complete" is the operative word in this description. Unklesbay goes into great depth on four main topics: global food production (including a discussion of population, food security, marketing and the role of foreign aid); agricultural production, processing, and consumption; nutrition; and current food issues, such as biotechnology, chemicals in the food supply and global warming. The book closes on an optimistic tone by discussing the role of multidisciplinary agricultural research and development programs in alleviating some of the grave problems facing global agriculture today.

Professors looking to assign a thorough overview of all the elements of global food production will find in this up-to-date and committed book a crucial resource. Their students, however, may find the exhaustive detail somewhat forbidding.

Gender

Afshar, Haleh, ed. *Women, Development and Survival in the Third World* (New York: Longman, 1991). 325 pp.

The fourteen studies of this volume explore the politics of production. The forging of industrial economies, it is argued, presents a vital opportunity to assimilate women into the workforce. The authors' particular contribution is to situate the informal sector of the economy as an intermediate stage between the home and the cooperative, factory or office. Fragmented home-based industries, such as lace making and tobacco rolling, are recognized as determinative in the successful integration of reproductive and productive relations under the same roof. Little understood because of their makeshift and concealed character, the home-based industries are appraised as essential preparatory organisms for women's economic autonomy and self-sufficiency.

This animated and challenging book will be an important resource to courses on women and development and on Third World regions. Upper-division students will profit the most from these polished and persuasive essays. The authors avoid excessive jargon and speak to the broadest possible audience in development studies.

Beneria, Lourdes, and Shelly Feldman, eds. *Unequal Burden: Economic Crises, Persistent Poverty and Women's Work* (Boulder, CO: Westview Press, 1992). 278 pp.

How did the widening gap between rich and poor in the eighties affect the dynamic of household economics and the empowerment of women? Beneria and Feldman's collection addresses this question by covering ground left unstudied by the UN and other agencies in recent years. The core concerns here are the painful burdens resulting from structural adjustment, burdens that the editors believe must be assessed in terms of gender and microeconomics. The contributors address the following questions: How do people cope with poverty on a household level and how can policies be adjusted to make coping easier? What ideological factors affect women's burden sharing? What are the differences between poor households in different countries? What is the relationship between class and structural adjustment burdens?

What is the role of micro-adjustment in the world economy? The book brings together general chapters on inequality and survival as well as specific nation-based studies (e.g., religion and gender in Bangladeshi households).

The global chapters offer fine fodder for discussion and can easily form the basis of students' own research. The more specific chapters will prove difficult for beginners. The editors include various compelling and often contentious themes in the collection. Contributors include Bina Agarwal and Helen I. Safa, as well as Beneria, director of the Program on International Development and Women at Cornell University.

Buvinic, Mayra, and Sally W. Yudelman. *Women, Poverty and Progress in the Third World* (New York: Foreign Policy Association, 1989). Headline series #289. 64 pp.

This is a book written specifically for students. It outlines "the economic contributions women make and their role in managing natural resources and promoting family health and welfare and examin[es] what international donors and national implementing agencies have and have not done" to assist them. In addition to writing chapters on WID as a discipline, women in the economy and women's relations with donor agencies, the authors offer a policy agenda for the nineties, containing recommendations for local and international policy changes. The book concludes with discussion questions.

This is a well-designed and effective introductory text on women and international development. The authors assume their readers have little or no acquaintance with the subject. Simple charts and occasional photographs help illustrate points.

Charlton, Sue Ellen M. *Women in Third World Development* (Boulder, CO: Westview Press, 1984). 240 pp.

An "advanced introduction to what development means for half the people in the world," *Women in Third World Development* grew from the author's teaching manual for development educators. The first section of the book describes the historical and political context from which WID derives. Part 2 examines specific aspects of development—technology, agriculture and education—using three case studies on the Green Revolution, cash crops and the baby formula debate. Part 3 critiques current approaches to development used by various agencies and offers alternative strategies for development in the Third World.

The book is not designed for beginners: Charlton assumes that her readers begin with some general knowledge of development issues. Supplementary reading lists after each chapter amply supply the more advanced student with research possibilities.

Charlton, Sue Ellen M., Jana Everett and Kathleen Staudt, eds. *Women, the State and Development* (Albany: SUNY Press, 1989). 248 pp.

In the attempt "to foster linkages between the development literature on the one hand and statist and feminist literatures on the other," the editors offer in-depth critiques of many current development theories. Two main points are emphasized here. The first is the need for development theories that consider the political and developmental role of women. The second is the desirability of nongovernmental activity as both a means for disenfranchised women to assert themselves and as a viable alternative to state action on all levels of development.

The essays are complicated, thorough and as critical of themselves as they are of the statist perspectives under review. Beginning students may be hard pressed to comprehend the debate, but advanced students of WID or political science will find the contributions solid, subtle and profitable.

Davies, Miranda, ed. *Third World—Second Sex*, vol. 2 (London and New Jersey: Zed Books, 1987). 284 pps.

Third World, Second Sex is a compilation of writings by, and interviews with, women participating in the struggle for women's liberation in the Third World. The topics of the various contributions included in the second volume vary greatly, from the role of women in the Guatemalan resistance movement to the organization of women workers in Sri Lanka, from women's health issues to violence against women and international prostitution. What comes across throughout is the vitality of feminist thought and political action in the Third World, and the tremendous strength of character of the women who fight to liberate themselves and others from the myriad forms of oppression, exploitation and abuse.

This volume will sensitize students to the social conditions of Southern women and inform them about the ways in which such women themselves are seeking change. Furthermore, it will provide a clear picture of grassroots political organization in the Third World and make clear the interdependency of social change and economic development. Because it offers a clear understanding of social and

political life in particular Third World countries, it should be introduced to students early on in their studies.

Deere, Carmen Diana, and Magdalena Leon, eds. *Rural Women and State Policy: Feminist Perspectives on Latin American Agricultural Development*
(Boulder: Westview Press, 1987). 282 pp.

The papers collected in this book were first presented at a 1985 symposium held in Bogota, Colombia, under the title "Agricultural Development Policy and Rural Women in Latin America: An Evaluation of
the Decade." Their purpose is to synthesize the results of the research
that had been carried out between 1975 and 1985 concerning the
effects on rural women of agricultural development. Case studies of
eight Latin American countries are included, along with comparative
analyses of agrarian reform, migration processes, integrated rural development, and income generation projects for women. Issues discussed
include "(1) the impact of state intervention in agriculture on rural
women, (2) the scope and consequences of 'women in development'
projects, (3) the impact of the economic crisis of the 1980s on women's
productive and reproductive roles, and (4) rural women's response to
agrarian change and economic crisis."

Taken as a whole, this volume provides a comprehensive picture of
the role of women in agriculture in the Latin American region. It is
also ideal for those students engaged in research on WID who wish to
focus on the conditions in one of the countries for which a case study
is included. This book will prove a useful resource for both intermediate and advanced students.

Hay, Margaret, and Sharon Stichter, eds. *African Women South of the Sahara*
(London and New York: Longman, 1984). 225 pp.

This volume amounts to a comprehensive survey of the role of
women in all aspects of African society, from the urban and rural economy to art, literature, religion, family life and politics. Designed for
undergraduate students, it includes information on precolonial, colonial, and contemporary conditions.

This is a solid introduction to the subject, incorporating the perspectives of a variety of disciplines. It includes an appendix of selected
statistics on African women, and an exhaustive bibliography which
will direct students to the resources required for further study.

Jaquette, Jane S., ed. *The Women's Movement in Latin America: Feminism and
the Transition to Democracy* (Boston: Unwin Hyman, 1989; reprinted by
the Westview Press, 1991). 215 pp.

The essays presented in this volume analyze "the role of women and of feminism in the transition from authoritarian to democratic politics in South America during the 1980's," looking at the part played by the women's movement in Brazil, Argentina, Uruguay, Peru and Chile. They thus serve to illuminate the vital contribution of women in the recent reshaping of the political and social life of Latin America.

This book can be used in a number of ways. Instructors lecturing on the transition to democracy in one of the Latin American countries with which the book deals may assign the relevant essay; courses surveying the political and social developments within Latin America as a whole may benefit from more extensive readings from it; and students of Third World feminism will certainly find much to interest them here. Solidly written and accessible, Jacquette's book effectively links two of the most current issues in contemporary development studies.

Leacock, Eleanor, Helen I. Safa et al. *Women's Work: Development and the Division of Labor by Gender* (South Hadley, MA: Bergin and Garvey Publishers, 1986). 300 pp.

The tripartite structure of this book reflects the three general topics that its essays address: historical changes in the structure of the division of labor by gender; effects on women of the shift from peasant to industrial society; and the impact on women's labor roles occasioned by the increasing integration of nonindustrial societies into the global market economy. As the editors write, "By bringing together scholars who have examined the origins of female subordination and the status of women in egalitarian societies and others who have raised issues dealing with women and development, this book ... yield[s] new insights into important questions regarding development policies and women's status today."

The contributors to this volume are indeed some of the foremost specialists in their fields. Instructors will want to pick and choose essays appropriate to their course, but this book is a must inclusion on any WID syllabus.

Mitter, Swasti. *Common Fate, Common Bond: Women in the Global Economy* (Wolfeboro, NH: Pluto Press, 1986). 184 pp.

"[I]t is in women everywhere that the large corporations find the promise of compliant labour," writes Mitter in the introduction to her study of the "background and the current manifestations of the struggle of women workers." Under particular scrutiny here is modern capitalism's increasing reliance on a flexible workforce, one kept off balance enough never to organize against its bosses. This reliance has led to the increased hiring of poor women at home and abroad. Technical fragmentation of industry has enabled corporations to hire out work to smaller shops with little union backing. And the unions themselves have, over the years, marginalized women and left them without recourse. The situation is not completely hopeless, however: Mitter's final chapter describes the international organizations of women workers currently finding solidarity across national and professional borders. Other portions of the book tackle such issues as women's role in capital flight and the use of minorities and guest workers in the European economy.

This is a simply written and compelling book that, while never running too long on data, brings enough facts to bear on its subject to present a vivid picture of the female industrial economy. While not specifically development oriented, *Common Fate* does draw the lines of interdependence clearly and will show American undergrads their potential role in empowering both Northern and Southern women.

Momsen, Janet Henshall, and Janet Townsend, eds. *Geography of Gender in the Third World* (Albany: SUNY Press, 1987). 424 pp.

This wide-ranging collection of case studies presents several aspects of women's roles in various regions of the developing world: the division of labor (on the farm, in the household and in industry); health care issues; family life. Of special interest are the chapters on women as consumers and heads of household.

Momsen and Townsend have gathered authors able to boil a wide range of experience down into well-written, self-contained segments. The broad scope of the volume provides a compelling picture of the role gender plays in daily life in the Third World. Those students who have come to grips with recent feminist thought will derive the greatest rewards from this book.

Monson, Jamie, and Marion Kalb, eds. *Women as Food Producers in Developing Countries* (Los Angeles: UCLA African Studies Center, 1985). 118 pp.

The essays in *Women as Food Producers* review the productivity of women in Third World agriculture, critique patriarchal data gathering methods, describe women's roles in various sectors of the food economy (using Ghana and Brazil as cases) and explore the politics of access. The collection concludes with a play by Nkeonye Nwankwo designed to teach the dynamics of life for women on African farms. Contributors include Kathleen Staudt and Susanna Hecht.

This slim volume deserves consideration for classroom use. Students new to WID or African studies will enjoy this book, both for its variety and its straightforward portrayal of African women's work. These women are not presented as passive victims, but as the breadwinners of the continent and agents of grassroots change. Politics, business and sociology all find space here. As the editors are concerned with alternative perspectives on African women, instructors can use this as a guide for students seeking to generate their own research methods.

Nash, June, Helen I. Safa et al. *Women and Change in Latin America* (South Hadley, MA: Bergin and Garvey, 1985). 372 pp.

A follow-up to *Sex and Class in Latin America* (which appeared in the seventies) *Women and Change* brings "new scholarship and some of the major issues confronting feminist research" to the table in order to "use women's [documented] contributions as leverage for change in Latin America." Part 1 brings feminist and developmental theories and methods up to date. Part 2 studies women's industrial production and biological reproduction roles. Part 3 consists of a series of articles devoted to women's status in farm and factory. Parts 4 and 5 are devoted to migration and political action, respectively. Specific peoples studied are Andean market women, Colombian and Dominican women in New York and women under the Cuban revolutionary government.

These essays are difficult reading, heavy with academic jargon. They are written by WID scholars for WID scholars. Instructors may wish to direct advanced students to this book, however, as it contains work by some of the best development scholars around, including Carmen Dianna Deere, Mary Garcia Castro and, of course, the editors. Chapter 2, "How to Study Women's Work in Latin America," will be a useful guide to instructors.

Parpart, Jane L., ed. *Women and Development in Africa: Comparative Perspectives* (Lanham, New York, and London: University Press of America, 1989). 345 pp.

Conceived in the conviction that a comparative focus is critical to feminist scholarship of development, this book faithfully spans the globe to place the African experience in context. The volume includes six essays on women in development in such countries as Canada, the U.S. and India, as well as the regions of the Caribbean, Latin America and the Middle East. Six essays treat the issue of women in development as it pertains to various African nations, including Tanzania, Botswana, Zambia and Nigeria.

The book is a proved classroom winner, versatile, accessible, effective. Perhaps best suited to the needs of second- and third-year students with a basic knowledge of issues pertaining to women in development, this book provides a comparative perspective on the subject and can play a role in introductory courses as well.

Parpart, Jane L., and Kathleen A. Staudt, eds. *Women and the State in Africa* (Boulder, CO: Lynne Rienner Publishers, 1989). 229 pp.

Parpart, Staudt and their colleagues set out here to describe "the particularity of women's relation to the state in Africa and . . . the need to study gender-state relations in order to understand both the nature of the state and women's place in it." The collection combines theoretical articles with case studies on a number of topics—militarism in Nigeria, peasant work in Zaire, urban Tanzanian society, Zambian development policies and the black market, and land distribution in Zimbabwe—all in terms of how they relate to women as political actors. Access to power, underrepresentation and coping mechanisms for politically marginalized (and empowered) women are all discussed.

This is an excellent second- or third-year reader for students of both politics and African issues. It is important for undergraduates to realize that oppression takes on different forms under different regimes, and in different cultures people respond to that oppression in different ways. *Women and the State in Africa* clearly illustrates these differences, bringing the reader step-by-step through difficult ideas without pulling any intellectual punches along the way. Contributors come from around the world and across the ideological spectrum.

Seager, Joni, and Ann Olson. Ed. by Michael Kidron. *Women in the World: An International Atlas* (New York: Simon and Schuster, 1986). A Pluto Press project. 128 pp.

The authors "ask not only *what* is happening between women and men (and between women themselves), but *where* it is happening." Their answers lie in dozens of colorful maps and charts, whose subjects range from the mortality rate of mothers in childbirth to the number of beauty contests held in the nations of the world. The point of this is to demonstrate "who has authority, who has power and who does not." Marriage and motherhood are the first two subjects studied cartographically, and subheadings include domestic violence and abortion. The section on work includes maps reflecting paid and unpaid labor. "Resources and Welfare" illustrates levels of health, numbers and distribution of refugees and poverty. "Authority" gauges women's influ-ence in politics, the military and the media. "Body Politics" covers rape and prostitution statistics. "Change" documents women's activity in governmental and nongovernmental activism.

While geopolitical change has rendered many of the lines on these maps out of date, this atlas is still a fine reference tool for development studies. The sheer number of topics mapped out and the skill and cre-ativity with which the authors present their material can only enrich a student's understanding of women in the world. The explanatory notes that accompany the maps are concise and opinionated, while those at the back of the book open avenues for further research. Country by country statistical tables are also included.

Sen, Gita, and Caren Grown. *Development Crises and Alternatives* (New York: Monthly Review Press, 1987). 116 pp.

Development Crises and Alternatives is the closest thing to a global feminist development manifesto that the world academic community has yet to produce. The authors, speaking on behalf of the Develop-ment Alternatives with Women for a New Era (DAWN), an informal collective of scholars, activists and fieldworkers, warn that "rather than improving, the socio-economic status of the great majority of Third World women has worsened considerably" since 1975. Chapter 1 describes why and how previous development strategies have been "inimical" to women. Chapter 2 explores ways that development analysis can be reoriented to serve men's and women's needs better, and how the empowerment of women would benefit all humanity. Chapter 3 documents the essential contributions that women make to the world economy as paid and unpaid workers and managers.

Written in a single voice, this short book speaks volumes about the dynamic heterogeneity of gender and development studies. To create a dialogue with their readers, the authors entertain many opinions, dis-missing few out of hand. Instructors are urged to use this important book in first-year classes to provoke discussion and debate among stu-dents, as well as to bring to undergraduates' attention the variety and importance of women's lives and work in today's world.

Sender, John, and Sheila Smith. *Poverty, Class, and Gender in Rural Africa: A Tanzanian Case Study* (London and New York: Routledge, 1990). 194 pp.

Analyzing their own research and that of others from a Marxian per-spective, the authors expose not only the close tie between gender roles and class status in Tanzania, but also the problems inherent in previous field data collected on rural Tanzanians. The book examines the process of capital accumulation and land distribution between 1973 and 1986, demonstrating that the Tanzanian peasantry is not nearly as homogeneous in terms of wealth, technology and status as previously believed.

Not only is this study itself original in its execution and provocative in its conclusions, but the authors have taken care to report on their own methodology in painstaking detail. Students in their first year of African studies or women's studies may benefit simply to familiarize themselves with the observations of the authors. More advanced undergraduates ought to learn quite a bit about fieldwork in general. The writing is clear and the writers are very confident with their findings.

Staudt, Kathleen, ed. *Women, International Development, and Politics: The Bureaucratic Mire* (Philadelphia: Temple University Press, 1990). 320 pp.

Many a development program has been designed with women's social and economic equality as a goal, but "policies are routinely ignored, contracted, and distorted in bureaucracies." The contributors to this volume assess the viability of achieving gender justice by working through the bureaucratic system. They examine women's political organizations, national and international agencies, as well as the nature of the internal bureaucratic process. Issues treated include feminism's impact on bureaucratic ideology; the hierarchy and class relations of women's organizations; the organizational factor in women's empowerment; the response of the World Bank to WID issues; and the ways bureaucracies collect and use data. These issues are discussed in reference to specific countries (Malawi, Cameroon, Nicaragua) and organizations (UN, FAO, SIDA, IAF), about which the contributors have first-hand knowledge.

Staudt's introductory and concluding essays pull it all together, lucidly describing the paradoxes that feminist development workers face in working through and for bureaucracies that are often less than supportive of their aims. Instructors of introductory WID courses will want to include Staudt's essays on their syllabi, while third- and fourth-year students should be directed as well to the more case-specific work of the other contributors.

Tinker, Irene, ed. *Persistent Inequalities: Women and World Development* (New York: Oxford University Press, 1990). 302 pp.

Persistent Inequalities is meant to be a basic book for development courses. It brings together such writers as Christine Obbo, Amartya Sen and Ester Boserup. Part 1 concentrates on politics and part 2 on microeconomics; part 3 presents four regions—West Africa, East Africa, the Caribbean and India—where patriarchy is under fire.

This extraordinary collection of scholarship and innovation is a welcome addition to any development course. Although the focus is strictly political and economic, and some of the material is rather polemical, the editor's admission that many of the essays contradict one another indicates how easily instructors will be able to engage their students in lively discussions of the material. *Persistent Inequalities* will add much to second- or third-year development syllabi.

"Women and World Development Series." London: Zed Books, 1991–1994.

This series of slim, informative volumes may well prove the best way to impart a good deal of WID knowledge in a quick, cost-effective way. Concise and attractive volumes, each fully illustrated, tackle women in reference to the world economic crisis; health issues; refugeeism; the environment; and several other categories.

The books are affordable, up-to-date, and accessible: they deserve serious consideration for use as foundation reading for a WID course or module.

Democracy and
Grassroots Power

Annis, Sheldon, and Peter Hakim, eds. *Direct to the Poor: Grassroots Development in Latin America* (Boulder, CO: Lynne Rienner Publishers, 1988). 226 pp.

The editors of *Direct to the Poor* decided to study the ramifications of the proposition that "the best way to help poor people is to give money to organizations that they themselves create and control." Does grassroots development work in practice? What do the poor invest in? Are the poor more effective agents of development? Why or why not? The essays profile individual grassroots developers; assess local development projects and organizations; describe the daily problems confronted in grassroots development; explore the cultural implications of grassroots development; and examine the possibility of implementing grassroots development strategies on a national level. The introductory essay searches for the "social energy" that sets grassroots development into motion.

Instructors ought not to let the Latin American basis of the study deter them from including this collection in a general course on grassroots development. It is handy, intermediate-level material for any course concerned with debates about empowerment in any regional political economy, especially since, in the words of the editors, "public agencies are more likely to absorb than distribute resources," and it is ultimately up to small, local organizations to change the world. (Ironically, the entire project was sponsored by the Inter-American Foundation—a U.S. government agency.)

Arat, Zehra F. *Democracy and Human Rights in Developing Countries* (Boulder and London: Lynne Rienner Publishers, 1991). 217 pp.

The central aim of this study is to explain the social, economic and political factors that lead to the breakdown of democratic institutions in developing countries. Three preliminary chapters are devoted to a critical review of the literature on the topic and to a reassessment of the conceptual framework employed by researchers in this area. Arat then examines such factors as the policy decisions of the democratic elite and the issue of dependency on foreign interests. Asking how they affect the maintenance of democratic political institutions, he argues that "civil and political rights cannot prevail if socioeconomic rights are ignored." The final chapter presents case studies of three countries—Costa Rica, India and Turkey—in order to demonstrate how the policy choices of newly established democratic governments contribute to the preservation or breakdown of democratic political processes.

The argument—no democracy based solely on civil and political rights to the exclusion of socioeconomic rights can survive—should prove provocative to a broad range of students.

Chambers, Robert. *Rural Development: Putting the Last First* (London, Lagos, and New York: Longman, 1983). 246 pp.

Addressing himself both to professionals working in the development field and to students, Chambers asks why existing development approaches have failed the rural poor, and how this failure might be ameliorated. Chambers defines the biases of development workers: they tend to spend an inordinate percentage of their time in urban centers, visiting rural areas only on short tours and avoiding the rainy seasons; wishing not to offend the governments on which their presence in any given country depends, they tend not to seek out the poor; a worker's given expertise may act as a blinder to the real needs of the people with whom he or she works; etc. Chambers identifies the gap between development practitioners and theoreticians, and suggests that a synthesis between the implemental attitude of the practitioners and the critical attitude of the theoretician is necessary in order to move farther towards the ultimate goal of development: improving people's lives. A key aspect of Chamber's own criticism of development approaches lies in the tendency of many Northern development workers and policymakers to assume intellectual superiority over the people whom they are assisting, thus closing themselves off to the wealth of knowledge the people possess.

In calling for a new breed of development worker who will venture out from the urban centers to live with, and get to know the needs of, the rural poor, Chambers challenges students and practitioners alike to reassess their motivations and goals in addition to their methodological assumptions. Students of development administration will find this book and its thesis most relevant to their studies.

Clark, John. *Democratizing Development: The Role of Voluntary Organizations* (West Hartford: Kumarian Press, 1990). 226 pp.

John Clark's *Democratizing Development* explores the duties and activities of NGOs—Northern and Southern—in the battle against poverty. Foremost on the author's agenda is the need for nongovernmental groups to empower those whom they are trying to assist. To explain the role of voluntary organizations in development, Clark adopts a broad, somewhat theoretical approach, carefully bolstered with ample anecdotal information, making *Democratizing Development* a fairly satisfactory introduction to development in general, although the brevity of the work prevents it from covering anything in any great depth. Part 3, the most interesting section for students and teachers alike, presents a laundry list of NGO failures (mostly restricted to the larger, Northern agencies) and a counterlist of successes won by smaller, grassroots groups to the South.

What *Democratizing Development* lacks, however, is a coherent plan of action. Clark tries to fit his many examples of helpful and hurtful NGO activity into a rubric of "ingredients of development" consisting of Development of infrastructure, Economic growth, Poverty alleviation, Equity, Natural resources protection, Democracy and Social justice (DEPENDS). Although he is clear on how things should be, Clark offers little instruction in how to make them so. Nevertheless, the DEPENDS approach is a useful window into development studies in any number of disciplines, and Clark's emphasis on self-help will benefit students raised on images of the world's poor as hapless victims. *Democratizing Development* is a beginner's text and is best read in conjunction with monographic studies of particular NGO projects.

DeSilva, Donatus. *Against All Odds: Breaking the Poverty Trap* (London: Panos Publications, 1989). 186 pp.

The Panos Institute, investigating grassroots development projects, asked a number of Asian and African journalists to answer these questions: Who created the projects? Do the people really benefit? And are the projects sustainable? The result is this collection of critical accounts of nine such projects, each written by a local journalist and illustrated lavishly with the works of Southern photographers. They describe "ordinary people and how they have broken through the poverty trap" in vivid detail. Homeless Indian women design and build their own low-cost housing. Clinics are built in Tanzania. Similar stories emerge from Zambia, Sri Lanka, Bangladesh, Kenya and Indonesia.

Although most of these stories are inspirational, this book is not merely a paean to pet projects. The contributors are skeptical and critical—of the project agents and their opponents. Effective self-help programs must effectively analyze themselves. These portraits of grassroots development from the inside offer compelling portraits of grassroots progress, hindrance and self-correction in a language and format that will entertain and inform beginning students.

de Soto, Hernando. *The Other Path: The Invisible Revolution in the Third World* (New York: Harper and Row, 1989). 271 pp.

This book is both an exposé of the underground economy in Peru and an analysis of the power structure which, the author concludes, excludes the majority of people from "legal" enterprise through inequality and bureaucratic mismanagement. In order to survive, Peruvians have created a massive informal economy or, as it is called by the state, a "black market." The author contends that it is only on account of this informal economy that people in Peru, as well as in other nations of the Third World, are able to meet their basic needs and even, occasionally, to flourish. Thus, in his eyes, the people themselves have laid the foundation for their own economic development—a more promising and organic approach than the many programs advocated by economists, development administrators and politicians.

The Other Path is something like a manifesto for informal economy and the need for reform. Translated into several languages and distributed broadly, this is a book that has made an impact. And it makes fascinating reading. But due to its length, instructors with limited space on their syllabi will probably want to assign only excerpts from the book. The contention that the black market is in fact the legitimate economy of the people will certainly spur heated debates between "law and order" conservatives and "people power" progressives, leading to a more enlightened consideration not only of economic development but also of power structures and their judicial apparatus.

Diamond, Larry, ed. *The Democratic Revolution: Struggles for Freedom and Pluralism in the Developing World* (New York: Freedom House, 1992). 254 pp.

This book is about democratic civil society, its institutions and its people. The contributors, all of whom have in one way or another participated in the struggle for democracy in their native lands, describe the role of various civil organizations in the bringing about of democratic reform in the developing world.

There is a sense of reality to these essays which is often lacking from more objective, third-party studies. At the same time, of course, they do not share the latter's idolatry of the principle of objectivity. For a ground-level look at the real circumstances of popular political participation in the developing world, however, this is an excellent collection, suitable for students of all levels.

Diamond, Larry, Juan J. Linz, and Seymour Martin Lipset, eds. (1) *Democracy in Developing Countries*, vol. 1–4 (Boulder: Lynne Rienner, 1988, 1989, 1990); (2) *Politics in Developing Countries: Comparing Experiences with Democracy* (Boulder: Lynne Rienner, 1990), 503 pp.

Democracy in Developing Countries is a four-volume work composed of twenty-six case studies, each of which examines the experience of an individual country with political democracy. Each study cuts deep, exploring the history of a country in order to understand its unique formulation of the principle of democracy and the form and function of its democratic institutions. Volume 2 covers democracy in Africa, with chapters on Nigeria, Ghana, Senegal, Botswana, Zimbabwe and Uganda; volume 3 focuses on Asia—India, Pakistan, Sri Lanka, Turkey, the Phillipines, South Korea, Thailand, Malaysia, Papua New Guinea and Indonesia—while volume 4 is devoted to the Latin American region: Argentina, Brazil, Chile, Uruguay, Venezuela, Colombia, Peru, Costa Rica, the Dominican Republic, and Mexico. Volume 1, subtitled *Persistence, Failure, and Renewal*, contains the theory and conclusions of the project as a whole.

Nowhere else has the political experience of so many countries been analyzed under the same methodological assumptions. Solid conclusions concerning the nature of the move towards (or away from) democracy remain elusive due to the large number of variables in each case, yet what one gains from this work is not only a panoramic view of the political and social reality of the twentieth century, but an appreciation of the diverse elements that go into the making of each nation's unique political culture.

Though an ideal reference work to which all students of political development should be directed, the size of *Democracy in Developing Countries* limits its usefulness in the classroom. Realizing this, the editors have issued another book, entitled *Politics in Developing Countries*, that includes ten of the country studies from the larger publication: those on Chile, Brazil, Mexico, Turkey, India, Thailand, South Korea, Nigeria, Senegal and Zimbabwe.

Of significance in this volume and the one reviewed above is the perspective most associated with Diamond himself: that democracy is a learned practice of behaviors, ideas and abilities, involving a battery of specialized bodies of knowledge and activity. This nuanced view, at variance with much development experience, implies that democracy is an exportable phenomenon, largely spread through contact with democratic systems. And as such it is an interpretation that can generate vigorous and fruitful classroom controversy.

Durning, Alan B. *Action at the Grassroots: Fighting Poverty and Environmental Decline* (Washington, DC: Worldwatch Institute, 1989). 70 pp.

In this straightforward pamphlet, Durning sets forth the linkages between poverty and ecological disasters. From this, he turns to descriptions of many grassroots initiatives to clean up and make better use of natural resources. While offering advice on "bottom-up" development activity and on fostering "top-down" aid, policy and management, the author also gives compelling examples of the best in local development organization.

Given the format of the Worldwatch pamphlet series, Durning can only write so much on the democratization of development. What is here, however, well serves the beginner and clearly states the human side of conservation and the actual and potential self-sufficiency of poor and threatened groups. It is suitable in classes on environment, grassroots activity and the study of NGOs.

Harley, Richard M. *Breakthroughs on Hunger: A Journalist's Encounter with Global Change* (Washington, DC: Smithsonian Institution Press, 1990). 169 pp.

Why do some development programs work while others fail? Harley studies the successes among grassroots development planners to discover "the processes of change these innovators set in motion" and "the kind of efforts citizens in the West should support." The portraits of the people and projects that work cover all the continents and many topics, including education, gender and empowerment. The writing is journalistic in tone and focuses on personalities, but the student can look to rather copious endnotes for more detailed bibliographic and statistical information. Each chapter begins with a short passage describing the broad development picture in the subject's region, followed by a detailed portrait of a particular project and the person (or people) responsible for it.

Harley's book performs a great service for students of development and development workers themselves. Beginners and advanced students can learn about the very human aspect of development and the courage and creativity that running a successful development project requires. Its only drawback is a lack of perspective on the larger forces that act as obstacles and, occasionally, midwives to development. But *Breakthroughs on Hunger* compensates for this with its clear-headed and compassionate rendering of the daily struggles of grassroots development everywhere.

Korten, David C. *Getting to the 21st Century: Voluntary Action and the Global Agenda* (West Hartford, CT: The Kumarian Press, 1990). 253 pp.

Korten's provocative reappraisal of the development process and the role of NGOs has greatly influenced the development profession in the early 1990s and may have an important classroom role to play as well. *Getting to the 21st Century* opens by pithily summarizing the development experience of the 1980s, drawing attention to the real failures in development as well as the substantial opportunities afforded by a rapidly changing geopolitical context. In part 2, Korten articulates his vision of people-centered development, "an economics for spaceship earth" which emphasizes improved quality of life over industrialization or increased economic output as the yardstick of real development. This vision will be realized through equity-led growth, with a preeminent role for Southern NGOs in creating equitable institutions of civil society and government, and important roles for Northern NGOs as enablers and constituent builders.

By turns description, prescription, and exhortation, Korten's book is truly indispensible for upper-division courses examining the role of NGOs in the development process. The author's insistence on "transformation" of individuals and institutions as prerequisites for development has sparked a lively debate within NGOs on the ethics of gradualism and compromise versus the more idealistic call for full-scale change, and may well spark similarly fruitful debate in introductory classrooms as well. As a book which evaluates the role of *everyone* in the development equation, it is liable to have impact on all students and deserves serious consideration for inclusion on development syllabi.

Lehman, David. *Democracy and Development in Latin America: Economics, Politics and Religion in the Post-War Period* (Philadelphia: Temple University Press, 1990). 235 pp.

This book explores the currents of Latin American economic, political and religious thought since 1948 and their effects upon the social structure of that region. It provides detailed analysis of such developments as structuralist economics, dependency theory, liberation theology and the grassroots theory of development, which the author has termed *basismo*.

The author is clearly impressed with the dynamism of Latin social thought—its capacity for adaptation and innovation—in the decades following the Second World War. By isolating in their generative contexts schools of thought which have greatly influenced the field of development, this book illuminates much that is unique in Latin American political culture and can be profitably read by any student of political science or development theory interested in the Latin American experience.

Lewis, John P., et al. *Strengthening the Poor: What Have We Learned?* (New Brunswick and Oxford: Transaction Books, 1988). 239 pp.

A product of the Overseas Development Council, this collection of twelve studies focusing on strategies for poverty alleviation include both case-specific material as well as more general evaluations. Topics considered include the efficacy of various grassroots approaches to development, the impact of agricultural growth on poverty, strategies for addressing the problem of urban, in contradistinction to rural, poverty, women and poverty, the effect of adjustment programs on the poor, and the changing role of Northern NGOs in the development process. In addition, there are examinations of Pakistan's rural development strategy, suggestions on how external intervention might best aid antipoverty campaigns in India and an emphasis on subsectoral planning for successful all-round development.

As a policy review, each chapter offers recommendations for policy adjustment. The studies provide concise assessments of the strategies and programs which have been adopted in the past fifteen years and thus would fit well into a syllabus relating to issues in development administration.

Montgomery, John D. *Bureaucrats and People: Grassroots Participation in Third World Development* (Baltimore: The Johns Hopkins University Press, 1988). 140 pp.

Reaching back as far as 1972, Montgomery has collected and updated a number of essays on grassroots development and, more precisely, on how bureaucracies—for better or worse—act as the fulcrum between government-level policy formulation and local implementation. The roots of the study began in Southeast Asia in the 1960s, when the author decided to "search for institutional means by which governments could bridge the cultural gap between peasants and their own officials" and how to link the expertise of development engineers to popular participation. The purpose of the collection is "to review the experiences on which [the author's] confidence in participation is based." The essays review land reform, water management, government activity and grassroots NGOs.

By no means a populist, Montgomery does not see participation as an end in itself but as a source of information for governments and a means by which citizens can improve their own welfare by circumventing bureaucratic stagnation. These essays will appeal to intermediate students of political economy and the democratization of development. Despite dated data, the conclusions remain relevant because they have been formulated over decades of experience in government, in the field and in the classroom.

Nelson, Joan M., ed. *Fragile Coalitions: The Politics of Economic Adjustment* (New Brunswick and Oxford: Transaction Books, 1989). 159 pp.

As the editor states in her introduction, "This volume focuses on the political dimensions of economic reform, particularly in Latin America and Africa." Articles address issues such as the relationship between political democratization and the success of economic reform, the prerequisites for economic adjustment programs that aid in poverty alleviation, and the effects that the political conditions prevailing within a developing country have on the outcome of adjustment programs negotiated with international financial institutions. All of the contributors agree on the premise that the desired goal for the Third World is twofold—economic and political liberalization.

Students with a strong background in both political science and issues of economic development will find this volume useful, particularly for studies that focus on the interrelationship in developing nations between politics and economic policy.

Owens, Edgar. *The Future of Freedom in the Developing World: Economic Development as Political Reform* (New York: Pergamon Press, 1987). 109 pp.

Edgar Owens considers "the conditions under which freedom can prosper in the developing world" and casts "'economic development' as a political reform process." This short book covers many disciplinary bases but seems especially concerned with the uses and misuses of history in explaining away despotism in the Third World—as well as our own apathy here in America. Corruption, the bane of many development programs, even in the freest of democracies, is also taken on as a subject of study, one that sees it not as a necessary evil or an argument for less bureaucratic authoritarianism but as a compelling reason to foster even more pluralistic regimes. Four specific cases are addressed, including the United States disastrous "democratization" of Vietnam. Taiwan, China and Yugoslavia are also studied.

Owens is passionate about his subject but does not allow his belief in democracy to get in the way of his logic. To him, government reform is, not a desirable side-effect of development, but a prerequisite. The book takes the form of an extended essay, and most of the statistics are relegated to the appendix. While this may be troublesome for more advanced readers, first-year students (for whom this book is quite appropriate) will enjoy the flow of the text uninterrupted by complex data. Furthermore, by drawing on the United States' own political literature (Jefferson and Adams) and its history in Vietnam, Owens gives the politics of development an immediacy for undergraduates that other, more advanced works do not.

Poulton, Robin, and Michael Harris, eds. *Putting People First: Voluntary Organisations and Third World Development* (London and Basingstoke: Macmillan, 1988). 178 pp.

The essays in this volume explore the aims and implementation of NGO programs in the Third World, providing readers with a clear picture of what it is that NGOs do. They argue that in order for economic development programs to affect the poor, the poor need to be able to participate in their formulation.

As one of the editors, Michael Harris, states, "The writers are not academics and do not pretend to be; their stories are personal and their tone is one of commitment . . . being field workers, they speak with great practical experience and an understanding of poverty."

Pourgerami, Abbas. *Development and Democracy in the Third World* (Boulder: Westview Press, 1991). 210 pp.

Contrary to the popular view that in order to achieve economic development Third World countries must sacrifice political freedom, Pourgerami argues that democracy and economic growth are "mutually reinforcing processes." He analyzes the relevant variables in 104 developing countries and examines the prospects for both sustained economic growth and the maintenance of democratic political institutions in the Third World. Different chapters focus on such issues as the performance of centrally planned economics, the influence of religion on the politics and economics of the Third World, and the impact of military spending on economic growth and political freedom.

The wealth of statistical data makes this book ideal for advanced students working on research projects in this area of study. The book is highly recommended reading for anyone tackling the increasingly voguish issue of the relationship between political liberty and economic prosperity.

Pradervand, Pierre. *Listening to Africa: Developing Africa from the Grassroots* (New York: Praeger, 1989). 229 pp.

Avoiding the already well-trodden ground of international and official relief efforts, Pradervand sets out to describe the effectiveness of peasant development activities in Burkina Faso, Kenya, Mali, Senegal and Zimbabwe. Topics include food production, literacy training and general self-help. The author also attempts to explore how gender roles in African peasant societies help and hinder grassroots relief work. (The appendix goes so far as to designate by gender-dominance the nonagrarian income sources of the five countries.)

Instructors may employ this book in two useful ways. First, *Listening to Africa* may be used in a course dedicated to the study of any of the five nations that the author concentrates on. Second, it may be employed in a general course on relief efforts that might otherwise exclude any Afrocentric literature. Beginning students learning about African peasants as initiators of their own relief can, in later years, avoid the pitfall of viewing underdeveloped societies as passive victims of widespread tragedy.

Randall, Vicky, ed. *Political Parties in the Third World* (London and Newbury Park, CA: Sage Publications, 1988). 198 pp.

The central aim of this book is to examine the variety of Third World political parties in an attempt to identify their similarities and differences and to discover patterns in the way they develop and function. The eight case studies presented are intended to serve as a sampling of "the main types of party systems on the one hand and the main Third World regions on the other." Particular countries examined include Zambia, Ghana, Iraq, India, Mexico, Brazil, Jamaica and Cuba. The contributors address themselves to a common set of questions concerning the origins, development and functions of a political party or party system. This approach makes *Political Parties in the Third World* extremely useful for comparative studies.

In addition, the historical material contained in each essay is presented clearly and succinctly, allowing students with little prior knowledge of the subject to gain a broad overview of the political history of the various countries treated. The book is thus appropriate for both intermediate and advanced students.

Rau, Bill. *From Feast to Famine: Official Cures and Grassroots Remedies to Africa's Food Crisis* (London: Zed Books Ltd., 1991). 213 pp.

Combining a "historical and analytical view of the food crisis in Africa" with a study of "the innovative efforts of African people to address food and development problems," this book presents a well-developed view of the successes and failures of recent relief efforts in Africa. The text is divided between a summary of official relief efforts—those of African national governments, foreign powers and international relief agencies—and an innovative study of peasant relief and reform efforts of recent years. It is, more than anything, a study in self-help.

Rau is not without his opinions, singling out especially the huge amount of time and money he sees as wasted on the cavalcade of "experts" who pour into Africa each year with little notion of what is best for its people. Rather than detracting from the effectiveness of the book, however, these views ought to inspire students, whether beginning (this is an easy read) or advanced, to examine their own goals. The text is peppered with observations from African journalists and peasant activists, offering any number of topics for papers and seminar discussions.

Sorenson, Georg. *Democracy, Dictatorship and Development: Economic Development in Selected Regimes of the Third World* (London: Macmillan, 1991). 214 pp.

A common topic of debate is the relationship between regime type and economic development. Sorenson uses four states—India, China, Taiwan and Costa Rica—as bases of study for these questions: Does a particular type of government help or inhibit development? And which regimes work best? Drawing on political science and political economy, the author addresses questions of welfare versus growth, authoritarian efficiency versus democratic laboriousness. In doing so, he finds different definitions of development from one regime to another and searches for a single defintion to apply to all. Furthermore, he reassesses regime types and creates new categories of government to assist his explorations.

This type of study is key to any course on development policy. Students of any of the areas specifically under study are especially fortunate to have such in-depth information at their disposal. The book is readable and relatively free of jargon. It deserves special attention from students of grassroots development.

Wasserstrom, Robert. *Grassroots Development in Latin America and the Caribbean: Oral Histories of Social Change* (New York: Praeger, 1985). 197 pp.

The Inter-American Foundation is a public corporation created by Congress in 1969 whose aim is to provide direct economic assistance to community-based enterprises in developing countries, bypassing bureaucratic and political obstacles to development by responding to the needs of the poor themselves. This book is a collection of interviews with participants in seven different organizations supported by the IAF, ranging from a computer store and marketing cooperative in Colombia to a women's theater group in Kingston, Jamaica. The foundation grantees describe the process of their empowerment as they worked to build up their enterprises and improve their own economic conditions.

Instructors will find that the personal accounts in this volume give a human face to the reality of poverty while demonstrating that successful ground-up development is possible. Students of all levels are bound to profit from reading these testimonials.

Interdependence

Brown, Janet W., ed. *In the U.S. Interest: Resources, Growth and Security in the Developing World* (Boulder, CO: Westview Press, 1990). A World Resources Institute book. 228 pp.

"How important are developing countries to broad U.S. interests and how important are resource management and population growth to these nations' economic and political futures?" Using the cases of Mexico, the Philippines, Egypt and Kenya—all nations with strong ties to the United States—the contributors unanimously answer that, to a greater or lesser degree, developing nations and the maintenance of their resources are very important to the well-being of the U.S. The introduction tells us why, in general, we should care. The case studies themselves show how specific foreign environmental interests are very much our own, drawing on the disciplines of history, politics, economics and resource management.

All of the material is simply presented, and each case follows a similar format. Beginning students will be comfortable with the level of difficulty, and the four parallel studies offer instructors the opportunity to engage students in discussions of the similarities and differences between different developing nations. Simple charts liven the pages by dramatically emphasizing the U.S. reliance on distant disappearing resources. Brown's text provides a fine introduction to environmental interdependency, particularly insofar as it personalizes the issues for American undergraduates.

Hamilton, John Maxwell. *Entangling Alliances: How the Third World Shapes Our Lives* (Cabin John, MD: Seven Locks Press, 1990). 204 pp.

Entangling Alliances documents the many ties of economic, environmental and cultural interdependence that closely link the work-a-day worlds and long-term interests of Americans and citizens of the Third World. Following a brief introductory essay, surveying U.S. attitudes towards interdependence, Hamilton presents three studies which serve as examples of his subject: global data entry business (economic interdependence), Costa Rican forestry (environmental interdependence) and the Kenyan tourist trade (cultural interdependence). While including the occasional anecdotal shocker—Swedish firefighters use data bases in Cleveland to trace street routes in Malmö—Hamilton investigates the ways that old conceptual categories of economic and political sovereignty are no longer viable in a changing technological context.

Hamilton pulls his three sketches together in a concluding essay which suggests that interdependence is an inexorable phenomenon demanding new approaches from U.S. policymakers and citizens. Here, he roots his argument in the context of U.S. interests and offers for consideration the ideas of thinkers who advocate grassroots activism and "continuous interaction" as constructive responses to the global changes that are taking place. Many faculty confront the complaint of students that issues in global development are remote or irrelevant given the economic and social crises of the U.S. In *Entangling Alliances*, Hamilton puts the global agenda where students will take note: on Main Street, America.

Kwitny, Jonathan. *Endless Enemies: The Making of an Unfriendly World* (New York: Penguin Books, 1984). 434 pp.

Endless Enemies is "a reporter's look at the world as it relates to America," a history of U.S. interventionism and its consequences on a microeconomic level—both at home and abroad. Kwitny provides anecdotal information along with fairly well researched contemporary history, covering Zaire, Angola, Iran, Grenada and many other countries. In addition, and perhaps of greatest interest, Kwitny offers an incisive critique of the American news media.

Endless Enemies is a fast, fascinating read. It can serve a number of purposes in the area of development studies. First and most obvious is its use as a thumbnail alternative history of American foreign affairs. Second, by focusing on local aspects of global activities, Kwitny's history indicates the rather complex perspective that peoples of developing countries have of American attitudes and intentions. Third, it clarifies much of the government's rhetoric about New World Order and what this really means to the Third World and America. Lastly, it will teach beginners to inspect their own sources—especially newspapers—more critically.

Maguire, Andrew, and Janet Welsh Brown, eds. *Bordering on Trouble: Resources and Politics in Latin America* (Bethesda, MD: Adler and Adler, 1986). A World Resources Institute book. 448 pp.

In this "book for North Americans by North Americans" the contributors examine "resource, environmental and population problems that touch on the United States." The interactions of American and pan-American institutions and policies are also studied in order to define the relationships between "resource management, economic health and orderly political change in Latin American countries." The United States' complicity in Latin American underdevelopment and environmental decline, as well as its helpful assistance to Latin American development are addressed as the contributors try to determine what actions are really in the best interests of the U.S.

Latin America is not a monolith politically, environmentally or developmentally, and the authors of these essays make it a point to illustrate the richness and diversity of South and Central America. Food, petroleum, forests and revolution are brought together in a lucid package accessible to the general reader or introductory-level student.

Novak, Michael, and Michael P. Jackson, eds. *Latin America: Dependency or Interdependence?* (Washington, DC: The American Enterprise Institute, 1985). 186 pp.

These essays fall into two distinct sections. The first, relying on contributions by American scholars and experts, seeks to discover and qualify the connections between the Latin American economy and the world economy. These essays include calls for more open trade, a modified assessment of dependency theory, reduced state protection of business and tax reform. The second section, consisting of Latin American contributions, is concerned with local issues: obstacles to development, putting the Medellín declaration into "proper context" and describing the cultural and historical realities of economic development. All of these articles have been collected in order to clarify, in the editors' eyes, questions of free trade, multinational corporations' interference in politics and, especially, the role of the Catholic church and other nongovernmental institutions in the Latin American economy.

The unabashed neoclassical conservatism of this collection may irritate some students, but, when paired with Munck's *Politics and Dependency in the Third World*, it will lead to lively discussion in the classroom. It is a text for intermediate or advanced students already familiar with the various theories and events in question.

Scott, Andrew M. *The Dynamics of Interdependence* (Chapel Hill, NC: University of North Carolina Press, 1982). 254 pp.

Dynamics is a theoretical and historical introduction to world systems of government, economics and social relations. Part 1 covers the evolution and dynamics of the modern world system; part 2, the problems of power politics in an interdependent world. Part 3 describes the relationship between constraint systems and global politics. The concluding section addresses various problems of managing global change in the world system.

Whereas Hamilton's *Entangling Alliances* relies on lively discussion of recent historical and anecdotal evidence, Scott's book is geared more to the undergraduate seeking a firm foundation in the study of global interdependence. The writing is simple but dry, and Scott takes great pains to put not just events but theories into their proper perspective, emphasizing systems over incidents. Instructors should begin any basic course on interdependency with this book before turning to more specific texts such as *Entangling Alliances*.

Sopiee, Noordin, B. A. Hamzah, and Leong Choon Heng, eds. *Crisis and Response: The Challenge to South-South Economic Co-operation* (Malaysia: Institute of Strategic and International Studies [ISIS], 1988). 450 pp.

Prepared in honor of the Second Summit of Third World Scholars and Statesmen held in Kuala Lumpur in 1988, this volume includes essays that address a broad range of issues relating to the need for cooperation among developing nations, in such areas as trade of manufactured goods and primary commodities, finance, technology and education. The statement issued at the end of the Kuala Lumpur summit is included as an appendix.

Contributors range from present and former Third World leaders to economists, academics and others who have worked both in and out of government. While much has been written about North-South relations, relatively little is available on the subject of the relations among developing countries. This book, therefore, offers a unique perspective on strategies for development that are based on the mutual interests of these nations and the need for cooperation among them.

Thomas, Caroline. *In Search of Security: The Third World in International Relations* (Boulder: Lynne Rienner, 1987). 228 pp.

The central theme of this book is "that most of the policies of developing countries can best be understood by reference to their grave need to increase their individual security in an extremely insecure world." After introducing the concept of nation building, Thomas considers the primary ways that Third World countries have sought to stabilize their position in the global order, from their relationship with the IMF and their search for a more equitable system of international trade to their attempts to provide food for their citizens. An analysis of the perspectives of Third World nations on the Nuclear Non-Proliferation Treaty and a case study of Jamaica in the 1970s are also included.

"This book has been written with the needs of Western students of the Third World in mind," and succeeds as "a basic international relations textbook dealing specifically with the Third World."

Watson, Keith, ed. *Dependence and Interdependence in Education: International Perspectives* (London: Croon Helm, 1984). 222 pp.

This is a study of national and international perspectives on education in the developing world. Of foremost interest to the editor is the extent to which educational systems are subject to dependency theory or interdependence. The collection consists of articles on theory, case studies and curricular suggestions for teaching development in Western classrooms. Topics of religion, culture and ethnicity are also touched upon. Specific topics include examination reform, education, and household life and obstacles to educational development.

Intermediate students of development will be able to compare their own ideas about education to those of the contributors, while at the same time learning how they might be able to bring their knowledge to the developing world. Instructors can use the theoretical material, as well as the suggestions in the final section, to improve their own curricula and better guide their students. The real benefit of this book, of course, is its illustration of how, like all other commodities, knowledge can and does circulate through an interdependent global marketplace.

Wennegren, E. Boyd, et al. *The United States and World Poverty* (Cabin John, MD: Seven Locks Press, 1989). 201 pp.

This book is a comprehensive introduction to the role played by the U.S. in the attempt to formulate and implement solutions to the problem of world hunger and poverty. It begins with an examination of supply and demand factors as they relate to food production and hunger, addressing such topics, among others, as population, technology and politics. This is followed by an outline of the history of U.S. foreign assistance from the Marshall Plan and the Point Four program to the present. A chapter on the relationship between U.S. economic assistance and international trade emphasizes the interdependence of nations within the global economy and demonstrates why it is in the interest of the U.S. to continue providing aid to the LDCs. The relationship of hunger to political instability is also explored. The last chapter provides suggestions, intended for application in a classroom environment, about how to demonstrate the impact of U.S./Third World interdependence on a local (U.S.) economy, and specifically the local impact of development assistance.

Designed as it is for Americans with little knowledge of economics and aid-related topics, this book will prove valuable for modules in introductory courses addressing the issue of foreign assistance.

Willetts, Peter, ed. *Pressure Groups in the Global System: The Transnational Relations of Issue-Oriented Non-Governmental Organizations.* (London: Frances Pinter, 1982). 285 pp.

Dividing the world of NGOs into eight discrete categories, the editors focus on those whose activities focus on political issues of a particularly international nature. These issue-oriented groups are discussed in a theoretical framework and evaluated as to the importance of their respective issues and the effectiveness of their methods. Among the NGOs dicussed—each with its own chapter—are the PLO, Amnesty International and Oxfam. Broader issues such as apartheid and women's rights also receive ample treatment. All of these chapters, except the one on the PLO, are written by individuals involved with the movements in question.

These articles are bound to stimulate heated discussion among students about the mission of particular groups and the usefulness of pressure groups altogether. Students already apprised of the facts surrounding the issues will be better rewarded by the editor's approach than will students studying nongovernmental issues for the first time. Instructors interested in a specific region or topic may pick and choose among the chapters. As a whole, this book can serve as a stimulating text for second- or third-year students of global development.

Wright, Moorhead, ed. *Rights and Obligations in North-South Relations: Ethical Dimensions of Global Problems* (Houndmills, Basingstoke, Hampshire and London: Macmillan, 1986). 196 pp.

All of the essays in this volume are concerned with the ethical aspect of the relationship between the rich nations of the North and the less developed nations of the South. Each looks at this question vis à vis a particular issue, such as the development of natural resources, foreign aid, and international sanctions. Additional chapters deal with the ethical implications of arguments for and against intervention in Third World conflicts, and the institutional framework of North-South relations, such as UNCTAD and NIEO.

The conflict between political self-interest and global humanitarian responsibility is unlikely to be resolved soon, but this volume points out the major issues and the theoretical models which characterize the debate over it. This book will probably prove most useful to students who have a background in development issues, international trade, and international relations.

Refugeeism

Camarda, Renato. *Forced to Move* (San Francisco: New Americas Press, 1985). 99 pp.

Haunting interviews of Salvadorans fleeing into exile in Honduras form the substance of this book. The graphic testimony of victims is copiously illustrated with photographs, poems and even children's drawings that bear further witness to atrocities inflicted on political refugees in Central America. Camarda's contribution is to have organized the mass of individual ordeals into broad categories of human experience. Condensed in newspapers as brief accounts of a mass exodus of six hundred thousand people in the early 1980s, the crisis is rendered here as flesh-and-blood trauma. In this book, the resettlement of refugees to a camp deep in Honduras emerges much less as a strategic decision to avoid subversion by guerrillas than as a ruthless dislocation involving the uprooting of innocents. Camarda sheds light in particular on the collaboration of the Honduran and Salvadoran military in "pacifying" the refugees. She has pieced together descriptions of scores of massacres on the border by troops trying to prevent migration. The reader will remember above all the searing testimony of priests, activists, and relief workers, who indict a cynical American foreign policy as deeply implicated in this tragic tale.

Courses on refugees, Latin American history, and U.S.–Latin American relations will be enriched by Camarda's book. Its generalist approach is most appropriate for introductory courses. The absence of excessively dogmatic language and few references to narrow policy debates makes Camarda's book timely even as this particular refugee crisis has ended. As a complement to statistical and conceptual studies of refugees, this volume could make vital reading in many courses.

Chierici, Rose-Marie Cassagnol. *Demele: "Making It"—Migration and Adaptation among Haitian Boat People in the United States* (New York: AMS Press, 1991). 333 pp.

There are any number of books available on the subject of Southeast Asian refugees' lives in the United States, but alarmingly few on the subject of Haitian immigrants. Chierici's book fills that lacuna quite satisfactorily. Not simply a portrait of Haitians' new American life, *Demele* provides historical background not found in comparable books. She reprises Haiti's tumultuous history as well as its record of refugee migrations to other regions of the American continents. Her study uncovers root causes of mass migration and places them in a "periphery-to-core" context. And, of course, she paints a vivid picture of life in the States, relating the stories of Haitian settlers in Rochester in their own words, touching on topics of employment, religion, race and gender relations.

Demele, despite the richness and sophistication of its approach, is surprisingly easy to read. This may derive from the author's reliance on the personal accounts of refugees, in addition to the care with which Chierici introduces new terms and ideas. Much like Griddle and Nam's *To Destroy You Is No Loss* (reviewed below), *Demele* relates the refugees' odyssey from root cause to final settlement, although Chierici's tone is more scholarly.

Criddle, Joan D., and Teeda Butt Nam. *To Destroy You Is No Loss: The Odyssey of a Cambodian Family* (New York: The Atlantic Monthly Press, 1987). 289 pp.

To Destroy You is the autobiography of Teeda Butt Nam, a middle-class Cambodian woman who survived America's bombing, the Khmer Rouge's devastation and Vietnam's invasion of her homeland. Her story covers a number of aspects of refugee life, including work and the difficulties of raising a family while on the move. In her story, Nam and coauthor Criddle portray a woman who, although victimized often, is also the agent of her own and her family's survival. Indeed, after escaping to Thailand, Teeda Butt Nam made her way to California where she found a job in Silicon Valley and eventually received United States citizenship.

The tone of the book is far from scholarly. It is a gripping narrative that weaves in strands of Southeast Asian history with those of the author's own life. What emerges is a vivid portrait of the everyday life of a refugee. Include this in modules concerned with the region, with peace and world order studies and, most of all, in segments concerned with the narrative history of refugees. The literature for the latter is vast and compelling; Teeda Butt Nam's contribution is certainly one of the best of recent years.

Ferris, Elizabeth G., ed. *Refugees and World Politics* (New York: Praeger, 1985). 224 pp.

This collection "seeks to contribute to a broader understanding of refugee issues by analyzing refugees in the context of their domestic and international political environments." Topics addressed include: refugees and state formation; U.N. responses to the refugee crisis; the political role of NGOs and U.S. and Canadian refugee policy. In addition, there are studies of four regional refugee situations: the Middle East, Africa, Southeast Asia and Central America.

Refugees and World Politics is a nonspecialist's guide to the best-known issues in refugee studies. Its political bent and emphasis on the policies of large institutions gives a false impression of the sophisticated crisis of forced migration. Similarly, shoehorning the entire African continent into a single chapter is somewhat misleading. Nevertheless, the collection is accessible to students and offers more critical analysis than can be found in similar nonspecialist texts. This book will come in handy in survey courses seeking a basic text to anchor a segment on refugee issues or interdependence but is best used in conjunction with more subtle studies of refugee life.

Forbes, Ann Armbrecht. *Settlements of Hope: An Account of Tibetan Refugees in Nepal* (Cambridge, MA: Cultural Survival Inc., 1989). 170 pp.

Beginning with a brief description of the circumstances surrounding the Tibetans' evacuation of their homeland, this book proceeds to discuss the social, political and economic adaptations within the Tibetan settlements in Nepal. The relationship between the exiled Tibetans and their host country is explored, as well as the role played by foreign relief organizations after the exodus from Tibet. Subsequent chapters examine the establishment of local industries which provide the economic means for the support of the settlements, and the difficulties involved in keeping traditional culture alive outside the homeland.

As the author writes, "Unlike other refugee groups whose communities are increasingly characterized by violence, suicide attempts, and cultural fragmentation, the Tibetans' story is largely marked by cultural integrity, economic success, and a call for nonviolent efforts to regain independence." This concise, readable account will fit well into a syllabus structured around the experience of refugee communities.

Gallagher, Dennis. *The Era of Refugees: The Evolution of the International Refugee System* (Washington, DC: Refugee Policy Group, 1989). 81 pp.

This brief essay begins with a historical outline of European refugee migrations before, during and after the World Wars, setting the stage for a discussion of the apparatus developed to deal with the vast new refugee movements in the developing world. Given central position among the actors on the new system's stage is the United Nations High Commission on Refugees (UNHCR). Gallagher describes how the agencies adapted to the new situation—and how they often failed to adapt. Each region that bore witness to massive forced migration since the mid-fifties is given separate assessment.

The Era of Refugees carefully notes that while refugees have existed at all times in human history, never before our own era have so many people been forced out of their homes in so many places for such a wide variety of reasons. The facts are laid out clearly enough for beginners to discover their own specific interests in the broader realm of the refugee problem. Instructors note that, as this is an outline of systems, the author's greatest concerns are institutional rather than social or economic.

Gordenker, Leon. *Refugees in International Politics* (New York: Columbia University Press, 1987). 227 pp.

Refugees in International Politics tells the story of the international refugee relief system—its development, its operations, its limitations. Gordenker also provides an excellent overview, divided into short, clearly organized subsections which concisely address the issues raised in the specialized scholarly literature on refugees. He concludes that renewed attempts to define absolute international legal standards for asylum are not only impractical but could undermine the very flexibility that underlies the success of the current system. But he does emphasize that certain normative standards of human rights could and should be integrated into current response mechanisms. Gordenker offers no panacea for global ills; he simply seeks to alleviate the misery of the disinherited.

This succinct summary of the origins, nature and scope of the refugee crisis will be particularly useful to undergraduates familiar with such issues.

Jacobson, Jodi L. *Environmental Refugees: A Yardstick of Habitability* (Washington, DC: Worldwatch Institute, 1988). Worldwatch Paper #86. 46 pp.

This brief, illuminating essay describes the development of a different sort of refugee community that flees, not hostile regimes, but hostile lands: an enormous migrant army of the environmentally disinherited, retreating from a toxic, arid countryside toward bloated slums and refugee camps. Jacobson locates most of these people in a "self-reinforcing cycle of land deterioration." Africa stands out among all threatened continents as being under most serious environmental stress. Jacobson also places natural cataclysms in their proper social context, noting that their devastating consequences are often the result of human agency.

The case of environmental refugees is an excellent way to teach students about the interconnectedness of politics, society and the economy within the developing world. But whichever connections are drawn in the classroom, the plight of "tens of millions of persons permanently displaced from their homes" will motivate otherwise unconcerned undergraduates. Jacobson's provocative and accessible report is an excellent starting point for any classroom exploration of the interdependence of industrial and agricultural development, environmental crisis and involuntary human migration. Free of dense statistics and daunting models, this concise explanation of global interconnectedness is supported by clear and compelling examples from both industrialized and developing societies.

Koehn, Peter H. *Refugees from Revolution: U.S. Policy and Third World Migration* (Boulder, CO: Westview Press, 1991). 463 pp.

Approaching his material on both the social-structural and the individual levels of analysis, Koehn focuses on the South-North flow of refugees following Third World revolutions. He examines the factors that lead to refugee formation and the mechanisms that facilitate migration to the industrialized North, and he presents an assessment of U.S. immigration policy and foreign policy towards the Third World in general. Koehn considers the reception of refugees in the U.S. and profiles five exile communities. A further issue is repatriation. Koehn emphasizes the role of refugee migrations in contemporary international relations and explores the future implications of current trends.

This comprehensive study is bound to become a staple of any class concerned with refugee issues. It provides a clear picture of the general trends of South-North migration as it pertains particularly to refugees from revolution, as well as a cogent analysis of the ambiguities of U.S. policy on the issue. Students with an interest in this area of study will profit greatly from this work regardless of their level of prior learning, although it may be best suited to those who have at least some prior knowledge of the subject.

Loescher, Gil, and Laila Monahan, eds. *Refugees and International Relations*
    (Oxford: Oxford University Press, 1989). 430 pp.

The essays in this volume present a comprehensive picture of the
contemporary global refugee problem and the strategies that have been
developed to deal with it. They examine a variety of issues, from the
European response to refugees and settlements of refugees in third-
party countries to state-sponsored, armed attacks on refugee camps in
many parts of the world, and the status of refugee women. Part 1
describes the international framework for refugee issues, while part 2 is
devoted to examinations of specific conditions faced by refugees and
part 3 analyzes various international approaches for aiding refugees.
The influence of refugees on international relations is stressed
throughout.

The reference guide to refugee organizations and documentation
centers, as well as the selected bibliography suggested for further reading, make this book a valuable resource for students new to the study of
refugee issues.

Loescher, Gil, and John A. Scanlan. *Calculated Kindness: Refugees and Amer-
    ica's Half-Open Door, 1945 to the Present* (New York: The Free Press,
    1986). 346 pp.

Calculated Kindness traces the evolution of postwar American
refugee policy, presenting a critical review of the Northern response.
The work of Loescher and Scanlan is forward looking: "only by examining the politics which shaped the American response to refugees
over the past forty years can we begin to understand the forces shaping
American policies today and standing a good chance of influencing
them in decades to come." Ideals of protectionism persist; Congress
and the American public continue to recoil from any perceived threat
of an insupportable influx of the underprivileged. The authors conclude that the humanitarianism of the United States is informed by "a
tradition of generosity, sacrosanct and sanctimonious," and a "heritage
of guilt."

Well written, thoroughly researched, packed with fascinating detail,
this book performs a critical service: it cuts through the rhetorical haze
surrounding the refugee question and provides the facts necessary to
push analysis past the barriers of fear and prejudice.

Miller, Jake C. *The Plight of Haitian Refugees* (New York: Praeger, 1984). 223 pp.
    This book serves as a spirited reminder of the perils of historical

ignorance in the treatment of refugee issues. Published almost a decade ago, it denounces the treatment of Haitian "boat people" interred in Florida and Guantanamo Bay; it vividly illustrates the fallacy of an American policy that isolates "economic" from "political" refugees; and it follows the brutal reception of Haitians forcibly repatriated in their homeland. But Miller goes beyond an exposé of the political oppression of Haitians. He examines, as well, immigration within its cultural context. He discusses religious practices, ethnic differences, and other issues that raise the stakes for Haitians who flee their homeland. This book, in sum, seeks to speak directly not only to the material conditions of Haitian immigrants, but to their hopes and dreams as well.

This book is recommended for two purposes: First, it is an excellent primer for first- and second-year students interested in Haitian immigration. Second, Miller's book is a superb example of the methodology of development studies for undergraduates who cannot engage in fieldwork. Its source material comprises exclusively newspaper articles and easily available reports by private and public institutions. The book's utility on these grounds outweighs its drawbacks: occasional awkward and jargon-swollen prose, dated references to the contemporary politics of Duvalier and Reagan.

Nanda, Ved P., ed. *Refugee Law and Policy: International and U.S. Responses* (New York: Greenwood Press, 1989). Studies in Human Rights #9. 225 pps.

Written by a variety of experts from the academic and NGO communities, *Refugee Law and Policy* combines the insight of field experience with the analytical perspective of theology, ethics, law and political science. The first set of articles examines international responses to the refugee crises, focusing on the myopia of American and European policy; the tightening of borders; and the domestic xenophobia and global power struggles that politicize humanitarian policy in Northern nations. A second group of essays focus on America's role in specific refugee situations. The thrust is critical, but conservative, using a forceful demonstration of interconnectedness to support a demand for policy reformulation. The Southern migrants clamoring for entrance are the direct social cost of U.S. foreign policy: through misguided foreign intervention, massive military assistance and inappropriate economic investment, the U.S. precipitates the migration it wants so desperately to staunch. Other selections consider

the ethical dimensions of American policy and critique the Machiavellian justification of restrictive immigration laws. The book ends
with a chapter on the continuing search for durable solutions, including a series of national, international and nongovernmental goals.

In a concluding remark that speaks directly to educators, Nanda
calls for a multidisciplinary approach and argues that the dissemination of accurate information is the critical first step toward "mobilizing
public support for the implementation of effective measures necessary
to provide durable solutions." Education is of singular importance in
an issue so highly politicized and so greatly influenced by the attitudes
of Americans and the government which represents them.

Scott, Joanna C. *Indochina's Refugees: Oral Histories from Laos, Cambodia and
Vietnam* (Jefferson, NC, and London: McFarland and Co., Inc., 1989).
312 pp.

Members of the Laotian, Vietnamese and Cambodian refugee communities within the Philippine Refugee Processing Center in Bataan
provide the sources for this collection of oral histories. They are farmers and clerics, soldiers and housewives, students and civil servants,
and each relates his or her own personal story in the context of the
recent political history of their native land. The book is divided into
three sections, corresponding to the three countries from which the
refugees have come. The section on Vietnam includes stories by those
who fled their country illegally, as boat people, as well as by those who
departed legally through the Orderly Departure Program. The Cambodian section deals primarily with life under Pol Pot's regime.

The stories contained in this volume amount to eyewitness
accounts of the political turmoil of Indochina and provide a ground-
level perspective on events. In conjunction with a more systematic
text it will serve well as an introduction to the contemporary political
history of the region, as it will provide students with a clearer understanding of what that history means for the people who are living it.

Sutter, Valerie O'Conner. *The Indochinese Refugee Dilemma* (Baton Rouge:
Louisiana State University Press, 1990). 256 pp.

Hannah Arendt articulates the premise of Sutter's impassioned
work: In our century, "what is unprecedented is not the loss of a home
but the impossibility of finding a new one." Sutter focuses on the myriad reasons why two million refugees fleeing war and famine in
Indochina since 1975 are refused the opportunity to find new homes.

Viewing the crisis as acutely political, Sutter studies the "national interests" that transform refugees into outcasts. Internecine struggles among nations that systematically refuse migrant Indochinese are rooted in geopolitical calculation, she argues. This volume avoids blaming only the inhumanity of the West, as she also finds culpable the Machiavellian ambitions of states neighboring Indochina. Demonstrating an impressive grasp of the issues, she analyzes the perceived threats to regional stability that migrants bring with their misery. Her conclusions are guardedly optimistic: Political realism will ultimately dictate that the West act to alleviate the migrants' flow to asylum states closest to Indochina. The organization of these states into the Association of Southeast Asian Nations (ASEAN) will bring political and economic pressure to bear where moral persuasion has thus far failed.

While this is a masterful work, it can be recommended only for upper-level political science seminars on Indochina or on immigration issues. The scope of Sutter's inquiry is relatively narrow. Her insistence on the primacy of politics makes for a compelling analytical framework, but at the expense of broader considerations of social, economic, and cultural issues. Sutter has achieved an insightful monograph, albeit one with only limited classroom application.

Yundt, Keith W. *Latin American States and Political Refugees* (New York: Praeger, 1988). 236 pp.

Yundt's work analyzes "the practices of Latin American states toward political refugees within the context of international, regional, and national asylum and refugee law," using regimes—international regimes in particular—as his analytical method. Much of his information derives from governmental and nongovernmental organizations' legislation, policy and documentation, which gives the book a distinctive political-scientific flavor. Yundt surveys activities from the time of the League of Nations to the rise of international refugee organizations in the fifties. He also places inter-American bodies such as the OAS in the greater context of the global refugee regime. South and Central America each receive separate studies that outline distinctive, interactive regime development from the fifties to the present.

Any development text that limits itself to a particular discipline (here political science) and to a particular method within that discipline (regime systems) is bound to appeal only to a narrow audience.

Nevertheless, this is a book for those who have some acquaintance
with political science. Instructors seeking a picture of Latin American
refugee systems as broad as this one is deep should pair *Latin American
States and Political Refugees* with a comparable work of political economy, human ecology or the like.

Zolberg, Aristide R., Astri Suhrke and Sergio Aguayo. *Escape from Violence:
Conflict and the Refugee Crisis in the Developing World* (New York: Oxford
University Press, 1989).

In *Escape from Violence*, the authors examine the unprecedented
refugee flows generated by political and ethnic conflicts in Asia, Africa
and Latin America. The first chapter surveys the types of conflicts that
have traditionally inspired migrations. Later chapters look into early
modern European history to document the evolution of refugee law
and practice in the West. Case studies are followed by a theoretical
reconsideration of the role of social conflict in the generation of
refugees.

Escape from Violence, without minimizing the horror of homeless-
ness, portrays refugees as the miserable detritus tossed up by the shifting plates of structural transformation: they are "a by-product of social
change" which constitute "only one item on a much broader canvas of
suffering and progress." These are all difficult and provocative ideas.
Beginning students will have difficulty following the immense amount
of evidence brought to bear on this exercise in theory building. But the
richness pays off in more advanced classes, where the basics of refugee
systems, policy and history are better understood, and where the students themselves are better equipped to assess new paradigms and draw
their own critical and theoretical conclusions.

CONTRIBUTORS

CONNER BAILEY is Associate Professor of Rural Sociology at Auburn University. He received his Ph.D. in Development Sociology from Cornell University and has long-term field experience in Malaysia, the Philippines and Indonesia, working on upland and lowland agriculture as well as coastal and marine fisheries. His research interests focus on the human dimensions of resource and environmental management. Among his publications are *The Sociology of Production in Rural Malay Society* (Oxford University Press) and articles in a diversity of journals, including *Marine Policy* and *World Development*.

RUTH C. BUSCH is Associate Professor Emeritus of Anthropology at Auburn University. She received her Ph.D. in Anthropology from the University of Arizona and has extensive field research experience in Turkey, Peru, Senegal and Egypt. She has served as a consultant to the Food and Agriculture Organization on the role of women in agriculture. Her research interests are in the fields of kinship and development. Among her publications are *Family Systems* (Peter Lang Publishers) and articles in anthropological journals, including *American Anthropologist* and *Human Organization*.

PETER CENEDELLA has served as the Associate Director of the Interfaith Hunger Appeal Office on Education since 1990. He also served on the advisory committee for the Panos Institute's educational module on the HIV pandemic and developing societies. He has written extensively on politics and culture, has tutored English to international students at the Hunter College Writing Center, and has been active in a number of grassroots educational and environmental research and action groups.

STEPHEN K. COMMINS is Advisor for Policy and Planning at World Vision International. His previous position was Director of the Development Institute at the UCLA African Studies Center. He is the editor of *Africa's Agrarian Crisis: The Roots of Famine* and *Africa's Devel-*

opment Challenge and the World Bank: Hard Questions, Costly Choices. He has regularly taught courses on hunger and development at UCLA and other universities.

LILLIAN RAE DUNLAP is Assistant Professor of Broadcast News at the University of Missouri-Columbia School of Journalism. She has extensive international experience including two years of teaching at the Institut Teknologi MARA/MUCIA in Shah Alam, Malaysia. She is a former television news reporter/anchor and was consultant to the award-winning documentary "Eyes on the Prize II."

WILLIAM F. FISHER is Assistant Professor of Anthropology and Social Studies at Harvard University. From 1990 to 1992, he was Director of the Program in Economic and Political Development at Columbia University's School of International Affairs.

JAMES K. GENTRY is Dean of the Donald W. Reynolds School of Journalism at the University of Nevada-Reno. He is also Executive Director of the Society of American Business Editors and Writers. Gentry frequently works with news media organizations to improve the quality of their business and economics reporting, and works with corporations, associations and professional groups to help them deal with the media. His articles appear in many journals, and he has written chapters for several books.

ROBERT KEESEY is Professor in the Department of English at SUNY-Potsdam. For the past two decades he has been involved with interdisciplinary team-taught programs and courses, among which are ongoing efforts in world food and hunger and environment issues. His most recent passion is an integrated course in film, literature and music of the contemporary Third World.

GABRIEL G. MANRIQUE is Professor of Economics at Winona State University in Minnesota, where he also teaches courses in International Studies and Women's Studies. His area of specialization is in economic development, particularly in questions of trade and world hunger. He is currently working on a research project on immigrants from the developing world who teach in U.S. colleges and universities. He has served as a fellow in the U.S. Congress, working with Rep. Tim Penny and the Select Committee on Hunger.

MARY J. OSIRIM is Assistant Professor of Sociology and Coordinator of the Africana Studies Program at Bryn Mawr College. Her teaching and research interests have focused extensively on gender and the role of entrepreneurship in African development, a topic on which she has conducted field work in southwestern Nigeria and Zimbabwe. Her publications include "Characteristics of Entrepreneurship in Nigerian Industries: Primary Results from the Lagos Case," in *Perspectives in International Development* (Mtewa, ed.); "Gender and Entrepreneurship: Issues of Capital and Technology in Nigerian Small Firms," in *Privatization and Investment in Sub-Saharan Africa* (Ahene and Katz, eds.); and "The State of Women in the Third World," in *Social Development Issues.*

TOM RIDDELL teaches in the Department of Economics and the American Studies Program at Smith College in Northampton, Massachusetts. He sits on the steering committee of the Five College Program in Peace and World Security Studies (PAWSS), and was a cofounder of the Center for Popular Economics.

GODFREY ROBERTS is Associate Dean for Undergraduate Education of the Faculty of Arts and Science at Rutgers University. He is also an Adjunct Professor at New York University, teaching courses in environmental biology. His professional interests are population and food policy.

WILLIAM SAVITT has been Director of the Office on Education of the Interfaith Hunger Appeal (IHA) since 1989. In that capacity, he oversees IHA's Curriculum Development Program, including biennial summer institutes for college faculty. He teaches intellectual history at Columbia University.

KAREEN B. STURGEON has pursued studies in the fields of both public health and biology, receiving her Ph.D. from the University of Colorado at Boulder. She has published extensively on the genetics of forest trees and bark beetles and is the coeditor of *Bark Beetles in North American Conifers: A System for the Study of Evolutionary Change* (University of Texas Press). She is Professor of Biology at Linfield College, where she has taught since 1982.

JAMES H. WEAVER is Professor of Economics at The American University and is on the faculty of the Institute for International Research. He is also a student at Wesley Theological Seminary. Weaver coauthored *Economic Development: Competing Paradigms* (1981) and has written numerous articles on the subject of development economics. He is coauthoring the forthcoming volume *Capitalism with a Human Face: Achieving Broad-Based Sustainable Development*, to be published in 1994.

KATHLEEN MAAS WEIGERT is the Faculty Liaison/Academic Coordinator at the Center for Social Concerns, Concurrent Associate Professor in the Department of American Studies, and Faculty Fellow at the Joan B. Kroc Institute for International Peace Studies at the University of Notre Dame. She has written and lectured on justice and peace issues, experiential learning, and the development of social concerns among college faculty and students.

EDWARD WEISBAND holds the Edward Singleton Diggs Chair in the Social Sciences, Department of Political Science, at Virginia Polytechnic Institute and State University. He was recently awarded the Philip and Sadie Sporn Award for Outstanding Undergraduate Teaching of Introductory Subjects. In 1987, while Distinguished Teaching Professor at the State University of New York, Binghamton, he was named as the State of New York Professor of the Year. His publications include the widely adopted reader/text, *Poverty amidst Plenty: World Political Economy and Distributive Justice* (1989), and, with Lev S. Gonick, *Teaching World Politics: Contending Pedagogies for a New World Order* (1992).

INDEX